FARM FRESH
FLAVORS

Over 450 Delicious Recipes Using Local Ingredients

Randall L. Smith

B
BETTERWAY HOME
CINCINNATI, OHIO
www.betterwaybooks.com

Other fine Betterway Home Books are available from your local bookstore, online, or direct from the publisher. Visit our website, www.betterwaybooks.com.

15 14 13 12 11   5 4 3 2 1

Distributed in Canada by Fraser Direct
100 Armstrong Avenue, Georgetown, Ontario, Canada L7G 5S4, Tel: (905) 877-4411
Distributed in the U.K. and Europe by F + W Media International
Brunel House, Newton Abbot, Devon, TQ12 4PU, England, Tel: (+44) 1626 323200,
Fax: (+44) 1626 323319, E-mail: postmaster@davidandcharles.co.uk
Distributed in Australia by Capricorn Link
P.O. Box 704, S. Windsor NSW, 2756 Australia, Tel: (02) 4577-3555

Edited by Candy Wiza
Cover designed by Clare Finney
Interior designed by Hotiron Creative
Production coordinated by Mark Griffin

For Heidi...

INTRODUCTION

After twenty years cooking professionally, I am always amazed at the reluctance of most people to cook; I started cooking to make some beer money in college. If a hopelessly lazy young man can do it, I know the ambitious and enlightened readers of this book can as well.

This is a cookbook and, as such, it is simply a how-to on using fresh ingredients with a little flair. Most of the recipes can be prepared with tools that most of us have in our kitchens and with ingredients easily found in any neighborhood. I have tried to explain any ingredients that are unusual and give directions on how to find them. The main ingredients are the items you get from your local farmers, CSA share or your own backyard and these are the centerpieces of the book. I have consciously tried to keep the instructions light and not weighted down with formulas and rigid chemistry. I have steered away from recipes with a lot of moving parts and long lists of ingredients. The point of the book is to make eating fresh food simple so that you will choose it over the processed trinkets found on store shelves.

A couple of things this book is not: It is not a handbook on nutrition; any reference to nutritive value is purely accidental. If you eat a wide variety of fresh food and avoid processed food, the amount and types of nutrients you get should take care of itself. It also is not a chemistry textbook. Nearly every ingredient has an alternative, and learning to be flexible with those ingredients is part of learning to cook. The best recipe is just a starting point for you to experiment. Please change anything you want according to taste. It is also not a screed for vegetarianism, but it is loaded with primarily vegetarian recipes. I'll let the reader investigate independently the thousand reasons we should eat more plant-based food. I don't want to preach but I became a vegetarian during the writing of this book. Take that for what it is worth.

Acknowledgments

This book would not have been possible without the help of Candy Wiza who shepherded me through an unfamiliar and arduous process and Pamela MacDonald who was a much needed second set of eyes. Both of these women have as much ownership as I do in this book. I thank them sincerely.

Eating fresh seasonal products from someone you know brings a little magic. A weekly CSA box, a trip to the farmers market or a few steps to your backyard garden filled with items that are constantly arriving, departing, changing and offering up their wonders will require focus and attention. It will demand that you treat two of the more important activities of your life, cooking and eating, with respect. It will help you take yourself more seriously and install meaning in what has become a meaningless exercise — take-out is so much easier. Bringing meaning to your life is the only real reason to do anything. If we eat food grown by men and women we respect, make love to those we love and do work that doesn't require compromise, we can't help but have full, meaningful and important lives. My wish is that this book, in some small way brings you closer to that goal.

And you thought it was just dinner!

—*Randy Smith*

TABLE OF CONTENTS

LOCAL RESOURCES

TOOLS TO GET YOU STARTED

RECIPES FOR FRUITS, VEGGIES AND HERBS A TO Z

THE SEASON AS IT COMES

MULTI-PURPOSE RECIPES

COOKING TECHNIQUES

PRESERVING THE FLAVORS

LOCAL RESOURCES

1

There is a movement afoot to develop a more personal relationship with food. A small but vocal minority has shouted "hell no" to the anonymous bread mill that delivers our daily bread. Many are concerned about the environmental degradation that institutional farming and food processing engender. The endless monocultures of chemically sustained corn and soybeans that carpet Middle America leaves our soils barren and require enormous petroleum inputs to sustain. Vast feedlots of cattle, hogs and chickens produce mountains of manure that pollute our waterways and groundwater.

Some are concerned about the questionable wholesomeness of the Western diet with nutrients processed out and complex and sometimes dangerous chemicals processed in. The Western diet has largely been reduced to various combinations of corn, soybeans and chemicals.

The welfare of factory-farmed and processed animals is also troubling, including the unseen cruelty they endure in order to be brought to our table. Cattle, hogs and chickens are confined in teeming enclosures and force-fed unnatural diets. These practices cannot be sustained and enlightened people are looking for alternatives. They are seeking a more intimate and significant relationship to the food we eat and the universe that produces that food. We have attempted to co-opt natural rhythms with science and need to return to sustainable consumption — searching for a way to balance our food karma. A way of eating that allows us to join in a timeless cycle of natural renewal and to participate rather than exploit.

Part of finding a more connected way to cook and eat is dealing with abundance when you are blessed with it and scarcity when nature demands it. The traditional coming and going of scarcity and abundance linked us with timeless rhythms of nature, the earth and ourselves. We had to think and plan ahead. We had to treasure and conserve the abundance. We had to manage and endure scarcity. We had to take what the world gave us and it taught us discipline, reverence and humility. These lessons are harder to come by when we can get anything we want, anytime we want, already prepared, for a few bucks and a small amount of time. I think this convenience and plenitude has made our lives less interesting. We all eat the same things and we eat them all year long. We follow the same diets and talk about food in the same ways. We aren't forced to change our tastes at all. It is entirely possible and, way too common, for a person to eat the same breakfasts every morning, every day of their life. We eat Hot Pockets and microwave dinners and the same frozen vegetable blends in December, June and October. We don't cook anything fresh because that would require understanding and commitment; understanding what we were meant to eat at any given season of the year and commitment to using that food with good sense and integrity.

Eating, loving and work is the three-legged stool that our life is built on. You wouldn't let a marketing director in Omaha decide whom you should love. You wouldn't take a job without knowing anything about the people you will work for. Why would you let strangers thousands of miles away decide what you will eat? We've decided that that part of our life is insignificant or out of our control. But what choice do most of us have?

The choice we have is to ask questions and take action. Attempt to know the pedigree of what you eat. Awaken to the fact that food is of the dirt and moisture and magic of the earth. Attempt to get to know the personalities that have built their life studying that magic and digging in that dirt and drinking in that moisture. This book is an advocacy for human relationships. A return to the understanding of the human effort required to bring you dinner.

A respect for that effort and a respect for the simple act of eating are the prerequisites to enjoying these recipes. The farmer, like all of us, has a life of affections and conflict. It's a life she wants to sustain due to a fulsome love of the earth's magic. She brings the result of that life to your table and asks you to give it the same love she has. When this happens, each bite is pregnant with meaning and flavored with significance.

Farmer's markets are everywhere now. In many urban areas there are markets available within a reasonable distance nearly every day of the week. The best of them demand that vendors sell items locally produced and many of them demand that they are certified organic. No matter what type of market it is, you will be able to acquire fresh seasonal items from the farmer who actually grew it. Your groceries will come with a pedigree and personality. Here are some tips for taking the best advantage of farmer's markets.

Farmer's Market Tips

1. Study and learn what to expect throughout the season. Plan several recipes with the items you expect to be in high season. Prepare the best food at its peak.

2. Go early to get the best selection. Go late to get the best deals when farmers are breaking down and willing to sell at a discount and avoid losing the produce.

3. Try new things. If you see something unfamiliar, ask the farmer how you might prepare it — or buy this book.

4. If you have time and inclination, consider volunteering for the market. Seek out the market manager and ask if there is a role for you. You will learn a lot about seasonality and get to know your group of local farmers.

5. Bring your own bag, basket or cart. Many markets won't allow plastic bags and it will surely be difficult to lug armloads of turnips and sorrel.

6. Bring cash. It's unlikely you will find a credit card machine.

Community Supported Agriculture (CSA)

I think the handle CSA is unfortunate. It stands for community supported agriculture, which is fine, but the term does not communicate any of the import and romance of what a CSA is — a community of people that includes producers and consumers in a synergy that cultivates each individual and the land. A group of people freely coming together to share the rewards of a specific patch of ground crafted by God and nurtured by man.

A CSA works by offering a share in the produce of a farm or collection of farms for the season. You pay a fixed amount at the beginning of the season and receive weekly shares of what has become available that week. In late spring you may receive asparagus, fresh greens, baby beets and small tart strawberries. In mid-summer green beans, baby carrots and the first of the tomatoes may be in your box. By late summer, your share is bursting at the seams with summer squash, beautiful large tomatoes, cucumbers, cabbages, and crisp head lettuces. The share money allows the farmer a cash infusion early in the season when cash is tight that will carry him through to the point where he can cash crop his goods in markets and restaurants. It truly allows the farm to be "sustainable;" able to stand on its own without hidden environmental costs or public subsidies. It is an imminently sane and earth-tender system.

The consumers acquire enough value from this arrangement to pay the farmer an amount that sustains him. There is a certain amount of humanity that is natural to that type of arrangement that is not expressed in an acronym. I don't know what would be a better phrase, but encourage anybody interested to come up with one.

CSAs come in all shapes and sizes and most CSA farms also sell in farmers markets and to restaurants. They can focus primarily on identifiable familiar produce or they may focus on unusual varieties and heirloom treats. Some work off of rented land, some off of very old family farms. Some are proudly certified organic and many don't feel the need to be certified. Some raise meat and eggs, some raise only vegetables. And in many cases, several farms will combine in order to allow for a broader selection. They are all a running commentary on seasonality and, as such, bring that beautiful synergy to our lives that I described in the introduction.

You can find CSA resources at your local university extension or by doing a little legwork online. A great starting point for information is http://www.LocalHarvest.org. Or ask around at your local farmers market. In the Midwest, a share typically is $400 to $600 a season and in many cases it is broken into two payments. Over the course of a season, this truly is a bargain for the freshest, most flavorful and healthful food available. This book is designed to help you to take advantage of every bit of food you might receive in a CSA farm share over the course of a season. With some commitment and a little work you can feed your family for the better part of a year.

Tips on CSAs

1. Be prepared to try new things. Buying this book is a great start. You must get out of the habit of eating what you want — when you want — and eat what's available when nature dictates. Most CSAs will have a list of available items from prior years.

2. Many CSAs have a late season storage share that contains potatoes, onions, winter squash, turnips etc. Give some thought to how you will keep this.

3. Make sure the pick-up times and places are convenient for you and find out what happens when you miss a pick-up.

4. It's okay to contact other members and ask them for an evaluation of the farm to help you determine if the farm is right for you. You might also want to visit the farm.

5. Many farms offer a discount on your share if you work on the farm. If this interests you, don't hesitate to ask the farmer.

6. Some CSAs allow a certain degree of choice in you share. If you want have the most choice, be early.

7. Learn how to make vegetable stock (Techniques) and to compost. The stock allows you to capture the flavor and nutrients of even the trimmings and scraps from your share and the compost provides rich fertile soil for another season or for your indoor plants.

8. Take care of your share once you get it. Most produce will degrade in warm conditions once out of the ground. Get it into storage temperature as quickly as possible.

TOOLS TO GET YOU STARTED

2

Most of what you need to prepare the recipes you likely already own. This is a quick overview of the tools, machines and gadgets you might need.

Knives

The knife is the most important cooking tool you have. If you are serious about cooking or just want to be better at it, buy quality knives. Don't go to the department store, don't buy them from a multi-level marketer and don't buy any knife from a guy with an infomercial. Go to a decent gourmet store or restaurant supply warehouse and ask the shop owner for some suggestions and buy quality knives. Most of the recipes in this book can be easily prepared with two knives — a paring knife and an 8 to10-inch chef's knife. There are myriad of knives available and they all have specific uses but these two are the most important and should be purchased first.

Cutting Board

Many will argue about whether to use wood or plastic cutting boards. The evidence concerning sanitation does not point to a clear choice. Wooden boards are thought to wick bacteria away from the surface where they die and are rendered harmless. Many prefer plastic because they are easier to clean and sanitize. Wooden boards are a little easier on your knives and with care will last forever. Plastic boards can go in the dishwasher. I prefer wooden boards because I think they look cooler and are more traditional. Either is a good choice. You should choose the largest possible that you can fit in your sink. A small cutting board is next to useless and ends up leaving a big mess on your counter top.

Pots and Pans

Pots and pans have almost gotten to be status symbols. Go in any suburban kitchen and you may see several thousand dollars in anodized 12-piece sets or brilliant stainless steel cooking ornaments. Even I have a beautiful $200 La Crueset enamel Dutch oven on display in my kitchen (Would you like to see it?).

Don't fret; you don't need all that. One large skillet, a couple of small skillets, a couple of saucepans, and a large soup kettle will be enough for most of the recipes in this book. The saucepans and soup kettle can be of inexpensive stainless steel. The choice of skillets is a little more complex. Life with a nonstick skillet is easy, but there are very valid concerns about the toxicity of nonstick cookware. The least troublesome nonstick skillets are anodized. They are sturdy and relatively safe, but they do degrade over time and leach some toxic chemicals. Cast-iron cookware is inexpensive, looks cool and is reliably safe, but is heavy and takes some finesse to season and care for (look online for detailed care instructions). The expensive alternative to cast iron is enamel cookware; these are more nonstick than cast iron and easier to care for, but, I repeat, they are expensive (though they come in dazzling colors).

Mixing Bowls

You should have several sizes of stainless steel mixing bowls. Stainless steel is durable and non-reactive; it won't flavor your foods. For most uses a bowl with a flat bottom is easier to use and keep steady when whisking briskly. Glass bowls are fine as well and if you are hand mixing baked goods, they will be steadier on the countertop. They are usually more expensive and it may be difficult to find smaller sizes.

Whisk and Whip

There are several styles of whisks and whips. Any of them will work but experience tells me that a balloon-style whisk is the most useful. The rounded end allows you to scrape the sides of round bowls and more fully mix your ingredients. For the home cook a whisk with the thinnest wire possible is best. Rarely will you be whipping the heavy product that a stiff whisk is made for. The usual mistake is to use a whip that is too big. An 8 to 10-inch whisk is best for most uses.

Mortar and Pestle

You can live without this, but for certain preparations crushing with a mortar and pestle brings a flavor you cannot get any other way. Besides, they look very stylish on your kitchen counter. You can get inexpensive ceramic mortars and pestles but you will work much harder to crush your ingredients. A hefty stone mortar and pestle will bring you back to the communal kitchen of our ancestors.

Food Processor

You may be able to live without a mortar and pestle but you can't live without this. You should look for a machine with at least a 1/2 horsepower motor. You really only need one speed but a large and small basket is helpful. This will likely be the most expensive small appliance you own. It will cost you a few "pesos" no matter which one you buy, so please spend a little money for this. In order to fully use the goodies in your CSA box or to take advantage of produce at its peak you will need this tool. It is essential for sauces, pesto and spreads. The additional blade attachments allow you to shred and grate easily. You might argue that grandma didn't need such innovations, but I think you will change your mind after spending 20 minutes chopping herbs for pesto.

Juicer

Most sections of this book have a juice recipe. Juicing is a great way to enjoy fruits and vegetables. Juicers are expensive but well worth the investment. When choosing a juicer, buy the most powerful machine you can afford. Other features to consider: noise and ease of cleaning.

Zester

A zester is a small hand tool that is used to remove the fragrant peel from citrus fruits. There are many styles and they all work well. It is important not to dig too deep with the zester. You only want to remove the very outside peel. The white inside pith will be bitter.

Fryer

If you don't want to eat fried food don't buy this. There are many styles available and they all do the job. Fry shortenings are problematic for health and environmental reasons. Good organic oils can be found and oil can be re-used several times. Let's face it, fried foods taste good and as a limited part of a varied diet bring some valuable enjoyment.

③

APPLES

When the apple fell on Newton's head, we may not have known where it was, but we sure knew when it was. Gravity was discovered in the autumn. Autumn is apple season and, after rubbing his melon and reinventing mechanical physics, Newton likely went home and enjoyed a glass of hard cider and a slice of pie. If you've ever had an apple tree in your yard, you know the smells of overripe apples and fallen leaves are a sure reminder of the end of summer. They are one last sweet gift that nature gives us just before entering a long winter slumber.

Apples come in many varieties. Some make great hand fruit. Some are perfect for baking and some make superior applesauce and juice. In most recipes, peeling is required. I've found that the easiest way to peel is to square the top and bottom of the apple and cut the peel off in thin vertical strips with a paring knife. It is very important that you toss the apples with lemon juice or vinegar as soon as you expose the apple flesh. Otherwise it will brown quickly and be very unattractive. I offer many recipes for apples because you will have a glut of apples late in the season. Farmers' stalls will be full and your CSA share may leave you a prodigious pile to deal with. There are many options for preserving apples, so take the late season apple glut as a gift and set some aside for leaner times.

Brown Rice Risotto With Apples

Risotto is typically made with short-grain arborio rice. The brown rice is more nutritious and will lend a distinctive nutty flavor that pairs well with the apple. It takes a little longer to cook but the results are worth the extra time. This is a satisfying entree alone or it can be paired with pork chops, a simple grilled chicken breast, or fresh trout.

Serves: 5 to 6 main course servings or 10 to 12 sides

Ingredients

1 medium onion, dice
1/2 cup red pepper
1/2 cup green pepper
2 cups cored and diced apples (any type)
1 stick plus 2 tablespoons butter
1 teaspoon Chinese five spice powder
   (available in most grocery stores)
2 cups vegetable or chicken
   stock (see Techniques)
1 cup apple cider or juice
1/2 cup cider vinegar
1 cup grated Parmesan cheese
Salt and pepper to taste

Directions

Melt 2 tablespoons of butter over medium-high heat in a large stock pot. Add onions and peppers. Cook until onions are translucent. Add remaining butter and melt fully. Add rice, salt and pepper and stir until well mixed. Reduce heat to medium-low. Add 1/2 cup stock and cook, stirring occasionally, until liquid is absorbed. Continue to add liquids, 1/2 cup at a time, stirring occasionally, until they are absorbed. This process may take 45 minutes.

When last of liquids (stock, cider, vinegar) are absorbed, taste rice to check for tenderness and seasoning. Add water if rice is not tender and continue to cook until rice is fully cooked and creamy. Stir in apples and Parmesan cheese and serve immediately. This is a large batch. Risotto can be reheated, but it is best to add a little water when you reheat.

· · · · · · · · · · · · · · · · ·

Chilled Apple Mint Salad

Any apple will work in this salad. Try mixing varieties for added interest.

Serves: 6

Ingredients

1/2 cup plain yogurt
1/4 cup chopped fresh mint
1/2 cup blanched almonds
1/4 teaspoon ground cardamom
2 lemons or limes
6 medium-size apples, core and dice
1 cup halved grapes

Directions

Zest lemons or limes into a small dish and set aside. Pulse yogurt, mint, almonds, cardamom and the strained juice from the lemons or limes in a food processor. The almonds should be chopped but still visible. Combine yogurt mixture, apples, grapes and zest in a mixing bowl and toss until well mixed. Chill for one hour before serving.

· · · · · · · · · · · · · · · · ·

Apple Compote

This is beautifully simple. It's great by itself, but really shines as an ingredient in turnovers or with ice cream.

Yields: 2 quarts

Ingredients

- 5 cups peeled, seeded and chopped/sliced apples
- 1/4 cup lemon juice
- 3 cups water
- 1-3/4 cups sugar
- 1 cinnamon stick
- 2 cloves
- 1/2 teaspoon grated nutmeg
- 1/4 cup brandy

Directions

Toss apples with lemon juice to keep them from browning. Bring water, sugar, and spices to a boil in a large pot over medium-high heat. Stir mixture to dissolve the sugar completely. Add apples and reduce heat to simmer. Cook until apples are soft. Stir in brandy and cook 2 more minutes. Remove from heat. Remove cinnamon stick and cloves. Serve warm or cold.

. . . .

Douillons or Apple Dumplings

A chilly fall night, someone you love, a glass of Riesling and a warm apple dumpling…

Serves: 8

Dough Ingredients

- 4-1/2 cups flour
- 1-1/2 cups soft butter
- 2 eggs
- 3 tablespoons milk
- 1-1/2 tablespoons sugar
- 1 teaspoon salt

Apple Filling Ingredients

- 8 small apples, sweet or tart
- 3 tablespoons butter
- 1 tablespoon sugar
- 1/2 teaspoon cinnamon

Egg Wash Ingredients

- 2 tablespoons milk
- 1 egg yolk

Directions

Preheat oven to 375 F. Place all dough ingredients into a large mixing bowl. Mix with a hand mixer until it forms a smooth dough. Roll into a ball and refrigerate for at least 30 minutes.

Peel and core the apples; keep whole. Mix together butter, sugar and cinnamon. Stuff a nugget of butter into each hollowed out core. Place in baking pan and bake for 10 to 12 minutes. Remove from the oven and cool completely.

Roll out dough into a 1/8-inch sheet, dusting with flour to keep from sticking when necessary. Cut sheet into roughly 8 equal pieces. Place an apple in the center of each piece. Pull and stretch the dough until you are able to pinch seams together with damp fingers. Squeeze dough around apple to completely seal. Cut 4 small vertical slits in the dough with a sharp knife. Mix together the egg wash and brush on the outside of the dumplings. Bake for approximately 30 minutes or until crisp and golden brown. Serve warm or cold with whipped cream or sour cream.

. . . .

Apple Fritters

The egg white folded into this batter gives the fritter a golden delicate crust.
This recipe calls for rum or calvados (yummy apple spirit). These are
optional, but lend an elegant flair to this familiar comfort food.

Note: Use caution when deep-frying.

Serves: 4 to 6

Batter Ingredients

- 2-1/4 cups flour
- 3/4 cup lukewarm water
- 2/3 cup beer
- 1/4 teaspoon salt
- 2 tablespoons melted butter
- 3 egg whites
- 1/4 cup calvados or rum
- 1-1/2 teaspoon sugar

Note: Batter keeps one week in the refrigerator.

Directions

Beat egg whites with a hand blender until stiff and peaky. Set aside.

Sift flour into large mixing bowl. Stir in water, beer and salt. Mix thoroughly with a whip or hand blender making sure to scrape flour off of the sides of the bowl. Blend in melted butter and rum or calvados. Gently fold in whipped egg whites with a wooden spoon or rubber spatula. Do not whip or blend.

. . . .

Apple Filling Ingredients

- 4 apples
- Lemon juice
- Calvados or rum

Directions

Preheat deep fryer to 350 F. It is always safest to use a commercial deep fryer. Peel apples and core with an apple corer or by hand. Slice apples into round donut-shaped disks about 1/8-inch thick. Sprinkle apple slices with lemon juice and soak for 30 minutes in rum or calvados.

Drain apple slices and dip into batter. Drop the apple slices into hot oil in batches. Do not overfill fryer. Fry the apple slices until crisp and golden. Scoop from fryer into a pan lined with paper towels to absorb excess oil.

Arrange fritters on a serving platter and dust with powdered sugar.

. . . .

Spiced Apple Chai

Chai is an Indian-influenced spiced tea. The pungent spices are relaxing and aid in digestion.
This is best with a very strong tea. I recommend a loose-leaf, eastern Mediterranean
tea, which has an earthy richness, but any black tea brewed strongly will do.

Serves: 4

Ingredients

1 cup strongly brewed black tea
8 apples, core and cut into wedges
1 fresh fennel bulb, trim stem end
   and cut into 2-inch pieces
1 golf ball-size piece ginger root, cut into chunks
1 cup milk or soy milk
1/4 cup brown sugar
1 teaspoon ground cinnamon
1/2 teaspoon ground allspice

Directions

Brew black tea in saucepan or teakettle. Stir in brown sugar and keep warm. Process apples, fennel and ginger through juicer as directed by manufacturer. Catch juice in a mixing bowl or pitcher. When the juicing is complete, stir in milk, cinnamon, allspice and tea. Serve immediately in 4 glasses garnished with apple wedges or cinnamon sticks.

Basic Applesauce

If you never had homemade applesauce, you are in for a revelation. The flavors are alive and
the sweetness is smooth. Experiment with different spice combinations and consistencies.
I like mine very roughly chopped; your infant may like it completely pureed.

Yields: 5½ pints

Ingredients

4 pounds apples
1 cup water
1/4 cup lemon juice
1/2 cup honey
Optional: 1 teaspoon cinnamon
Optional: 1 teaspoon ground cloves
Optional: 1 teaspoon ground nutmeg

Directions

Sanitize 5 half-pint (8-ounce) canning jars in a water bath. In a large pot, place all of the ingredients but the apples. Core and peel the apples. Cut them into large chunks and drop immediately into the pot. Bring to a boil over medium-high heat. Reduce heat and simmer, uncovered, for 20 to 25 minutes until apples are tender. Mixture can be canned or frozen at this point. If you would like a smoother applesauce, place in a food processor and process to the desired consistency.

Remove jars from water bath and fill with sauce to within 1/2 inch of top. Cover jars, seal, and process for 20 minutes in a boiling water bath as outlined in Chapter 7.

Gingered Apple Juice

Hoisin sauce is an Asian barbecue sauce with a hint of chili pepper and garlic. It can be found in the ethnic aisle of most supermarkets.

Serves: 2

Ingredients

6 red apples, core and cut into wedges
2 tablespoons sliced ginger root
2 teaspoons hoisin sauce

Directions

Process apple wedges and ginger through juicer as directed by manufacturer. Vigorously stir in hoisin sauce and serve in 2 glasses. This is very good over ice with a shot of brandy

From The Everyday Cookbook
· circa 1890 ·

Apple Charlotte

"Cut slices of wheat bread or rolls, and having rubbed the bottom and sides of a basin with bits of butter, line it with the sliced bread or rolls; peel tart apples; cut them small, and nearly fill the pan, strewing bits of butter and sugar between the apples; grate a small nutmeg over; soak as many slices of bread or rolls as will cover it; over which put a plate, and a weight, to keep the bread close upon the apples; bake two hours in a quick oven, then turn it out. Quarter of a pound of butter, and half a pound of sugar, to half a peck of tart apples."

Potato and Apple Soup

Serve with warm rye bread.

Serves: 5 to 6

Ingredients

- 2 onions, slice thin
- 1 pound tart apples, core, peel and roughly chop
- 2 pounds potatoes, peel and slice
- 1-1/2 cups cider
- 5 cups vegetable stock (see Techniques)
- 1 teaspoon dried oregano or basil
- 1 teaspoon ground coriander
- 2/3 cup plain yogurt
- Salt and black pepper to taste
- 2 tablespoons chopped fresh chives

Directions

Combine the onions, chopped apple and sliced potatoes in a large pot. Add the cider and bring to a boil over medium-high heat. Boil for 10 minutes, stirring occasionally. Add the stock, dried basil or oregano, and coriander. Bring back to a boil. Reduce heat, cover and simmer until everything is very tender, about 25 minutes. Pour hot soup into the bowl of a food processor and puree. You may have to do this in batches. Return to the cooking pan and stir in the yogurt. Serve very hot with a sprinkling of chives.

Sweet Apple Omelet

A hearty change of pace for a fall breakfast.

Serves: 2

Ingredients

- 2 large sweet apples, peel, core and slice
- 1/4 cup butter, divided
- 3 tablespoons sugar, divided
- 1/2 cup and 2 tablespoons heavy cream
- 3 tablespoons brandy or Calvados (French apple brandy)
- 6 large eggs

Directions

Heat 2 tablespoons of butter in a large skillet over medium heat. Add apple slices and 2 tablespoons of sugar and cook for 3 minutes until apples brown slightly. Add 1/2 cup heavy cream. Bring to a boil and then simmer until cream boils down to a thick sauce surrounding the apple slices. Add brandy or Calvados and mix thoroughly. Remove from heat and set aside.

Whisk eggs with 2 tablespoons heavy cream and 1 tablespoon of sugar in a mixing bowl. Continue to whisk eggs until they become light and frothy.

Heat remaining butter over medium-high heat in a 9-inch skillet. Pour in egg mixture and allow bottom of eggs to "set." Using a rubber spatula, push outside of eggs toward the center of the pan allowing liquid eggs to run under cooked eggs. Continue working your way around pan until most of the eggs are cooked. Carefully flip the eggs over and cook a further 2 minutes.

Pour apples on one side of eggs, fold over the other side and slide onto serving platter. Serve immediately with a sprinkling of cinnamon.

Pan-Grilled Apples With Maple Butter

Eat these alone or use to top waffles or ice cream.

Serves: 4 to 6

Ingredients

4 apples, core and cut into 1/4-inch slices
2 tablespoons butter
1 recipe maple butter (see p. 282)

Directions

Melt butter in a large skillet over medium-low heat. Add apple slices and cook about 10 minutes, stirring occasionally, until apples are soft and lightly browned. Add maple butter. Stir and toss apples until butter is melted and apples are well coated. Serve hot.

CHEF'S NOTES

1. Apples usually are categorized as eating or baking apples. Those in the former category are firm-textured and juicy but do not hold their shape well when cooked. Eating apples include Red Delicious and Gala apples. Those in the latter category tend to retain their shape and moisture when cooked. These include Golden Delicious, Bramley and Jonagold varieties. A few varieties, such as Granny Smith and Pink Lady, can do both duties.

2. Sliced apples with a selection of fine cheeses are as close to a perfect dessert as you can offer. Keep your gooey chocolate mess; I'll take fruit and cheese please.

3. Very few fruits lend themselves to savory preparations as well as apples. Add any sweet baking variety to soups, stews, meatloaf, roasts, sausage or casseroles. They blend well and carry the flavor of nearly any spice. Be adventurous and experiment.

4. Once an apple is bruised, it should be eaten immediately. It will spoil quickly. Trim off the bruised portion and eat or use in a recipe. Of course, you should always remember the "one bad apple" admonition.

5. Apples will keep for several months if stored in a cool, dry, well-ventilated place.

ARUGULA

Arugula has become synonymous with a sort of effete culinary experience. Regular folks eat salad; pretentious bores eat arugula. I'm not sure why pretentious bores should be the only ones allowed to enjoy arugula, but it may have something to do with the fact that arugula isn't really improved with the big scoop of ranch dressing, which is Joe six-pack's typical approach to anything green and not readily identifiable. Please! Please! Join us pretentious bores in the wonders of arugula. Put away your ranch dressing! Break free from the prison of iceberg lettuce and taste what has inspired all that snobbishness.

One of my favorite greens, it tastes like a funky mix of pepper and mystery. It can be used as a lettuce in a mixed salad, shredded with a knife as a garnish on fish or chicken, blended into a distinctive pesto, wilted in a hot pan for a side dish or blended into a tasty soup. Many chefs use it as a seasoning herb and its strong flavor allows that. It is available in most areas starting in late spring and remains available throughout the growing season. If your CSA grows arugula, you likely will get a lot of it. It will find a great home in any of these recipes.

Arugula and Carrot Juice

Juicing is not the best use of arugula. However, you may find prodigious quantities in your CSA box and this juice will allow you to capture its flavor and nutrients before nature reclaims them. The peppery flavor of the arugula brings a pungent jolt to plain old carrot juice.

Serves: 2

Ingredients
6 medium carrots
2 celery stalks
2 scallions, green and white
2 cups arugula, firmly pack

Directions
Cut carrots, celery and onions into pieces that will fit through your juicer. Run all ingredients through juicer according to the manufacturer's directions. Drink up and enjoy!

Wilted Arugula Sauté

Use this dish as a model for simple wilted green and pasta dishes. Nearly any lettuce or green can be substituted for the arugula and feel free to play around with different types of cheese, nuts, and other garnish ingredients.

Serves: 6

Ingredients

1 pound dry linguini
1/2 cup olive oil
4 garlic cloves, gently crush with the flat of a knife
4 cups arugula, firmly pack
1/2 cup pistachio nuts, roughly chop
1 cup grated Parmesan cheese
2 tablespoons finely-chopped basil

Note: You can use a garlic press to crush the garlic.

Directions

Bring a large pot of water to the boil over high heat. Cook linguine per package directions until tender but not soft.

While pasta is cooking, heat olive oil in a very large skillet over medium heat. Add garlic and cook for 2 minutes until it just browns. Add arugula and cook for about 30 seconds until leaves just wilt. Remove skillet from the heat.

Drain pasta completely in a colander and return to the pot. Add the arugula and garlic mixture, pistachio nuts, and 3/4 cup of the cheese to the pot; salt and pepper to taste. Toss well and serve in a decorative bowl. Top with the remaining cheese and the basil.

. . . .

Arugula Pesto

Arugula has a very distinctive flavor. Toss this pesto with fresh tomatoes and onions for a delicious fresh tomato salad. This recipe also uses pistachio nuts, which I think are the best-tasting pesto nuts, although you give up a little richness.

Yields: 3 cups

Ingredients

1-1/2 cups arugula leaves
1/2 cup basil leaves
2/3 cup shelled pistachios
8 cloves of garlic
1/2 cup stuffed green olives
3/4 cup extra virgin olive oil
1 tablespoon fresh lime juice
Dash of cumin
Dash of cayenne pepper
Salt and pepper to taste

Directions

Place all ingredients except oil in a food processor; process until smooth while drizzling in the oil. Will keep for several weeks in the refrigerator or up to a year in the freezer.

. . . .

Arugula, Fennel and Orange Salad

This might make a very interesting breakfast. Carving the orange takes a little practice; but, once you master the technique, you will find that the orange segments are a beautiful garnish on any salad.

Serves: 6

Ingredients

2 tablespoons minced shallots
3 tablespoons extra virgin olive oil
1-1/2 tablespoons lemon juice
1 teaspoon honey
2 oranges
7 cups arugula, firmly pack
1 fennel bulb
1 red onion, thinly sliced in rings
Salt and pepper to taste

Directions

Make the vinaigrette with the shallots, olive oil, lemon juice and honey as outlined in the Mulit-purpose Recipes. Set aside.

Cut a slice (the size of a half dollar) off opposite ends of the oranges with a paring knife. Stand the orange on one of the flat ends and cut away the peel and pulp from the orange with a curving vertical motion. Continue until the orange is completely peeled with very little pulp showing. Identify the segment membranes running the length of the orange and make straight cuts into the center alongside each membrane; two cuts along the inside of the membrane should free a single segment. Carefully remove the segment and set aside. Remove all segments from both oranges.

Cut the green stems with the fronds from the fennel bulb and set aside for future use. Cut the core end from the bulb and discard. Slice the bulb lengthwise in half and then slice each half again to make quarters. Slice fennel very thin across the quarters. Set aside.

In a large salad bowl, combine the arugula, fennel, red onions and half of the orange segments; salt and pepper to taste. Toss well with the dressing and pour into a decorative serving bowl. Garnish with the remaining orange segments.

. . . .

Arugula Verde Dip

You can spoon this onto a lettuce salad, but it really shines as a dip for roasted root vegetables.

Yields: 2-1/2 cups

Ingredients

3/4 cup sour cream
1/4 cup mayonnaise
1 clove garlic
1 green onion
1 tablespoon lemon juice
2 cups arugula, firmly pack
2 tablespoons tarragon
Salt to taste

Ingredients

Combine sour cream, mayonnaise, garlic, green onion, lemon juice, tarragon and 1 cup of arugula in the bowl of a food processor. Process until smooth and green. Add salt and the remaining cup of arugula. Pulse the mixture a few times, just enough to chop the arugula. Keep refrigerated.

. . . .

CHEF'S NOTES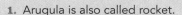

1. Arugula is also called rocket.

2. The Greek physician, Dioscorides, described arugula as "a digestive and good for ye belly." I really don't know if that's true, but anyone with that many syllables in his name needs to be taken seriously.

3. Arugula, like most greens, will not last long in the refrigerator. Use quickly or blend into a pesto (page 23) and freeze.

4. When using any green in a salad, dress at the last minute to keep the greens crisp. The salt in any dressing will quickly draw out the moisture in fresh greens.

5. Arugula's flavor is usually described as peppery and delivers a lot of flavor in a small package. Try chopping the greens fine and stuffing a pork chop or a tuna steak with a thin layer of the chopped arugula mixed with olive oil.

6. Arugula is an outstanding match with any rich strong-flavored cheese: bleu, gorgonzola, goat cheese or a well-aged Parmesan are great partners.

Arugula Salad With Blended Cucumber and Tomato

This dressing virtually is fat and sugar-free and it still tastes good. It's very good with the earthy taste of arugula, but it could be used with any leafy green.

Serves: 4

Ingredients

5 cups firmly packed arugula, tear into bite-size pieces
1 large cucumber
1 tablespoon rice wine vinegar
1 teaspoon lemon juice
2 tomatoes
1 red onion, finely chop
4 garlic cloves, mince
1 tablespoon chopped cilantro
1 tablespoon chopped basil
1 teaspoon chopped thyme
1 tablespoon Dijon mustard
Salt and pepper to taste

Directions

Peel cucumber and slice in half lengthwise. Scoop out seeds with a spoon and discard. Place in the bowl of a food processor and puree. Empty pureed ingredients into a mixing bowl.

Core the tomatoes, cut them in half and scoop the seeds out with a spoon and discard. Chop tomatoes with a knife until it is a mushy pulp. Place in the mixing bowl with the cucumbers.

Add vinegar, lemon juice, onion, garlic, cilantro, basil, thyme, mustard, salt and pepper. Stir gently until well combined.

Add arugula to the bowl with the dressing. Toss well and serve immediately on a large platter or on four individual plates.

ASPARAGUS

Asparagus once was thought to arise from ram's horns buried in the soil. It seems to me that the act of procuring ram's horns would be fraught with significant danger and sacrifice. Perhaps the bravest and noblest were required to help the asparagus along and, through these efforts, the value of asparagus was set. A trophy earned and revered.

Asparagus sits like a trophy on any plate. Where I come from, the spring finds the ditches filled with salivating wild asparagus hunters. While conflict is rare, latecomers usually are disappointed. My farmer friends tell me that it takes a real commitment to start an asparagus patch — It takes a few years to get established. But once established, it's nearly impossible to get rid of. I think the taste for asparagus develops much the same way. As children, it takes threats and negotiation to get us to nibble even small portions of asparagus. We choke it down with a frown and a screwed up face. When we grow up, we might stick a fork through someone's hand if they reach for that last stalk of asparagus on the platter.

It's appropriate that asparagus starts near the beginning of this book. It is one of the first treats that the good earth offers up to us. The season for asparagus is short, but fecund. Eat your fill — it will be gone soon.

Asparagus With Brown Butter

The French call it buerre noisette. A rich nutty toasted butter. There are few things better in the world than lightly steamed vegetables with brown butter. Asparagus is a star served this way.

Serves: 6

Ingredients
2 pounds asparagus, trim off white woody ends
1 recipe brown butter (see Index)

Directions
Bring a large shallow pan full of water to a boil over medium-high heat. Add asparagus and allow water to return to the boil. Boil for 3 to 5 minutes until asparagus is just tender. It should not collapse when squeezed between your fingers. Drain in a colander, shake dry and arrange on a serving platter. Spoon over warm brown butter and serve immediately.

Asparagus Feta Custard

This is a very rich and elegant offering that is perfect for a winter brunch or as a side dish at Thanksgiving or Easter. You might add shrimp, chicken, beef, or pork to turn this into a dinner item as well.

Serves: 8 (as a casserole or individually)

Ingredients

8 slices of French bread, 1/8-inch thick (day old if possible)
1 cup fresh asparagus, cut into ½-inch pieces
1/2 cup crumbled feta cheese
2 cups fresh chopped tomatoes
Custard
6 egg yolks
8 ounces heavy cream
1 tablespoon dried dill
Hot pepper sauce to taste
Salt and pepper to taste

Directions

Preheat oven to 350 F. Grill or toast slices of French bread until well-browned and crispy. Place slices in a single layer of a casserole dish or one in each ramekin or ovenproof bowl. Top the bread with asparagus, tomatoes, and feta cheese. Set aside.

Separate the eggs and place yolks into a medium-size mixing bowl; reserve the whites for another use. Add heavy cream and the remaining custard ingredients. Mix well with hand mixer or wire whisk for 5 to10 minutes to incorporate air into custard. This technique will make cooked custard light and airy. Fill pans with custard until all ingredients are covered. Bake, uncovered, until custard barely jiggles in the center when lightly shaken. Remove from the oven and allow cooling slightly and continuing to set. Top with sprigs of fresh dill.

. . . .

Pickled Asparagus

This will be great in February. Top with a mayo flavored with sorrel pesto.

Yields: 2 quarts

Ingredients

3 cups white vinegar
3 cups water
1/4 cup sugar
2 teaspoons salt
3 pounds of asparagus, cut to fit quart canning jars
4 cloves garlic
2 tablespoons pickling spice
12 whole black peppercorns

Directions

Sterilize quart jars in a boiling water bath. Combine vinegar, water, sugar, and salt in a saucepan and bring to a boil over medium-high heat. Boil for 3 minutes. Remove jars from boiling water and pack each jar with asparagus, tips facing up. In each jar place 2 cloves of garlic, 1 teaspoon pickling spice and 6 peppercorns. Pour vinegar mixture over the asparagus. Fill to within 1/2-inch of the top. Cover jars, seal and process for 20 minutes as outlined in Chapter 7.

. . . .

Asparagus Mousse

This is a very simple mousse recipe and can be prepared with all manner of vegetables from beets to tomatoes. This asparagus mousse is delicious and produces a beautiful pastel color that is perfect for canapés (small one-bite appetizers).

Yields: Approx. 24 ounces for about 30 canapé-size appetizers.

Ingredients

1 pound fresh asparagus
1/2 cup chopped green onion
1/4 cup mayonnaise
2 teaspoons lemon juice
2 teaspoons Dijon mustard
Salt to taste
1/2 cup heavy cream
1 egg white

Directions

Boil asparagus in salted water until tender — not mushy. Transfer asparagus to a food processor and add onions, mayonnaise, lemon juice, mustard, and salt. Process mixture until it is pureed and then transfer to a mixing bowl; cool in refrigerator.

While mixture is cooling, whip heavy cream with a hand mixer until it forms peaks that stand up in sharp points. Note: You will need to have a cold bowl and cold heavy cream to form sharp peaks.

In a separate bowl, whisk the egg white until it also forms sharp peaks. Gently mix in whipped cream and egg whites into asparagus mixture with a rubber spatula.

To serve, the mousse can be spooned out or piped out with a pastry bag (these are available in many department stores). Try any of the following, or invent a few of your own.

1. Cut cherry tomatoes in half and scoop out insides; fill with mousse and top with a sprig of cilantro.

2. Cut 1/4-inch slices of cucumber; top with mousse and plant a sliver of radish in it.

3. Cut little circles or triangles of toast; top with mousse and oven-wilted tomato (page 245).

4. Wrap mousse inside wonton skins and cook briefly in boiling water; dab with Chinese mustard.

Grilled Asparagus

This is the very best way to enjoy asparagus. For those of us in the upper Midwest, grilled asparagus is a special treat because it is one of the first items available as we unpack our outdoor grills each spring. It requires thicker spears so they don't burn and are less likely to fall through the grates. Many cookbooks will recommend peeling the stem end of the spear, but in most cases, I find this unnecessary. When prepared on the grill, the tougher skin chars very nicely and I find the crunch an exciting texture contrast to the tenderness of the tip.

Serves: 4

Ingredients

1 pound thick asparagus spears,
  cut off woody white part
1/4 cup olive oil
Kosher salt to taste
Fresh ground black pepper to taste

Directions

Preheat a gas, charcoal, or wood grill to a fairly high heat. Arrange asparagus on a baking sheet. Pour oil over spears and liberally sprinkle with salt and pepper. Allow the asparagus to marinate for an hour or so in the oil. Place the asparagus on the grill grate. Try to keep the tender tips on the outside where the heat is lower and the thick stalks on the hotter part of the grill. Turn once or twice with tongs and cook until they become a little charred on the outside and a little tender on the inside, about 10 minutes.

Remove the asparagus from the grill and arrange on a decorative platter. Top with fresh tomato bruschetta (page 246), hollandaise sauce or a little mayo mixed with herbs. Grilled asparagus is the perfect accompaniment to grilled steak, chicken, or fish.

· · · · · · · · · · · · · · · ·

Blended Asparagus Soup

This soup deserves to be shared with a very special person. It's rich, beautiful and comforting. Please don't waste it on people you don't like!

Serves: 6

Ingredients

2 pounds asparagus
4 tablespoons butter
1 cup diced onions
1 cup peeled and diced waxy potato
  such as any fingerling variety
6 cups chicken or vegetable stock (see
  Index); make sure it is relatively clear
1/4 cup chopped parsley
1 cup heavy cream

Directions

Cut off the tips of the asparagus. Boil the tips lightly in salted water, drain and cool with cold running water. Set aside for a garnish.

Cut the remaining asparagus into 2-inch chunks and cook in the same way as the tips. This will eliminate some bitterness.

Heat the butter over medium heat in a 4-quart pot and add the onions and potatoes. Cook the onions and potatoes for about 10 minutes, stirring occasionally. Add the stock, the asparagus spears (not tips), and the parsley to the pot. Simmer for about 15 minutes until vegetables are very tender. Puree the soup thoroughly in a processor or blender.

Return soup to the pot, mix in the heavy cream, and reheat. Ladle the soup into bowls and garnish with asparagus tips and chopped fresh herbs.

· · · · · · · · · · · · · · · ·

Asparagus With Egg Sauce

A rich side dish or hors d'oeuvre; this simple sauce can be used on any cooked vegetable.

Serves: 4

Ingredients

1 pound fresh asparagus, trim off white parts
Salt and black pepper to taste
2 hard cooked eggs, peel
1/4 cup salad oil (soybean or canola)
1 tablespoon rice wine vinegar
1 teaspoon Dijon mustard
1 teaspoon lemon juice
1 tablespoon chopped chives
1 tablespoon chopped parsley

Directions

Place asparagus in a large pan and cover with salted water. Bring water to a boil over medium-high heat. Once water boils, reduce heat to medium low and simmer for 5 to 10 minutes until the asparagus is just becoming tender, but still a bright green color.

Remove pan from heat, pour off water, transfer asparagus to a serving platter and set aside.

Slice the eggs in half and scoop the yolks into a fine wire sieve. Set sieve over a mixing bowl and push the egg yolks through the sieve with the back of a spoon to pulverize the egg yolks. Finely chop the egg whites with a knife or hand chopper and set aside.

Add the vinegar, mustard and lemon juice to the egg yolks. Slowly add oil while rapidly whisking the egg mixture. Continue whisking until smooth and creamy. Stir in the chopped egg white, chives and parsley.

The asparagus can be served in individual dishes or serve on a platter buffet or family style. Spoon the egg sauce over asparagus. This dish can be served warm or at room temperature.

. . . .

CHEF'S NOTES

1. The white, woody part of the stalk is good for nothing but compost.

2. Asparagus is great added to any salad or as a simple salad all its own. It should be blanched and shocked and dressed with any simple vinaigrette (see Index).

3. Don't store asparagus in a plastic bag. Store unbundled in a paper bag in the refrigerator or tip-side up in a large glass of water.

4. I don't necessarily agree with the school that claims that vegetables should always be under-cooked and crisp, but I would join that school when it comes to asparagus. Do not overcook.

5. You likely will eat all of your asparagus before your conscience demands you freeze it; however, if you do freeze, cut the asparagus into sizes to fit your containers. Blanch, shock and freeze asparagus in a single layer on a cookie sheet. After the asparagus has hardened, place in freezer containers for storage.

6. Thick asparagus are best for grilling and as a side dish. Thinner works best in chilled preparations or salads.

BEETS

I have to share that I have a queasy, emotional relationship with beets. My feelings stem from the days when I worked in a vegetable cannery while putting myself through school. The beet processing equipment would weep a gory red liquid that ran onto the floor and formed small rivulets snaking toward the floor drains. I always expected to see a chalk outline on the cannery floor. I thought of them less as food and more as victims of the machine.

Many people's exposure to beets — the perfectly spherical or geometrically round slices of unidentifiable crimson lugged out to fill an empty spot on the Thanksgiving table — is similarly impersonal. But, they really do come out of the ground and share their taste and personality with anyone willing to pay attention.

Color is one of the challenges of cooking with beets. They tend to want to dye anything they come in contact with. You'll have to keep this in mind if you mix them with any other ingredients. That being said, the dark red color is kind of sexy and exciting in its own right and the beet can be a real visual focal point on a salad or blended into a sauce. The greens are outstanding wilted or braised and are a real bonus that can be had when you procure your beets at a farmers market, CSA, or your own backyard.

Beet Salad With Mint

Voila! A roasted beet recipe.

Serves: 6

Ingredients
2 pounds roasted beets, precook according to instructions on page 32.
1 minced garlic clove
3 tablespoons olive oil
2 tablespoons red wine vinegar
Salt and black pepper to taste
1/4 cup fresh chopped mint

Directions
Place the garlic, red wine vinegar, salt, pepper and half of the mint in a large mixing bowl. Whisk all together rapidly while drizzling in the olive oil. Add the beets and toss well. Place in a serving bowl and sprinkle with the remaining mint.

Roasted Beets

Roasted beets are great by themselves but also are the starting point for many beet recipes.

Serves: 4 to 6 (as a side dish)

Ingredients
    1 pound fresh beets
    2 tablespoons olive oil
    Salt and fresh ground pepper to taste

Directions
Preheat oven to 400 F. Scrub the beets well, remove the green tops and cut the large beets so that the whole batch is about the same size. This will help ensure even cooking. Arrange in a single layer on a shallow baking sheet. Drizzle olive oil over beets and sprinkle with salt and pepper to taste. Lightly toss beets to coat with the oil. Place in oven and roast for 1 to 2 hours until the beets are soft like a baked potato.

Remove from the oven and allow cooling until the beets can be handled. Peel the beets by rubbing off the skin, or slice off with a paring knife. Use the beets in a recipe or reheat and serve drizzled with a little butter or olive oil.

. . . .

Beet and Chickpea Dip

Serve this with hunks of torn pita bread.

Serves: 6

Ingredients
    15-ounce can chickpeas with liquid
    1 large onion, diced
    3 large beets, peel and cook
    1/2 cup tahini (sesame seed paste)
    3 cloves garlic, mince
    1/4 cup lemon juice
    1 tablespoon ground cumin
    1/4 cup olive oil
    1 tablespoon fresh chopped parsley

Directions
Place all ingredients except olive oil in the bowl of a food processor. While blending, drizzle in the olive oil. Process until very smooth. Transfer to a shallow serving dish. Drizzle with olive oil and chopped fresh parsley.

. . . .

Beet Coulis

The color of this is stunning. For a simple "Wow" presentation, fill the bottom of a plate with beet coulis, place a piece of grilled sole or flounder in the center and drizzle little dots of heavy cream on the beets.

Yields: 1 quart

Ingredients

2 pounds fresh beets, peel and
  cut into 3/4-inch pieces
Water or vegetable stock (see p. 289)
1 teaspoon sugar
1 tablespoon cider vinegar
Salt to taste
White pepper to taste

Directions

Place the beets in a medium saucepan. Add just enough water or stock to cover beets. Bring to a boil over medium-high heat and cook until beets are very tender. You may have to add a little water to keep beets covered.

Place cooked beats and cooking liquid in the bowl of a food processor. Add sugar and vinegar. Process until very smooth. Add salt and black pepper to taste. If coulis is too thin, return to stove and reduce to desired thickness. If too thick, add a little stock or water.

. . . .

Beet Curry

This is a cook-friendly vegan curry with very few ingredients. Add or subtract chilies to bring the desired heat. Serve over basmati rice.

Serves: 8

Ingredients

2 cups dried red lentils, rinse and remove debris
8 cups vegetable stock (see p. 289)
10 small/medium beets, peel and
  cut into 3/4-inch cubes
5 cloves garlic
1 tablespoon turmeric
2 tablespoons cumin
1 tablespoon coriander
2 small dried chili peppers (4 inches long), crush
1 tablespoon salt
2 tablespoons oil

Directions

Bring lentils and stock to a boil in a large pot over medium-high heat. Reduce heat and simmer, stirring occasionally. While lentils simmer, heat olive oil in a large skillet over medium-high heat. Sauté garlic in oil, add beats and reduce heat to medium low. Continue to cook, stirring occasionally, for about 5 minutes. Add contents of the frying pan to the simmering lentils. Add cumin, coriander, dried red chilies and salt to taste. Simmer for about 20 to 30 minutes, until the lentils start to disintegrate.

. . . .

Beet Risotto With Chard

You easily could substitute beet greens for the Swiss chard in this recipe. This risotto would be a gorgeous accompaniment to simple grilled sole.

Serves: 6

Ingredients

2 tablespoons olive oil
1 cup chopped onion
1 cup uncooked Arborio rice
1 tablespoon minced fresh ginger
2 teaspoons finely chopped fresh rosemary
1/2 cup dry white wine
3 cups peeled and finely chopped beets
1/4 teaspoon kosher salt
2 -1/2 cups vegetable stock (see p. 289)
6 cups finely sliced Swiss chard
1/2 cup crumbled goat cheese
1/4 cup chopped and toasted walnuts

Directions

Preheat oven to 350 F. Lay chopped walnuts in a single layer on a cookie sheet. Toast until lightly browned, about 10 minutes.

Heat oil in a large stockpot over medium-high heat. Add onions and cook until soft. Add rice, ginger and rosemary; stir to coat with oil and cook 2 more minutes. Add wine; cook 3 minutes or until liquid is nearly absorbed, stirring constantly. Add beets, water, salt, pepper and stock; bring to a boil. Cover, reduce heat and simmer 20 minutes or until beets are tender, stirring frequently. Add water if necessary. Stir in chard; cook 5 minutes. Add cheese, stirring until blended. Sprinkle each serving with toasted walnuts.

· · · · · · · · · · · · · · · ·

Sautéed Baby Beets With Onions

Consider this as an alternative to potatoes at breakfast.

Serves: 4

Ingredients

1 pound baby beets, remove greens
1 medium onion, dice or slice
1/4 cup vegetable stock (see p. 289)
2 tablespoons butter
Salt and pepper to taste

Directions

Par-cook beets in salted water 3 to 4 minutes until just tender on the outside. Remove from heat, drain and run under cold water to stop cooking.

Melt 1 tablespoon of butter over medium-high heat in large skillet. Add beets to the skillet. Salt and pepper to taste. Cook beets until tender and brown. Add onions and cook until soft. Add vegetable stock and bring to a boil. Remove from heat and stir in remaining butter to thicken sauce. Serve immediately.

· · · · · · · · · · · · · · · ·

Chlodnik

The Polish version of chilled beet soup. All of the ingredients for this soup should be available in early summer. This dish initially may be arresting to an American pallet, but I promise a nice surprise for your senses if you try it. It's refreshing and distinctive. Serve this with a bowl of hard-cooked eggs and kosher salt for an Old World lunch.

Yields: 2 quarts

Ingredients

1 pound fresh beets, peel and grate
1 pint vegetable stock (see p. 289)
5 radishes
2 red or green scallions
2 tablespoons chives
1 tablespoon chopped fresh parsley
1 lemon
1-1/2 cups plain natural yogurt
1/4 cup sour cream

Directions

Bring stock and grated beets to a boil in a saucepan over medium-high heat. Cook until beets are soft. Remove from heat and allow to slightly cool. Place cooled saucepan in refrigerator to chill completely for at least 2 hours. Meanwhile, dice (1/4-inch thick) radishes, scallions, chives and parsley. Once beets are chilled, blend in yogurt, sour cream and lemon juice. Stir until well mixed. Stir in chopped vegetables. Return to refrigerator for at least 30 more minutes. Serve in shallow bowls, garnished with a wedge of hard-cooked egg and a sprinkling of chives or a few chive flowers.

· · · · · · · · · · · · · · · ·

Beet Greens Stewed With Drippings

This certainly is not a particularly healthy dish, but it is rich and comfortable. Cook the beet greens in the fat and juices from roasted chicken, pork or beef. Yummy!

Serves 4

Ingredients

1/4 cup beef, pork or chicken drippings
1 pound beet greens
1 tablespoon cider vinegar
Salt and pepper to taste

Directions

Trim the stems from the greens. Remove roast from the pan, set aside and keep warm, leaving the oven on. If the drippings have dried while the meat was cooking, simply pour 1/4 cup of water into the hot roasting pan and scrape with an egg turner. Add the greens, cover the pan and cook for 10 minutes. When greens are wilted, transfer to a serving bowl, season with salt and pepper and sprinkle with vinegar. Serve as a side to the roast.

· · · · · · · · · · · · · · · ·

Minted Beet Juice

I was reluctant to try beet juice, but I must admit this didn't entirely suck.

Yields: 2 servings

Ingredients
4 small beets (not baby beets)
2 oranges, peel and cut in wedges
2 tablespoons mint leaves

Directions
Scrub beets and cut into large chunks that will fit into juicer or blender. Process beets, oranges, and mint leaves through juicer. Serve in 2 glasses garnished with a sprig of mint.

. . . .

Ukrainian Borscht

During beet season, compare this soup with chlodnik. There are countless borscht recipes. This one is hearty with a mild sweetness. Many borscht recipes include cooked meat. Try leftover pieces of chopped breakfast sausage or pot roast.

Yields: 3 quarts

Ingredients
4 white or yellow onions, chop
2 cups diced potatoes (any kind)
1 cup grated carrots
2 cups diced tomatoes
2 cups chopped or shredded cabbage
2 cups grated beets
4 cloves garlic, smash and roughly chop
1 tablespoon lemon juice
1/4 cup canola oil
1 tablespoon sugar
Salt and pepper to taste
3 tablespoons chopped fresh dill
Sour cream for garnish

Directions
Heat oil in a large skillet over medium-high heat. Add onions and cook until soft. Add carrots, tomatoes and beets. Add lemon juice, stir and cook for 2 more minutes. Cover and cook for 5 to 10 minutes. Remove from heat and set aside. Place potatoes in a large pot and cover with water; bring to a boil. Cook until potatoes are soft. Add cabbage, beet mixture, garlic, sugar, and salt to taste. Add enough additional water to cover all vegetables. Bring back to a boil for 5 minutes. Turn off the heat, stir in the dill. Cover and allow soup to steep for 2 hours. Reheat to serve or store in refrigerator for up to 3 days. Serve hot, garnished with a dollop of sour cream.

. . . .

Beet Puree With Yogurt

An interesting dip or sauce for poached fish.

Yields: 1 quart

Ingredients

1 pint plain yogurt
8 small beets
1 tablespoon tahini (available in the ethnic section of a good grocery store)
1 garlic clove
2 tablespoons lemon juice
Salt and pepper to taste

Directions

Line a sieve or colander with a couple of layers of cheesecloth. Place the colander over a sink or bowl and while yogurt is draining, scrub the beets well and cut them into roughly 1-inch chunks. Place in a food processor and add the garlic, tahini, lemon juice and salt and pepper to taste; process until smooth. Add yogurt and pulse until well combined. Serve immediately or chill.

· · · · · · · · · · · · · · · ·

Warm Beet Slaw With Toasted Nuts

This simple one-pan recipe makes a very nice side dish to accompany beef or pork. Use pine nuts if you want to add some elegance, but walnuts, or even peanuts will work as well.

Serves: 4

Ingredients

1 pound beets, remove greens
2 tablespoons nuts
2 tablespoons butter
2 teaspoons balsamic or red wine vinegar
Salt and pepper to taste

Directions

Peel the beets with a vegetable peeler or knife. Grate the beets using a hand grater or a food processor and set aside. Heat a large skillet over medium-high heat. Add the nuts and cook, stirring occasionally, for 1 to 2 minutes until nuts are lightly browned. Remove the nuts from the pan and set aside. (You may skip this step if you use nuts that are already roasted or toasted.) Reheat the skillet over low heat and melt the butter. Add grated beets, 2 tablespoons of water and a little salt. Cover and cook for about 10 minutes, stirring occasionally, until the beets are tender. Remove from heat and stir in the vinegar. Salt and pepper to taste. Pour into a serving bowl and top with the toasted nuts.

· · · · · · · · · · · · · · · ·

Smashed Beets With Bleu Cheese Butter

A savory side that goes well with roast beef or chicken.

Serves: 4

Ingredients

1 pound fresh beets, remove tops
  and cut into 1-inch chunks
2 tablespoons butter, room temperature
2 tablespoons crumbled bleu cheese
2 tablespoons chopped fresh cilantro
Salt and pepper to taste

Directions

In a small bowl, gently mix together butter, bleu cheese, and cilantro and set aside. Cook beet chunks in boiling salted water until tender enough to mash with a fork. Drain beets and place in serving dish. Quickly mash with the back of a fork before they cool. Drop spoonfuls of the bleu cheese butter on top of the beets and sprinkle liberally with fresh ground black pepper.

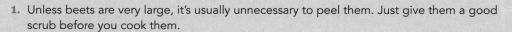

CHEF'S NOTES

1. Unless beets are very large, it's usually unnecessary to peel them. Just give them a good scrub before you cook them.

2. Beet greens can be used as a salad lettuce, but there are better choices for the greens. Beet greens cooked quickly in a very hot pan with a little butter, salt and pepper is a far better choice.

3. While beet greens will be palatable after a stay in the fridge, they are truly a revelation prepared as soon as possible after they are harvested.

4. Small beets can be frozen whole after a short (5 to 10 minutes) bath in boiling salted water.

5. Much like potatoes, beets can be microwaved. Simply place them in a bowl covered with plastic wrap and microwave on high for 5 minutes. Turn beets over, recover, and cook a further 3 to 5 minutes. Let them sit in the covered bowl until cool enough to handle.

6. Beets are typically red, but golden and marbled "Chioggio" varieties are turning up at many farmers markets and in CSA shares.

BELL PEPPERS

Bell peppers are indispensable in cooking. The pungent sweetness delivered by bell peppers in both long and short cooking dishes is key in many ethnic cuisines from Cajun to Italian to Eastern European. They can improve any salad, soup or stew and are also a very common salad ingredient. Roasting peppers brings them near perfection and, in my mind, is the best way to use them in most preparations. They are now found in an array of colors that can really bring life to any dish you use them in. Peppers will be available in bunches from mid-summer on.

Down on the Farm

While my apprentice, Brent, and I were setting irrigation systems in the back garden, a gopher ran out into the open, looked over his shoulder at us and (this part is my imagination at work) hollered, "Watch this," and dove under the row cover that I thought was hiding my corn. He emerged some minutes later and ran over to disappear down his hole. Gophers 1, Humans 0. When I took up the row cover today to look at my baby beets in one of the middle gardens, I discovered a gopher bored a hole under the cover and enjoyed a smorgasbord of six kinds of beet greens, eating them down to within a quarter inch of the ground. I had moved the beets to the back garden so the chipmunks wouldn't steal them. Gophers 2, Humans, 0. The chipmunks up front, while still eating the oats in the mulch, have turned to strawberries for dessert. Only last week, the resident black cat demonstrated his ability to catch and dispatch chipmunks. Today, however, when the chipmunk, who resides under the north porch, returned to his abode from the strawberry patch across the driveway carrying a strawberry as big as his head, the same cat, who lay lounging not six feet away, watched the larceny with bemused boredom. It's not always easy to find good help.

— David Peterson, Maplewood Farms

Chicken a la Bohemienne

This is a simplified version of a French version of chicken with rice. It's a fine late-summer supper. Farmers markets and CSA food boxes should have beautiful peppers, tomatoes, and fennel available in abundance and variety.

Serves: 4

Ingredients

4 medium-size (5 to 6 ounces) boneless, skinless chicken breasts
3 tablespoons olive oil
3 medium peppers (sweet or hot), slice in strips
1 onion, dice
1 small fennel bulb, slice in strips
2 cups diced fresh tomato
2 cloves garlic, mince
1/4 cup dry white wine
1/4 cup tomato juice
Salt and pepper to taste
2 cups warm prepared rice

Directions

Preheat oven to 350 F. Liberally season both sides of chicken breasts with salt and pepper. Heat 2 tablespoons olive oil in a large skillet over medium-high heat. Place chicken in hot oil and cook until well browned. Turn chicken and brown the other side. Remove partially cooked chicken from pan and place in an ovenproof casserole dish. Set aside.

Add the remaining olive oil, onions, peppers, and garlic to hot skillet and cook until soft. Add white wine and tomato juice to pan and allow to a boil vigorously while stirring for a minute to loosen browned bits off the bottom of the pan. Add tomatoes and warm through. Pour mixture over chicken and bake uncovered in the oven until chicken reaches an internal temperature of 180 F, about 15 to 25 minutes.

Serve over rice on individual plates or family style on a large platter. Sprinkle with fresh herbs.

Green Pepper and Thyme Juice

If available, lemon thyme is perfect with this. You could also use several sprigs of rosemary in place of the thyme.

Serves: 2

Ingredients

3 large green peppers, remove stems and seeds
1 cup green grapes
2 stalks celery
6 sprigs of fresh thyme

Directions

Cut peppers and celery into pieces that will fit into your juicer or blender. Process peppers, grapes, celery, and thyme in juicer. Serve in 2 glasses and garnish with a sprig of thyme.

Eggs Piperade

*A Basque version of scrambled egg — serve this when your CSA
share or garden is full of tomatoes and bell peppers.*

Serves: 4

Ingredients

1 pound fresh tomatoes, core and roughly chop
1/2 pound red or green bell peppers,
    remove seeds and cut into strips
2 cloves garlic, roughly chop
2 tablespoons olive oil
Salt and pepper
1/2 cup diced ham
4 large eggs

Directions

Heat 2 tablespoons of olive oil in a large skillet over medium heat. Add peppers, garlic, tomatoes and ham; season with salt and pepper. Bring to a boil, reduce heat and cook slowly for 30 minutes, stirring occasionally, and adding water a little at a time if mixture gets too dry.

Beat 4 eggs together in a bowl. Increase heat on tomato mixture and pour eggs into pan. Gently stir until eggs are set but still a little soft. Serve immediately with a sprinkling of fresh chopped parsley.

Bell Pepper and Eggplant Relish

*Serve on an antipasto platter or on toasted slices of French bread for
an elegant appetizer. This also makes an attractive gift jar.*

Yields: 2 pints

Ingredients

6 Asian eggplant, slice into 1/2-inch slices
6 bell peppers, any color
1 cup olive oil
3/4 cup cider vinegar
4 cloves garlic, lightly smash
    with the flat of a knife
1/2 teaspoon pickling salt
1 red chili, split in half and remove seeds
12 basil leaves

Directions

Preheat broiler or barbecue grill. Lightly brown slices of eggplant on both sides over flame of grill or on cookie sheet under broiler, about 10 minutes a side. Set aside. Do the same with peppers, but make sure the skin blisters all the way around all peppers. It should take about 30 minutes. Place peppers in a plastic bag and seal (see roasted peppers on p. 288). Let sit 20 minutes. Remove from bag, and gently remove the skin, discard the stem, remove the seeds and quarter the peppers. While the peppers are sweating, heat the oil in a skillet. Add vinegar, garlic, salt and red chili. Bring to a boil, reduce heat and simmer for 5 minutes. Remove from heat. Arrange eggplant slices, bell peppers and basil leaves in alternating layers in 2 sterilized, and still hot, pint jars. Pour hot oil mixture over eggplants and peppers leaving a 1/2-inch gap between the top of the liquid and the lid of the jar to allow for expansion. Cover and jars and process in a water bath for 20 minutes (see Chapter 7). Let flavors marry for 14 days before serving.

Bean and Bell Pepper Ragout

A ragout is a thickened stew. You can use any type of bean for this dish; 1 cup dry yields about 2-1/2 cups canned. If you prefer not to cook the beans, you will need to make that adjustment.

Serves: 4 to 6

Ingredients

1 cup dried beans (flageolet, black, cranberry or adzuki are examples)
2 tablespoons olive oil
2 cloves garlic, mince
1 red onion, cut into 1/2-inch thick strips
2 bell peppers, any type, remove stems and seeds and cut into 3/4-inch chunks
3 tomatoes, core and roughly chop
2 tablespoons tomato paste
2 cups vegetable stock (see p. 289)
2 tablespoons chopped fresh basil
1 cup stuffed green olives
2 teaspoons brown sugar

Directions

Cook the beans as directed (see p. 287). Heat olive oil in a large skillet over medium heat. Add onions and garlic and cook until onion is soft, 2 to 3 minutes. Add the peppers and cook, stirring occasionally, for 5 minutes. Add the tomatoes, paste, and stock. Stir, and return to a boil. Reduce heat, cover and simmer for 30 minutes. Remove cover and stir in beans, basil, olives and brown sugar; season with salt and pepper. Serve warm with crusty French bread or warm flat bread.

- - - - - - - - - - - - - - - - -

Red Pepper Coulis

This coulis can be made with fresh or roasted red peppers (see p. 288). The fresh coulis will be brighter but the roasted coulis will have a richer taste.

Yields: 1 quart

Ingredients

1 pound sweet red peppers, dice into 1/2-inch pieces
Water
Salt
White pepper

Directions

If peppers are fresh, place in a saucepan and add just enough water to boil them. You may skip this step if the peppers are roasted. Boil peppers until soft. Scoop peppers from water and place in bowl of food processor. Process until very smooth adding a little water if necessary. Season with salt and white pepper.

- - - - - - - - - - - - - - - - -

Romesco Sauce

There are many recipes for this sauce made of red pepper and nuts. It is truly an all-purpose sauce. This is a simple and rich version.

Yields: 2 cups

Ingredients

1 cup roasted red peppers (see Appendix)
1/3 cup almonds
1 clove garlic
1 cup mayonnaise
1 tablespoon red wine vinegar
Salt

Directions

Place the almonds and garlic in a food processor and process until the nuts are finely chopped but not pasty. Add remaining ingredients and process until well blended.

· · · · · · · · · · · · · · · · ·

Warm Grilled Bell Pepper Salad

In this dish, the peppers are the star not just an ingredient — An easy and soulful barbecue side.

Serves: 6

Ingredients

4 large bell peppers, any color
1 recipe Criolla sauce (see p. 246)

Directions

Get a charcoal or gas grill very hot; a little flame coming off the coals is preferred. Place whole peppers over the hottest part of the flame. Grill each side until well charred and blackened. It should take 10 to 15 minutes to grill on all sides. Once all of the peppers are well charred, remove them from the grill and seal in a large plastic bag. Let the peppers sweat in this bag for 20 minutes. Remove the peppers. Peel the peppers but don't be too fussy about it. It's all right to leave some of the char on. Cut each into 4 large quarters. Discard the stem and place in a large mixing bowl. Add the Criolla sauce and toss until completely mixed.

· · · · · · · · · · · · · · · · ·

Down on the Farm

July 28

Our four-legged and furry friends have been behaving reasonably well this last week, although a brazen deer walked right down the middle of an ex-garlic bed that we had weeded, raked, out and planted to oats as a cover crop — only about 30 feet from the house. Yesterday I found a small, very excitable and more than a little confused rabbit, who had entered garden one through a hole in the deer fence and, under the pressure of my presence, couldn't seem to remember where the hole was. To his credit, he seems to have found his hole again and during the night slipped in and chewed on the tops of a bunch of beets. Today when my intern saw him back inside the fence, either his memory had improved or she was less terrifying than I — he found his portal and exited forthwith.

— David Peterson, Maplewood Gardens

Shrimp With Tomatoes and Bell Peppers

A quick, simple shrimp dish for a quick supper

Serves: 4

Ingredients

3 tablespoons olive oil
1/2 red onion, dice
1 tablespoon minced garlic
1 cup cored and chopped fresh tomatoes
1 cup chopped roasted red peppers (see p. 288)
2 tablespoons chopped fresh cilantro
1 pound medium (21 to 25 count)
    shrimp, peel and devein
1 teaspoon olive oil
Salt and pepper to taste
2 cups cooked rice

Directions

Heat 2 tablespoons olive oil in a large skillet over medium heat. Add the onions and cook for 2 minutes, stirring frequently, until onions are soft. Add the tomatoes and cook for 5 minutes, stirring frequently. Stir in roasted red peppers and fresh cilantro and cook for 2 minutes. Remove from heat and set aside. Heat the remaining tablespoon of oil in separate skillet over medium-high heat. Add the shrimp and cook for 2 to 3 minutes, stirring frequently, until shrimp are cooked through. Pour the pepper mixture into the pan with the shrimp. Allow to come to a boil, drizzle in the teaspoon of olive oil and salt and pepper to taste. Serve warm over rice.

CHEF'S NOTES

1. If kept cold, bell peppers can keep for up to two weeks.

2. Bell peppers come in a rainbow of colors, and that is one of their assets. Try various colors of pepper to enliven the visual appeal of any dish.

3. To freeze peppers, simply remove the core, seeds and inner membranes. Dice, slice or leave whole as you desire and freeze in freezer bags. They may be blanched briefly to allow easier packing.

4. The best way to store a glut of bell peppers is to roast them and can or freeze them. The uses for roasted peppers are endless and you will be sure to consume them well before the start of the next season.

From *The Everyday Cookbook*
· circa 1890 ·

Piccalilli

"One peck of green tomatoes; (if the flavor of onions is desired, take eight, but it is very nice without any); four green pepper; slice all, and put in layers, sprinkle on one cup of salt, and let them remain over night; in the morning press dry through a sieve, put it in a porcelain kettle and cover with vinegar; add one cup of sugar, a tablespoon of each kind of spice; put into a muslin bag; stew slowly about an hour, or until the tomatoes are as soft as you desire."

BLACKBERRIES

The good people of northern Wisconsin have a term of endearment for the weekenders from Chicago and Milwaukee that swarm the ditches and woods around state and county roads in late summer hunting wild blackberries. They call them "pickers." This may seem innocent enough until you realize that the term lyrically replaces a slightly less endearing term in casual speech. Nonetheless, the wild blackberries are so good that our "pickers" are more than happy to endure this native scorn.

Sparkling Blackberry and Mango Juice

For an elegant brunch treat, replace the sparkling water with champagne.

Serves: 4

Ingredients
3 pints blackberries
4 mangoes or 2 cups frozen mangoes
1/2 peeled lemon
1-1/2 cups sparkling water

Directions
Peel mangoes and cut into 2-inch slices. Discard the stone. Process blackberries, mangoes and lemon through juicer. Pour juice into 4 glasses. Stir 3 ounces of sparkling water into each glass and serve immediately.

Minted Blackberries

This is a simple and effective way to dress any fresh berry. Serve small portions of these as a first course at lunch or as a light dessert.

Serves: 6

Ingredients
3 cups fresh blackberries
2 tablespoons sugar
1 tablespoon finely chopped mint
2 teaspoons lemon juice

Directions
Gently toss all ingredients in a mixing bowl. Let rest at room temperature for at least 30 minutes to allow flavors to marry.

Blackberry Preserves

Fruit and sugar — uncomplicated and very good.

Yields: 4 pints

Ingredients
3 quarts blackberries
6 cups sugar

Directions
Place a large saucepan over medium-low heat. Rinse berries under cold water and place in pan. Cook berries, stirring occasionally, until they burst and the juice is extracted. Add sugar, increase heat to medium-high and bring to a boil. Reduce heat and simmer, uncovered, for 25 minutes. Pour the preserves in sterilized pint jars leaving 1/3-inch space between preserves and top. Cover and seal the preserves. Process preserves in a hot water bath for 15 minutes according to the directions outlined in Chapter 7, preserving.

. . . .

Blackberry Coulis

A dramatic sauce on any dessert.

Yields: 3 cups

Ingredients
3 cups fresh blackberries
1/4 cup sugar
Lemon

Directions
The technique is the same as for strawberry coulis. Wild blackberries, if mature, are sweeter than strawberries and require less sugar. If you are a "picker" and, insist on picking immature berries early in the season, you will have to add more sugar.

. . . .

Blackberry Curd

Curd eats like a pudding but is a wonderful dressing for a piece of sponge cake or shortcake.

Yields: 2 cups

Ingredients

- 1-3/4 cups fresh blackberries
- 3/4 cup superfine sugar
- 1/2 cup butter
- 1 teaspoon lemon zest
- 1 tablespoon lemon juice
- 4 egg yolks

Directions

Sterilize a 1-pint canning jar in a boiling water bath. Combine blackberries, sugar, butter, zest, and lemon juice in saucepan over low heat. Gently stir until butter has melted and sugar has dissolved. Simmer for 5 minutes and remove from heat. Beat the egg yolks with a whisk. Slowly add the berry mixture a little at a time. Return pan to low heat and cook for 2 minutes, stirring constantly. Be careful not to let the mixture boil. Pour curd into sterilized jar. Cover and seal as outlined in Chapter 7. Will keep 2 months (unopened) in the refrigerator.

CHEF'S NOTES

1. Blackberries freeze well and will keep for months in a frozen state. To freeze the blackberries: rinse well; remove the tops; spread on a sheet pan; put into the freezer; and tumble into a freezer bag.

2. Blackberries will mold fast and should be eaten or used in a recipe within 2 days.

3. This is for all you "pickers" out there: Do not pick until berries are very black and soft. They will be very tart until then.

4. For a very simple dessert, marinate berries in champagne for an hour, place in small dishes or wine glasses and top with a dollop of mascarpone cheese.

BOK CHOY

I took my first cooking job to make a little beer money. I would like to say that it was a grand youthful ambition (that would have been to be an NFL running back, a dream dashed when I realized I was slow and lazy). But the truth is, I knew nothing about cooking, although I did appreciate eating when I first stepped into a professional kitchen. One of the exotic discoveries I made was bok choy. Bok choy was not wrapped in foil and did not come in a can. Plus, what a cool name! Later in the evening, while I was out spending my beer money on beer, I would try to get the attention of pretty young women by talking about bok choy with a pretentious air. It surprised me at the time that they did not find bok choy as interesting as I did, a puzzlement that continues to this day.

Bok choy has a sharp celery-like taste. It does well quickly stir-fried, yet is not so fragile that it can't take long slow cooking. The stems are crunchy and require longer cooking than the bright leaves. Many stir-fry recipes call for a two-stage cooking method to account for this. Baby bok choy starts to appear in late spring. It is outstanding braised whole and served as a side vegetable. The larger varieties appear later in the season and are particularly good in the fall.

Bok Choy With Butter and Oyster Sauce

Here's a tasty bok choy stir-fry. Oyster sauce lends this a distinctive richness and is available in the Asian section of most supermarkets.

Serves: 4

Ingredients
2 tablespoons white wine
1 tablespoon tamari
1 tablespoon oyster sauce
2 tablespoons salad oil
2 pounds bok choy, cut into 1/4-inch slices
2 tablespoons butter

Directions
Heat oil in a large skillet over medium-high heat. Add bok choy and sprinkle with salt. Cook, stirring constantly, for 2 to 3 minutes. Add tamari, oyster sauce and butter. Continue to cook for 2 more minutes, stirring constantly, until bok choy gets just tender. Serve immediately.

CHEF'S NOTES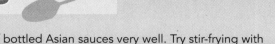

1. Surprise! — Bok choy carries the flavor of bottled Asian sauces very well. Try stir-frying with oyster sauce, fish sauce, or any variety of chili paste, black vinegar, hoisin sauce or sesame oil.

2. Bok Choy does not freeze well. If you would like to preserve it, you might make a pickle out of it. Use it in place of Napa cabbage in Kim Chee (page 63).

3. You can extend the storage life of bok choy by separating the stems and greens, keeping the stems in the crisper and soaking the greens in water. Bok choy should keep 1 to 2 weeks this way.

Braised Bok Choy

My CSA supplies me with delightful baby bok choy that are perfect for braising whole. The technique is similar in all of these recipes. You also can braise the larger sizes you might find in the supermarket, but you may have to remove the thick stalk end and shred for slaw or prepare separately.

Serves: 6 as a side

Ingredients

6 baby bok choy
2 cups vegetable stock
1 cup white wine
Salt and pepper to taste

Directions

Arrange the bok choy in a shallow baking dish. Cover with stock and wine. Bok choy should be about half covered with liquid. Season the bok choy with salt and pepper to taste. Seal pan with plastic wrap and seal plastic wrap with foil. Bake for 30 minutes to an hour. Stalk end should still have some crunch and the leaf end should be wilted but not falling apart. Serve hot as a side dish or room temperature as a unique salad.

Poached Bok Choy With Sesame

The Asian ingredients are readily available at a well-appointed supermarket.

Serves: 4

Ingredients

1 large bok choy
3 tablespoons Chinese black vinegar, red
   wine vinegar, or balsamic vinegar
2 teaspoons honey
1/2 teaspoon chili paste
2 teaspoons sesame oil
2 teaspoons sesame seeds
Salt to taste
2 tablespoons chopped cilantro

Directions

Cut 1 inch off of the stem end of the bok choy. Cut the leaves from the stalks. Cut the greens into 1/4-inch ribbons and cut the stalks into 1/4-inch slices. Keep them separate. In a mixing bowl, combine vinegar, honey, chili paste, sesame oil, sesame seeds, and salt. Stir until well mixed. Place bok choy stems in 1/2-inch deep water in a large skillet. Bring to a boil over medium-high heat, cover and cook for 4 minutes. Add the leaves and cook 4 minutes more. Pour off the water and transfer bok choy to the mixing bowl. Toss all together and serve immediately.

Bok Choy Ginger Stir Fry

This is best with baby heads of bok choy, but the result is still delicious with large heads roughly chopped. It requires a short period of focused attention, so don't walk away.

Serves: 6

Ingredients

1-1/2 pounds bok choy
2 tablespoons canola or peanut oil
2 cloves garlic, minced
1 teaspoon grated fresh ginger
3 tablespoons water, white wine, or
   vegetable stock (see p. 289)
Kosher salt to taste
1/2 tablespoon sesame oil

Directions

If using baby bok choy, trim off just the very bottom of the stem end and split the heads down the center lengthwise. If using larger heads, cut off bottom and chop across the width in 1/2-inch slices. Rinse and dry thoroughly.

Start with a cold wok or large skillet and add oil, garlic and ginger. Turn heat on to medium-high and stir in garlic and ginger as it heats up. This will allow you to infuse the oil with flavor without scorching the ginger and garlic. When garlic starts to sputter and sizzle, add bok choy.

Toss and vigorously stir the bok choy in the hot oil to coat each leaf for 15 to 30 seconds. Pour in water, wine, or stock; cover, and let cook for 1 minute. Transfer to serving bowl, season with salt and drizzle with sesame oil.

Down on the Farm

My love affair with bock choy began when I saw its round little seed, so much easier to plant than the flat seeds of lettuce ... and it germinated quickly and decisively, something no carrot could offer. In warm weather it presented itself upright and easy to harvest with knife or scissors. I quickly realized that when left to go to seed it produced lovely tall fronds of long thin pods that could hastily be gathered and effortlessly crushed to release their tiny seeds. The pods being long meant that one could gather a handful and drop it in a colander. With a few shakes of the wrist, seeds separated from chaff and you were done, and oh sooo much seed from a tiny patch. It didn't end there, but began again in November after the CSA was finished and I began to put the finishing touches on the late fall beds. The purple choy that was so tasty in October when I harvested it for the boxes had begun to sprout new leaves beneath its cover, oh the delight! This little gem was not done yet. After winters chill had past and March had come all blustery and wet, I pulled back a bit of flattened row cover, near the greenhouse, and what should be sprouting but perfect flat rosettes of dark green leaves. My god ... fresh greens for dinner, hungrily we gathered them, emerald against the dark soil and flaunting their color against the dried brown grasses and leaves. My love you have come home, and it is spring again!

— Andy Hazzard, Hazzard Free Farm, First Hand Harvest CSA

Fried Choy Greens With Cashews

This is an attention grabbing salad to unveil at your next dinner party.

Serves: 4

Ingredients
12 ounces bok choy greens, cut
    into very thin ribbons
2 cloves garlic, shave very thin
Salt to taste
1 teaspoon sugar
1/4 cup chopped cashews
Oil for deep frying

Directions
Preheat fryer to 350 F. Make sure bok choy leaves are very dry to avoid spatters. Drop greens, a handful at a time, into hot oil. Fry until they become a dark forest green, about 30 seconds. Drain each batch in a pan lined with paper towel. Fry greens a handful at a time until you get to the last batch. Add the shaved garlic to the last batch. Drain the last batch and place all in a large mixing bowl. Sprinkle with salt, sugar, and cashews. Toss well and serve in small bowls or soup cups.

BRUSSELS SPROUTS

Sprouts are believed to have been cultivated in the Roman Empire. They have a long tradition in European cookery and were first grown in large quantities in 16th century Belgium (which is why they are called "Brussels" sprouts). They are one of the vegetables most likely to get the stink eye from those that don't like them and often are used as a punishment for-ill behaved children. That is so unfair. These humble baby cabbages deserve more love than that. People who don't like vegetables always point to the Brussels sprout as the hellish experience they just can't revisit. The person who does not like vegetables will not likely be reading this book, but if this page somehow finds its way under the nose of a sprout hater, I would say to them "grow up." Sprouts are adult food and require you to embrace subtlety. The following recipes should help you to mature.

Brussels sprouts should be available from mid-summer on. They are one of the last vegetables available in late season markets and are truly outstanding after a late season frost has sweetened them up.

Brussels Sprouts With Gremolata

Simple and clean. Prepare this with very fresh sprouts.

Serves: 4 as a side

Ingredients
1 pound Brussels sprouts
2 tablespoons olive oil
1 recipe gremolata (see page 131)

Directions
Bring a pot of lightly salted water to a boil over medium-high heat. Add Brussels sprouts and allow the water to come back to a boil. Reduce heat and simmer, uncovered, for 8 to 10 minutes until sprouts are just tender. Drain in a colander and shake dry. While sprouts are cooking, prepare the gremolata. Stir olive oil into gremolata and mix completely. Place warm Brussels sprouts in a serving dish and spoon over gremolata. Serve immediately.

Pickled Brussels Sprouts

These are great right out of the jar, but they are usually found floating in a cocktail.

Yields: 4 pints

Ingredients

- 2 pounds Brussels sprouts
- 2 cups vinegar
- 1 cup lemon juice
- 1/2 teaspoon cayenne pepper
- 9 sprigs of dill
- 4 cloves garlic
- 1 teaspoon mustard seed

Directions

Sanitize 4 pint canning jars in boiling water. Bring 2 quarts of lightly salted water to a boil over medium-high heat. Peel loose outer leaves off of the Brussels sprouts and cut a 1/8-inch deep cross in the bottom of each sprout. Blanch sprouts in boiling water until just tender, 5 to 10 minutes depending on size, and shock (see p. 287) sprouts in ice water. In a separate pan, combine 2 cups of vinegar, lemon juice, cayenne and half of the dill. Bring to a boil over medium heat and cook for 5 minutes. Pack Brussels sprouts equally into hot sanitized jars. Place 1 clove garlic, 1 sprig of dill and 1/4 teaspoon mustard seeds in each jar. Fill each jar with the hot vinegar mixture to within 1/4 inch of the top. Cover, seal and process 15 minutes in a boiling water bath as outlined in Chapter 7.

. . . .

Sautéed Brussels Sprouts With Cinnamon and Grapes

This recipe was a favorite of a Haitian chef I once worked for. It has an unusual flavor combination to an American palette, but is a very unique way of preparing a vegetable that most often is just overcooked, salted, and poured in a bowl.

Serves: 6

Ingredients

- 1 pound Brussels sprouts, shred or shave
- 1 cup red grapes cut in half
- 1 tablespoon cinnamon
- 2 tablespoons chopped flat leaf parsley
- Salt and pepper to taste
- 2 tablespoons butter or olive oil

Directions

Shred or shave the sprouts in a processor or use a knife if you're skilled. Melt the butter or heat the oil on medium-high heat in a shallow thick-bottomed pan. Add the shredded sprouts and sauté lightly while stirring and tossing. It's okay to brown them a little, but the idea is to just warm them. Sprinkle in the cinnamon and season with salt and pepper. Toss with the cut grapes and chopped parsley. This side goes well with pork or lamb.

. . . .

Chilled Sprouts With Goat Cheese and Tomatoes

Use this as a model for creating your own "sprout salads."

Serves: 4 to 6

Ingredients

5 cups Brussels sprouts, trim for cooking
1 cup diced fresh tomatoes
1/2 cup goat cheese, cut into small nuggets
2 cloves garlic, minced
1/2 cup fresh basil, cut into ribbons
1/4 cup extra virgin olive oil
2 tablespoons white wine or sherry vinegar
Salt and black pepper to taste

Directions

Bring a large pot of lightly salted water to a boil over medium-high heat. Add the Brussels sprouts and allow water to return to a boil. Cook 3 to 5 minutes until sprouts are just cooked, but still bright green. Drain in a colander and rinse thoroughly with cold water to stop the cooking. Shake dry and allow sprouts to chill completely in the refrigerator. Whisk together vinegar and oil in a large mixing bowl. Add sprouts, tomatoes, garlic, basil, salt and pepper. Toss well. Add goat cheese and gently toss being careful not to mash the cheese too much. Serve immediately.

Seared Brussels Sprouts

The rich caramel brown on the sprouts from searing is magical. You can prepare this recipe using any skillet but the best results can be achieved with an old-fashioned cast-iron skillet.

Serves: 4 to 6

Ingredients

3 tablespoons butter
2 tablespoons olive oil
4 garlic cloves, slice thin
1 pound Brussels sprouts, cut in
    half through the stem
1/4 cup pine nuts
Salt and black pepper to taste

Directions

Heat 2 tablespoons of butter and the olive oil in a large skillet over medium heat. Add garlic and cook, stirring frequently, until lightly browned (about 3 minutes). Remove the garlic with a slotted spoon and set aside. Reduce heat to low and place sprouts, cut side down in a single layer. Sprinkle on pine nuts, salt, and pepper. Cook without turning for 10 to 15 minutes. The bottoms should turn crispy and brown while the sprout becomes warm and tender. Transfer sprouts to a serving dish. Add 1ttablespoon butter to the pan with the remaining pine nuts. Stir together and cook for 1 minute. Add garlic and pour over sprouts. Serve immediately.

CHEF'S NOTES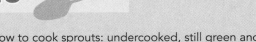

1. There are two schools of thought on how to cook sprouts: undercooked, still green and crunchy or well cooked, dark and mushy. Mushy is all right if you don't have teeth.

2. If you are cooking sprouts whole, peel the loose wrapper leaves and cut a shallow cross in the core end. This will allow the somewhat tough core to finish cooking the same time as the leaves do.

3. Brussels sprouts can be frozen. Blanch for 5 minutes and shock to stop the cooking (see p. 287). Freeze in airtight containers or freezer bags.

4. Toss warm or cold cooked Brussels sprouts with any vinaigrette (see Chapter 5) for a simple side dish.

5. Sprouts will last quite a long time in the refrigerator, but they become less sweet and bitterer with time.

BURDOCK

Burdock is something new to me. When I discovered that it is the root from the plant that grows those nasty little burrs that cling to and ruin so many pairs of my socks and cotton gloves after working in the woods, I vowed that my revenge would be to cook and eat it. Occasionally found at farmers markets it always can be found in any patch of trees with a fair amount of under-growth. A search online will give pointers on properly harvesting the root. Also known by its Japanese name Gobo, burdock has been consumed in Japan for centuries. Burdock has a distinct flavor, like a cross between parsnip and horseradish. It must be cooked and, once peeled, needs to be kept in water, like raw potatoes, to avoid browning. It can be used just like any root vegetable, and brings its own personality to a braised pot roast or stew.

Roast Pork With Burdock and Leeks

This is a simple pot roast. You could substitute beef or game meat for the pork.
The earthiness of burdock is perfect for stews, braised meats and pot roasts.

Serves: 6 to 8

Ingredients

2 pounds pork loin or pork butt
2 tablespoons dried thyme leaves
1 cup sliced leeks
2 cloves garlic smash with the flat of a knife
2 tablespoons butter
2 tablespoons flour
2 cups burdock root, dice into 1/2-inch pieces
2 cups carrots, dice into 1/2-inch pieces
4 cups vegetable stock (see p. 289) or water
Salt and pepper to taste

Directions

Liberally rub the meat with salt, pepper and thyme. Heat a large Dutch oven over medium-high heat. Place the meat in the pan and sear thoroughly on all sides. Don't be afraid to get the meat very brown and for bits to burn on the bottom of the pan. When roast is well browned on all sides, remove from pan and set aside.

Reduce heat to medium and melt the butter. Add leeks and garlic. Cook both, stirring occasionally, until leeks are soft. Add flour, salt and pepper to cooked leeks and stir until well mixed forming a thick paste. Raise heat to medium-high. Pour in stock or water and bring to a boil, stirring vigorously to break up flour lumps. Scrape the bottom of the pan to loosen the tasty burned bits. Remove pan from heat and replace the roast in the center of the pan. Spread burdock and carrots around pan.

Cover and place in a 350 F oven for 2 to 3 hours until meat is very tender. Serve roast pork sliced and smothered with the sauce.

Sweet and Spicy Burdock

This is the classic Japanese technique for burdock. The key to success with this dish is to cook down the finishing sauce until it becomes a syrupy glaze.

Serves: 4 as a side

Ingredients

- 2 medium burdock roots
- 1 tablespoon toasted sesame oil
- 1 tablespoon tamari or soy sauce
- 1 teaspoon rice wine vinegar
- 1 tablespoon honey
- 1/4 teaspoon crushed red pepper

Directions

Mix together tamari, vinegar, and honey in a small bowl and set aside.

Scrub burdock with a nylon brush to remove any soil. Whittle thin sticks of burdock, as though sharpening a pencil. Try to keep them a consistent thickness to ensure even cooking. Heat the sesame oil over high heat in a wok or large skillet. Add the burdock and stir-fry for 3 to 4 minutes until it just softens. Add the crushed red pepper and the tamari mixture. Continue to stir-fry over high heat until the sauce becomes a shiny glaze on the burdock. Serve immediately.

Burdock Refrigerator Pickle

This is an interesting alternative to pickled ginger with sushi.

Yields: 1 quart

Ingredients

- 4 cups burdock, scrub well and whittle into small matchsticks
- 1 cup cider vinegar
- 1 cup water
- 2 tablespoons allspice
- 2 bay leaves
- 2 tablespoons thinly sliced fresh ginger
- 1 teaspoon ground cloves
- 1 teaspoon Dijon mustard
- 1 teaspoon salt

Directions

Bring 2 quarts of water to a boil over high heat. Add burdock, reduce heat, and simmer uncovered for 20 to 30 minutes until burdock is soft enough to bite through easily. Drain the burdock in a colander and place in a glass quart jar. While the burdock is cooking, bring the water and vinegar to a boil over high heat. Add the remaining ingredients and stir to combine. Pour mixture into the jar with burdock. Cover jar and refrigerate for at least 1 day before serving. Will keep refrigerated for several months.

CHEF'S NOTES

1. For an interesting side or garnish, shave the burdock into thin chips with a vegetable peeler and fry in hot oil until golden and crisp. Season with salt.

2. It is not necessary to peel burdock, but you should scrub the root with a scrub brush until all the dirt and soil are removed, unless you like the taste of dirt.

3. Unless using in a long-cooking stew or braise, burdock needs to be sliced thinly or chopped in small pieces to cook completely. It is fibrous and requires a fair amount of cooking.

CABBAGE

The Romans believed that cabbages rose from Jupiter's sweat when confronted with a difficult riddle. That legend reminds me of a story told regularly during holidays at my mother's house. It related to my brother-in-law having dinner with our family for the first time and being served some type of cabbage soup. He hated cabbage, but thought it politic to quell his nausea and swallow the whole bowl. I'm sure he sympathized with Jupiter and his beads of sweat that day and, perhaps, wished that Jupiter had sweat chocolate chip cookies or beer instead. If you're like him, you might want to skip this chapter. The rest of us will enjoy cabbage without you.

Whether used in a slaw, sauerkraut, or Asian stir-fries, the versatile cabbage can take on very different personalities. We stuff cabbage leaves and stuff things with cabbage leaves. They are familiar, comfortable, abundant, inexpensive, and keep for a long time. The humble cabbage has sustained and enriched folk populations the world over for centuries. Cabbage deserves a book of its own. Alas, we only have space for these few recipes.

Braised Red Cabbage

Braised red cabbage is the classic sidekick to wild game. Pair this with duck, venison or pork roast.

Serves: 8

Ingredients

1 head red cabbage (3-1/2 pounds), shred with a knife, food processor or cabbage shredder
1 tablespoon butter
2 onions, slice thin
1/2 cup red wine vinegar
3 tablespoons brown sugar
Salt and pepper to taste
Optional: 4 slices chopped bacon or 2 tablespoons olive oil

Directions

Cook bacon in a large pot over medium-low heat until crisp, about 8 minutes. Scoop out bacon with a slotted spoon and set aside (if you would like a vegetarian dish, replace the bacon with 2 tablespoons olive oil). Add butter to the pan, increase heat to medium and add onions. Cook onions, stirring occasionally, until browned (about 12 minutes). Stir in cabbage, vinegar, brown sugar, salt and pepper. Bring to a boil, reduce heat, cover and simmer 1 to 1-1/2 hours, stirring occasionally, until cabbage is tender. Remove from heat and transfer to a serving bowl. Garnish with cooked bacon.

Simple Sauerkraut

When I was a boy, I remember being terrified by the whispering crock of sauerkraut residing under my Polish grandmother's basement stairs. I'm still not sure that sauerkraut doesn't have a soul, but you don't have to be Dr. Frankenstein to bring it to life — just mix a little cabbage and salt.

Yields: 25 pounds

Ingredients
    25 pounds fresh cabbage
    3/4 cup pickling salt

Directions
Clean any wilted wrapper leaves from cabbage heads. Quarter or halve the cabbages, remove the core and shred very thin with a knife or processor. Mix cabbage and salt in batches — 3 pounds cabbage to 2 tablespoons salt — and let wilt for a few minutes before packing. This allows you to pack cabbage without bruising or breaking the cabbage.

Pack batches into a large crock or jar. Tamp down each batch with a spoon or your hands until liquid comes to the surface. Fill the container with cabbage to within 4 inches of top.

Tuck a few sheets of cheesecloth over surface of cabbage to keep off pests and set a plate or cover on top that just fits inside, exposing as little of the cabbage to air as possible. Place just enough weight on cover to bring level of brine up to, but not over, cover and store to ferment in an out of the way place (like under grandma's stairs) with a room temperature of 65 F to 75 F.

The whispering gas bubbles signal that fermentation is occurring. Adjust weight occasionally to make sure cover is not submerged. Let it ferment until bubbling stops, about 5 to 6 weeks.

Once fermentation is complete, kraut will keep in the refrigerator for several months and can be frozen indefinitely. Kraut also can be preserved using the hot-pack canning method (see Chapter 7).

. . . .

Cabbage and Apple Salad

Make this salad with red or green cabbage. The apples add a natural sweetness to this slaw.

Serves: 8

Ingredients
    1-1/2 pounds red or green
        cabbage (1 small head)
    3 green apples
    2 tablespoons lemon juice
    6 scallions, thinly sliced
    1/2 cup packed mint leaves
    2 cloves garlic, roughly chop
    1 teaspoon sugar
    3/4 cup olive oil
    Salt and pepper to taste

Directions
In the bowl of a blender, combine lemon juice, scallions, mint leaves, garlic, sugar, salt, and pepper. Blend mixture until smooth. While blender is on low, slowly drizzle in olive oil. Set aside.

Cut cabbage into quarters and remove the woody core. Shred cabbage with the shredding attachment of your food processor or cut into very thin ribbons with a sharp knife; place into a large mixing bowl.

Cut the apples into quarters and trim out seeds. Slice quarters into thin 1/8-inch slices and add to the cabbage. Pour in dressing and toss until cabbage and apples are completely coated. Set aside one hour in the refrigerator to allow the flavors to marry. Serve well chilled in a decorative bowl.

. . . .

Alsatian Fried Eggs

Try this for a new twist on breakfast or brunch.

Serves: 4

Ingredients

2 cups prepared sauerkraut
8 to 12 ounces ham steak, slice
    into 1/4-inch thick pieces
4 large eggs
6 ounces brown, cream, or sausage
    gravy (see Chapter 5 for recipes)
2 chopped green onions
Salt and pepper to taste

Directions

Heat the sauerkraut on the stovetop, in the oven, or in the microwave. Pan-fry the ham in a large skillet over medium-heat until warm and lightly browned. Set aside and keep warm.

Fry eggs in butter to desired doneness; salt and pepper to taste.

Place sauerkraut on shallow serving platter. Alternate ham and fried eggs in shingles over sauerkraut. Surround platter with a border of your favorite gravy. Garnish with chopped green onions.

. . . .

Bigos

Bigos is the Polish national dish. You can make this simplified version in your crockpot. Traditionally, it was made with large kielbasas and wild game. Any meat that can hold up to long cooking is acceptable. This version uses beef shoulder and kielbasa. The measurements are approximate and amounts are largely determined by the size of your pan or crockpot.

Yields: 4 quarts

Ingredients

2 pounds sauerkraut, drain and rinse
1 medium onion, dice
2 granny smith apples, peel, core, dice and
    sprinkle with lemon to inhibit browning
1 pound beef chuck, cut into 1-inch cubes
1 pound Polish kielbasa, cut into 1/2-inch slices
1 cup dried or fresh mushrooms (any type)
4 to 6 cups meat or vegetable stock (see p. 289)
Black pepper to taste
1 stick butter
1/2 cup all-purpose flour

Directions

Preheat oven to 350 F. Mix the sauerkraut with diced apples and place a layer of the mixture into the bottom of a large Dutch oven or casserole dish. Place a layer of beef and sausage chunks on top of kraut. Sprinkle a few of the mushrooms over meat and pepper liberally. Continue to layer sauerkraut, meat, and mushrooms in this manner until pan is nearly full, finishing with sauerkraut. Add stock until it just covers the sauerkraut. Cover and cook in the oven for 3 hours until meat is very tender.

While dish is cooking, melt butter in a heat-proof bowl and mix with flour to form a paste. Set aside.

When dish is done, remove the pan from the oven and add 2 cups of liquid from the pan to butter and flour mixture. Stir until smooth and pour back into the pan. Gently stir this gravy into the whole pan and return to the oven for 30 more minutes.

. . . .

Cabbage Kofta

Kofta are Indian vegetable fritters. They come in countless varieties and an enterprising cook could find a home for almost any vegetable in a golden kofta once the ingredients and technique are mastered. Some of the ingredients may require a little legwork, but Indian spices and ingredients are becoming much easier to find in decent markets and co-ops.

Serves: 4

Ingredients

3-1/2 cups finely shredded cabbage
2 jalapeno peppers, mince fine
1 tablespoon fresh grated ginger
1/4 cup grated coconut
1 teaspoon turmeric
1 teaspoon garam masala*
3 tablespoons chopped fresh cilantro
Salt to taste
1 teaspoon baking powder
1 cup chickpea flower*
Oil for frying
* Chickpea flour and garam masala are Indian ingredients available in the ethnic section of many supermarkets and specialty stores.

Directions

Preheat fryer to 375 F. Combine cabbage, jalapenos, ginger, coconut, turmeric, garam masala, cilantro, baking powder and salt. Toss ingredients together until well mixed. Add chickpea flour and knead mixture together by hand. Working quickly, form mixture into 8 portions and roll each into nuggets about 1-1/2-inches long. Slip the koftas into the hot oil and fry for about 8 minutes. The koftas will sink at first and then return to the surface. Turn them with a wooden spoon to make sure all sides fry. Remove from fryer and drain on paper towel. Serve with Spiced Tomato Gravy (see p. 247).

Kimchee

A spicy Korean sauerkraut; I love this stuff in place of lettuce on tacos. This version is a refrigerator pickle, but many canned kimchee recipes are available for the curious cook.

Yields: 1 quart

Ingredients

1 pound Napa cabbage leaves, slice into 1/2-inch wide strips
1 carrot, cut into 1/8-inch slices
1 pound radishes, cut into 1/8-inch slices
2 scallions, thinly chop
1/4 cup soy sauce
2 tablespoons honey
3 tablespoons cider vinegar
1 teaspoon fresh grated ginger root
4 cloves garlic
4 dried cayenne peppers, snap in half

Directions

Combine cabbage, carrot, radishes, scallions, soy sauce and 1/2 cup water in a bowl. Toss ingredients and cover with a loose fitting piece of plastic wrap. Let set at room temperature overnight.

Sterilize a 1-quart canning jar in a boiling water bath. Drain liquid from cabbage mixture into a separate bowl. Add honey and vinegar to the liquid and stir together. Add ginger, garlic and peppers to the cabbage mix and toss together. Remove jar from water bath and fill with vegetables. Pour liquid over vegetables. Add water if needed to cover vegetables. Cover jar but don't screw lid tight. The seal must breathe a little. Allow to ferment at room temperature for 4 to 5 days. The liquid should bubble and sour. Cover jar tightly and refrigerate. Kim Chee will keep for at least 2 months.

CHEF'S NOTES

1. Freeze the whole head of cabbage overnight when using the leaves for stuffing. It saves time and when you thaw the next day the leaves will be tender and ready to roll.

2. If kept in a cool dark place, cabbage can keep for several months. However, it will emit strong odors during storage..

3. To freeze, blanch either shredded cabbage or wedges until the desired tenderness and shock in ice water (see p. 287). Freeze in proper containers or in sturdy freezer bags.

4. While red cabbage is colorful and tasty, be mindful of the fact that it will leach that red color into slaws and salads overnight.

5. To shred cabbage with a knife, first quarter the head and cut diagonally across the base to remove the thick core. Hold cabbage firmly against cutting board with the flat side down. Cut cabbage as thin as possible along the cut sides. You may have to rotate the wedge to the other side to finish shredding. Repeat with all four quarters. Or just use the shredding attachment on your food processor.

CARROTS

Imagine you were given a carrot for the very first time as an adult. It would be a revelation. It's a vegetable that we don't have to force children to eat and even macho carnivores have been known to crunch happily away at a plate of carrots. Because they are so popular, carrots are also taken for granted and seen as boring. But we should all shake off our carrot ambivalence and realize that the carrot is an ingredient in more recipes than any other vegetable but onions and garlic. It has an almost fruitlike sweetness, bold, exciting colors and an exciting toothiness and texture. Carrots come in many colors and are available in many sizes. You will see small carrots about mid-summer and they remain available well into the fall. Rarely will you see the large carrots you find in the supermarket in your CSA box or at a farmers market, but that's all right, smaller carrots are more flavorful and versatile. They are wonderful raw, cooked, juiced, pureed, roasted and steamed and they freeze and can well. It might be the perfect vegetable.

Butter Poached Carrots With Raisins

Try this as an alternative to green bean casserole or scalloped corn at the next family gathering. You can make it ahead and reheat it slowly in the oven just before serving.

Serves: 4

Ingredients

- 1 pound carrots, cut into 1/2-inch slices
- 2 tablespoons butter
- 2 tablespoons flour
- Water
- Salt and pepper to taste
- 1/2 cup raisins
- 1 tablespoon chopped fresh mint

Directions

Melt butter in a large saucepan over medium-high heat. Add carrots and stir-fry for approximately 2 to 3 minutes. Sprinkle flour into pan and stir until carrots are well coated. Fill pan with enough water to just cover carrots. Salt and pepper the carrots to taste. Stir carrots to mix flour and water, cover and reduce heat. Simmer for 15 minutes. Remove cover and stir in raisins. Continue to simmer until carrots are tender, adding more water if sauce gets too thick.

Serve piping hot with a garnish of chopped mint.

Charred Carrot Soup

Serve this soup in late summer when wonderful sweet carrots and fresh cucumber are plentiful. This recipe is most successful with the small multi-colored carrots that are common at farmers markets, your backyard garden and in your CSA box. It is unnecessary to peel the carrots before you grill them. The char from grilling adds a robust perfume to this very sensuous soup and the cucumber garnish adds great contrast in both color and texture.

Serves: 6 to 8

Ingredients

2 pounds small carrots
3 medium cloves garlic
1 onion, diced
1 cup diced celery
1 cup peeled and diced kohlrabi
4 tablespoons butter
1/4 cup flour
5 cups vegetable or chicken stock
1 bay leaf
2 whole cloves
1 cinnamon stick
1 cup heavy or light cream
Salt and pepper to taste
Optional: 1/4 cup sherry

Directions

Grill or broil carrots until well charred. Roughly chop carrots after they have cooled and set aside.

Wrap the bay leaf, cloves and cinnamon in a small piece of cheesecloth and tie securely.

Melt butter over medium-high heat in a thick-bottomed 5-quart saucepan. Add garlic, onion, celery, and kohlrabi and sauté until onions are soft. Sprinkle flour into the pan and stir until vegetables are covered. Continue to cook flour for a few minutes stirring constantly. Add stock while stirring until the flour dissolves. Add bay leaf, cloves, cinnamon bundle and sherry (if desired) to the saucepan. Bring to a boil and simmer for 20 minutes.

Add the chopped carrots including as much of the char as possible, bring back to a boil, and simmer 10 more minutes. Remove seasoning bundle. Puree mixture in a blender or food processor until smooth and return to saucepan. Heat the soup to boiling and stir in the cream. Salt and pepper to taste.

Serve immediately in shallow bowls and garnish with a spoonful of cucumber pistachio relish (see p. 107).

· · · · · · · · · · · · · · · · ·

Carrot Slaw With Oranges

A simple buffet or potluck salad

Serves: 6 to 8

Ingredients

3-1/2 cups fresh carrots, peel and shred
3 large oranges
2 red onions, slice in thin rings
1 cup lemon vinaigrette (see p. 279)

Directions

Peel and separate orange segments. Clean out as much pith as possible and clean out any seeds. Dice the oranges. Place orange pieces and carrots in a large mixing bowl. Add vinaigrette and toss well. Transfer mixture to a serving bowl and top with red onion rings. Sprinkle with chopped fresh mint or parsley.

· · · · · · · · · · · · · · · · ·

Carrots Vichy

"Vichy" describes a method of cooking carrots with sugar and baking soda. The baking soda gives it an interesting sharp flavor but I think it softens the carrots too much. I'll stick with regular old salt for seasoning.

Serves: 8 as a side dish

Ingredients

2 pounds baby carrots with a little green left on (you may leave the peel on)
Water
1 teaspoon salt
1 teaspoon sugar
2 tablespoons butter
1 tablespoon chopped parsley

Directions

Place the carrots in a large skillet. Fill the skillet with water to just cover the carrots. Add salt and sugar. Place skillet over high heat until water boils, reduce heat to medium-low and continue to simmer until the water completely cooks away. Remove skillet from heat and place carrots in a serving dish. Scatter small pieces of butter over carrots and sprinkle with parsley.

Down on the Farm

July 21

The cool-weather plants are doing exceptionally well. The spinach has been the best I have ever seen, the lettuce keeps on producing, cutting after cutting, and the potatoes are amazing. I traded garlic for the potatoes in your CSA box this week. A fellow certified organic farmer, who has grown potatoes all his life, tells me that this might be the best crop he has ever grown. Carrots are a lot less impressed with the conditions than the potatoes. I have planted four times in six different locations in three different gardens, and none of the plantings have germinated normally. I have never experienced this much lack of success with carrots in my 26 years of gardening, but it seems that there is a first time for everything.

— David Peterson, Maplewood Gardens

Curried Carrot Dip

Sweet and spicy, spread this on crackers or serve with warm pita bread or tortillas.

Yields: 4 cups

Ingredients

3 large or 6 to 8 baby carrots
1 onion, diced
2 oranges
1 tablespoon prepared curry powder
1 tablespoon water
3/4 cup plain yogurt
1/4 cup chopped fresh basil
2 tablespoons lemon juice
Hot pepper sauce to taste
Salt and black pepper to taste

Directions

Place the diced onion in a large skillet. Peel and grate the carrots with a hand grater and place in pan with the onions. Zest both oranges into the pan, slice them in half and squeeze in the juice. Add curry powder and water. Bring ingredients in pan to a boil. Boil over high heat, reduce heat, cover, and simmer for 10 minutes or until carrots are tender.

Remove carrots from heat and scoop into a food processor. Process until mixture is smooth. Transfer to a mixing bowl, cover with plastic wrap and chill in the refrigerator for an hour.

Stir in yogurt, basil and lemon juice. Season to taste with salt, pepper and hot pepper sauce.

Dip will keep up to 7 days in the refrigerator.

CHEF'S NOTES

1. To maintain the crispness of peeled or cut raw carrots, immerse them completely in cold water. Carrots will stay crisp for several weeks.

2. At the market look for carrots with the greens attached. If the greens look fresh you can be sure the carrots are fresh. The leafy fronds from the greens can be chopped up and used like a fresh herb.

3. If you've never had fresh vegetable juice, start with carrot juice — it's wonderful.

4. Carrots can be stored like potatoes and onions for several months, but you can also freeze them for extended storage. Peel, cut into your preferred shape, blanch and shock (see p. 287). Freeze in appropriate containers.

5. Experiment with the various sizes and colors of carrots available at your market. They have subtle differences and the variety of colors can be stunning in a medley or salad.

CAULIFLOWER

"Cauliflower is nothing but cabbage with a college education."
— *Mark Twain*

It's sometimes hard to love cauliflower. Too many tired vegetable platters and overcooked bags of frozen florets have chased away any romance cauliflower may have once had in our personal vegetable mythology. That's unfortunate because its subtle musky flavor is truly noble. Much of our ambivalence is due to its drab whiteness. It only becomes visually stimulating as a counter point to other more vibrant colors and, perhaps appropriately, its flavor functions much the same way — a sturdy carrier for flashier more gregarious flavors. In that role, the cauliflower stars. It absorbs sharper flavors and mixes its own humble perfume into surprising experiences. The recipes for whole heads of cauliflower may reawaken that dormant love. They can make wonderful culinary conversation pieces on the family table or at a cocktail party buffet.

Eat cauliflower raw or cooked, pureed, piping hot, chilled or at room temperature. It is very forgiving to inexperienced cooks and lends itself to experimentation for the more adventurous. In high season, cauliflower is abundant and one may be challenged to find a use for all of it. The following recipes will help overcome that challenge

Oven-Roasted Cauliflower

This is so simple that I'm hesitant to call it a recipe. It works best with smaller heads of cauliflower that can be roasted whole or cut into halves. Once roasted, you can serve as a side or cool and use as the centerpiece for a simple salad.

Serves: 6 to 8

Ingredients
4 small or 2 large heads cauliflower
Olive oil
Coarse salt

Directions
Preheat oven to 400 F. Trim leaves and stalks from cauliflower and cut larger heads in half. Arrange on a baking sheet, brush with olive oil and sprinkle with coarse salt.

Roast until soft and well browned, 20 to 30 minutes. Serve. It's that simple!

Whole Cauliflower With Curried Tomato Sauce

You may see snow-white softball-size heads of cauliflower at your market or in your food box. These are perfect for cooking whole and displaying with a savory sauce. Carve wedges and serve for a very dramatic presentation.

This attractive centerpiece vegetable can be served with dinner or as part of a buffet. The seasoning ingredients in the tomato sauce are a form of garam masala, which is an Indian spice blend. You can find many variations of garam masala in a well-appointed grocery store or you can make your own.

Serves: 4 to 6

Ingredients

1 medium-size cauliflower
1-1/4 pounds fresh tomatoes, core and quarter
1/4 cup water
1 bay leaf
12 whole peppercorns
4 tablespoons melted butter
1/2 teaspoon cumin
1 teaspoon ground coriander
1/4 teaspoon cayenne pepper
1/4 teaspoon ground fennel
1/4 teaspoon mustard powder
1/4 teaspoon turmeric
1/2 teaspoon salt
1/2 teaspoon brown sugar
1/2 cup plain yogurt
2 tablespoons chopped cilantro
Kale leaves or leaf lettuce for presentation

Directions

Trim base leaves and stems from cauliflower. You may leave the small leaves that are wrapped tight in the heads. Take a paring knife and carve a wedge out of the stem, being careful not to pare so deep as to detach the florets. This will allow the florets to finish cooking at the same time as the interior of the head. Place stem-side down in a pot of cold salted water covering the head. Bring water to a boil, cover and simmer for 15 to 25 minutes until cauliflower is nearly tender.

While cauliflower is cooking, place the tomatoes in a shallow pan with 1/4 cup water, bay leaf and peppercorns. Simmer for 10 to 15 minutes until tomatoes break down into a bubbly sauce. Force this mess through a fine strainer with the back of a ladle or spoon to extract the sauce and separate out the peel, seeds, bay leaf and pepper. Set sauce aside and discard the remainder.

Remove the cauliflower from the pot and drain in a colander. Mix ground spices in a dash of water to from a paste. Heat butter over moderate heat in a saucepan and add spice paste. Fry this mixture, stirring constantly for about 30 seconds to enhance the spices. Add the tomato sauce and cook until sauce is the thickness of your average salad dressing.

Arrange kale leaves or leaf lettuce on a round serving platter and place cauliflower in center. Spoon tomato sauce over cauliflower head and top with a dollop of yogurt mixed with chopped cilantro. Cut and serve in wedges like a cake.

Cauliflower and Penne Sauté

Green cauliflower is particularly attractive, if you can get it, but the recipe works just as well with white cauliflower or even with broccoli. The strong flavors from the garlic and anchovies bring alive the more subdued cauliflower, so if you don't like anchovies, you will have to replace them with a similar bold taste — capers or perhaps feta cheese.

Serves: 4 to 6

Ingredients

1 pound cauliflower or broccoli,
   break into large florets
1/3 cup extra virgin olive oil
6 anchovy fillets, minc
4 cloves garlic, mince
1/4 teaspoon crushed red pepper
1 pound penne or similar tube pasta
Salt and pepper to taste
2 tablespoons chopped fresh parsley
1/4 cup shredded Parmesan cheese or
   seasoned bread crumbs (for topping)

Directions

Bring a large pot of salted water to boil and cook large cauliflower florets until they are tender, but not soft. Remove from heat, fish out cauliflower pieces with a slotted spoon and immerse in ice water to stop cooking. Bring water back to a boil and add the pasta, cooking until al dente.

Roughly chop cauliflower into ¼-inch pieces and set aside.

While pasta is cooking, heat olive oil in a large skillet over medium heat and add minced garlic, anchovies and crushed red pepper. Brown garlic slightly. Add cauliflower pieces and toss to coat with oil and warm through. Salt and pepper to taste. Add a splash of water to pan and keep warm over low heat until pasta is done.

Drain pasta in a colander and add immediately to cauliflower sauce. Add chopped parsley. Toss or stir gently until pasta is well coated. Plate immediately and top with Parmesan cheese or bread crumbs.

· · · · · · · · · · · · · · · ·

Braised Cauliflower With Olives

You can use any type of olive but a flavorful kalamata or gaeta will really make the cauliflower sing.

Serves: 4

Ingredients

1 pound cauliflower florets, remove core
   and stems; reserve for another use
3 tablespoons olive oil
2 garlic cloves
1/4 cup water
1/2 cup pitted and roughly chopped olives
Pinch of salt
2 tablespoons chopped fresh parsley

Directions

Gently smash the garlic with the flat of a knife and roughly chop. Set aside.

Heat a large skillet over medium heat. Add olive oil and cauliflower and cook, stirring occasionally, for 5 minutes until cauliflower browns. Add the garlic, salt and water. Reduce heat to low, cover the pan and cook for 10 minutes. Add olives and cook, uncovered, stirring occasionally for 3 more minutes.

· · · · · · · · · · · · · · · ·

Cream of Cauliflower and Gorgonzola Soup

You will see cream soups throughout this book. They are usually pureed, so it is a great way to use those vegetables that may have been stored too long. Cauliflower tends to rust pretty quickly and become unattractive for other uses. You should trim off the worst of the rust, but a small speckle or two will not harm this recipe.

Serves: 4 to 6

Ingredients

6 cups cauliflower stems and florets,
    roughly cut in 1/2-inch pieces
1 cup small cauliflower florets (for garnish)
1 cup chopped leeks
3 tablespoons butter
3-1/2 cups vegetable stock
1/2 cup heavy or light cream
3 tablespoons chopped fresh herb (any will do)
8 ounces Gorgonzola or bleu cheese crumbles
Salt and pepper to taste

Directions

Poach small florets in salted water until tender but not soft. Drain and rinse with cold water to stop cooking.

Melt butter over medium heat in a large thick-bottomed pot. Add leeks and sauté until soft. Add cauliflower and stock, bring to a boil, and simmer 15 minutes until cauliflower is very soft. Puree in blender or processor and return to pot.

Bring back to a boil. Add cream and 6 ounces of the cheese. Add salt and pepper to taste. Simmer for 5 minutes while stirring occasionally. Remove from heat and stir in fresh herbs.

Serve in shallow bowls and garnish with a spoonful of the cooked florets and a sprinkling of cheese.

Maple Roasted Cauliflower

Here is another recipe calling for a whole head of cauliflower. You must sense a pattern. Oftentimes, you get a box full of cauliflower from your CSA. They become like turkey at Thanksgiving." What the hell am I gonna do with these cauliflower?" Perhaps prepare whole heads and give them as gifts.

Serves: 4

Ingredients

1 head of cauliflower
1/2 cup maple syrup
1/2 teaspoon ground cumin
2 tablespoons fresh grated ginger
1 tablespoon lemon juice
2 crushed bay leaf
1 tablespoon sesame oil
Salt and pepper to taste
1 cup water

Directions

Preheat oven to 400 F. In a mixing bowl, combine maple syrup, ground cumin, ginger, lemon juice, bay leaf, sesame oil, salt and pepper. Blend well and set aside.

Cut a 1/4-inch cross in the bottom core of the cauliflower to ensure that it cooks evenly. Place it in a small cake pan core side down. Pour the maple mixture over the head and spread evenly. Add water to the bottom of the pan and place in oven. Roast 30 minutes until well browned. To serve, break into florets or carve with a sharp knife.

Du Barry Salad

"Du Barry" refers to a number of preparations that are garnished with cauliflower. Usually, it's an arrangement of cauliflower and potatoes broiled with cheese and served with grilled or roasted meat.

Serves: 8

Ingredients

4 cups small cauliflower florets
1 cup sliced radishes
Dressing
1/4 cup extra virgin olive oil
1/4 cup lemon juice
1 tablespoon Dijon mustard
1 clove garlic, minced
1 tablespoon chopped fresh tarragon
1 tablespoon chopped fresh parsley
Salt and pepper to taste

Directions

Cook cauliflower in boiling salted water until tender. Drain and chill in an ice water bath to stop cooking. Drain again and let dry thoroughly.

Place all dressing ingredients except oil in a mixing bowl. Slowly add oil while stirring vigorously with a whisk. Toss cauliflower, radishes and dressing in mixing bowl until well coated with dressing. Pour into serving bowl and garnish with tarragon sprigs.

CHEF'S NOTES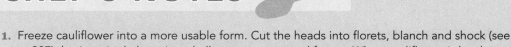

1. Freeze cauliflower into a more usable form. Cut the heads into florets, blanch and shock (see p. 287), lay in a single layer in a shallow pan, cover and freeze. When cauliflower is hard, transfer to a freezer bag and store indefinitely.

2. Roasting and frying brings out the natural sweetness of cauliflower. In many cases, roasted cauliflower will be interchangeable with steamed or boiled in recipes and bring added texture. Boiling and steaming are better options for recipes that require some marinating. The boiled or steamed cauliflower will absorb the marinade more readily.

3. There are purple and green varieties that you may discover. The flavors are subtly different, but the big distinction is the color. Mix with the white varieties for a rainbow cauliflower salad.

4. The best way to separate the florets is to remove the leaves by hand and cut the core as close to the base as possible. Take a paring knife and cut out the core in a cone shape. The large florets should easily separate. Break into smaller florets by hand.

5. Well-cooked and pureed cauliflower makes a wonderful low-fat alternative to cream or milk in cream-style soups. Simply replace part or all of the cream with the pureed cauliflower.

6. It is best to cook cauliflower in a stainless steel, glass, or enamel pan. Aluminum or cast iron may discolor the cauliflower.

Cauliflower Au Gratin

This chapter would not be complete without this recipe. Few things are more comforting than vegetables bubbling in a rich cheese sauce with a dotting of brown on the surface. This recipe calls for cheddar cheese but it works equally well with any cheese that melts well. Gruyere (a type of Swiss cheese) is a classic gratin cheese and is well worth the extra expense.

This recipe calls for a béchamel sauce. Béchamel is simply seasoned, thickened milk or cream. The recipe is on page 277.

Serves: 8

Ingredients

3 pounds large cauliflower florets
2-1/2 cups béchamel sauce
1 cup grated sharp cheddar, divided
1/4 teaspoon grated nutmeg
1/2 cup grated Parmesan
1/4 cup bread crumbs
Salt and pepper to tast

Directions

Preheat oven to 350 F. Cook the cauliflower in boiling salted water until tender but not mushy. Drain and place in a single layer in a buttered ovenproof pan. Set aside while you prepare the sauce.

Heat or prepare béchamel. Once boiling, add 3/4 cup cheddar, Parmesan cheese, nutmeg, and salt and pepper to taste. Stir until cheese melts. If the sauce is too thick, thin with a little milk. Pour cheese sauce over cauliflower and shake pan to get sauce to settle around cauliflower. Top with a mixture of the remaining grated cheddar cheese and the bread crumbs. Bake uncovered in oven until cheese bubbles and starts to brown, approximately 25 to 35 minutes.

. . . .

Pickled Cauliflower

A great snack right out of the jar.

Yields: 6 quarts

Ingredients

10 pounds cauliflower
8 cups vinegar
8 cups water
1/4 cup salt
1/4 cup mustard seed
12 cloves garlic
12 dill tops
12 red chilies, cayenne or Thai

Directions

Sterilize 6 quart canning jars in a boiling water bath. Remove green leaves from cauliflower. Using a paring knife, carve a cone out of the bottom of the cauliflower. Break apart heads with your hands and either pull apart or cut the cauliflower into pieces no bigger than a ping-pong ball. Bring a large pot of water to a boil over medium-high heat. Blanch and shock (see p. 287). Set aside.

Combine vinegar, water, salt, and mustard seeds in a saucepan and bring to a boil over medium-high heat. Boil for 5 minutes. Remove jars from water and pack each jar with 2 cloves of garlic, 2 tops of dill, and 2 chilies. Pack each jar with blanched cauliflower. Pour over vinegar solution. Fill to 1/4 inch from top. Cover, seal and process for 15 minutes in a boiling water bath as outlined in Chapter 7.

. . . .

CELERIAC

Celeriac, also called celery root, is a big, ugly lump of a thing that most people avoid with suspicion when they see it. Unlike shiny, happy tomatoes, strawberries and carrots, which can dazzle with visual charm, celeriac is the "Shrek" of vegetables and needs understanding to be loved. Once you peel back the layers of ugliness, a beautiful soul will be revealed. Celery root is flavorful and can be prepared in innumerable ways. It makes wonderful soups, can be eaten raw in salads, roasted for a satisfying side or even fried into chips. It has a flavor that reminds one of celery but is earthier and richer.

Celeriac will be one of the last seasonal offerings. It is often harvested well after the first frosty fall nights and can be stored for months in the right conditions.

Celery Root Chips

Fried root vegetables are a wondrous snack. These beauties eat like potato chips but actually taste like something other than salt.

Yields: A big bowl of chips

Ingredients
1 medium celery root (approx. 1-1/2 pounds)
Oil for frying
Sea salt
Black pepper

Directions
Preheat fryer to 350 F. Fill a large bowl with 2 quarts of water and mix in 2 tablespoons of lemon juice. Peel the celeriac and shave thin chips with a vegetable peeler into the water. Drain chips in a colander and shake dry removing as much water as possible. Fry chips in small batches that are not too tightly packed. Fry 5 to 7 minutes until chips float and are crisp on the edges but just a little tender in the centers. Drain on a paper-lined pan and toss each batch with salt and pepper to taste while still warm. Repeat until all chips are fried.

Celeriac en Remoulade

This is the traditional way of eating celeriac. Celeriac pairs well with creamy dressings and this slaw is distinctive and rich. Try it as a garnish on you favorite deli sandwich.

Yields: 2-1/4 cups

Ingredients

2 cups peeled and grated celeriac
1/4 cup prepared remoulade (see p. 284)
1 tablespoon chopped fresh herbs

Directions

Bring 2 quarts lightly salted water to a boil. Add celeriac and cook for 1 to 2 minutes. Drain celeriac and rinse with cold water. Dry thoroughly. Fold together remoulade and celeriac. Let stand for at least 1 hour. If salad seems dry, add more remoulade. Sprinkle with fresh herbs before serving.

. . . .

Curried Celeriac

A great side to any beans and rice dish at a vegetarian supper. Curry powder is a toasted spice mixture. The inexpensive ones are little more than turmeric and garlic. It is worthwhile to shop in gourmet shops or Indian groceries to discover the better blends.

Serves: 4

Ingredients

1 medium celeriac (1-1/2 pounds),
    peel and cut into 1-inch cubes
1 pound of carrots or butternut squash,
    peel and cut into 1-inch cubes
3 tablespoons butter
1 tablespoon fresh grated ginger
1 tablespoon prepared curry powder
2 tablespoon mango chutney or prepared
    rhubarb chutney (see p. 201)
1/4 cup whipping cream
Salt and pepper

Directions

Bring a large pot of water to a boil over medium-high heat. Add celeriac and carrots or squash. Cook until very tender, 15 to 20 minutes. Drain in a colander. While pot is boiling, melt butter over medium heat in a small skillet. Add ginger and curry powder. Cook mixture, stirring frequently for 1 minute to soften ginger and lightly toast curry. Place celeriac mixture, butter mixture, chutney, whipping cream, salt, and pepper in the bowl of a food processor; process until smooth. Serve immediately.

. . . .

Glazed Celeriac

Serve this as a side to roasted meats. Your guests will be delighted and gleeful requests for recipes and kitchen secrets will follow. Of course, you may want to eat it all yourself in which case you can serve them frozen carrots.

Serves: 4

Ingredients

1 large celeriac (approx. 2 pounds), peel
1 tablespoon butter
1 teaspoon sugar
Salt and pepper
1 tablespoon chopped fresh thyme

Directions

Cut the celeriac into roughly 2-inch by 1-inch pieces. You may cut them as uniformly as your obsessiveness requires, but they should all be about the same size to ensure even cooking. Arrange pieces in a skillet that will just fit them in a single layer. Add the butter and sprinkle on the sugar and salt to taste. Fill the pan with water until it covers the pieces, about half way up. Place pan over medium-high heat and bring to a boil. Reduce heat to medium-low and loosely set a piece of foil over pan to capture some of the steam. Cook for roughly 15 minutes until celeriac is tender enough to run a pick through but still a little dense in the center. Remove foil and turn the heat back up to medium-high. Cook the water out completely and allow celeriac to brown slightly on one side. Continue to stir and brown on all sides as though you were frying potatoes. Add 2 more tablespoons of water to loosen the caramelized sugar on the bottom of the pan and gently toss mixture while still in the pan. Remove from heat and season with fresh-ground black pepper. Serve immediately with a sprinkling of chopped thyme.

. . . .

Roasted Celery Root Soup

The carrots give this soup sweetness, the celery root sharpness, and the roasting smokiness. If there was anymore going on, your tongue you might get disoriented.

Serves: 6

Ingredients

2 tablespoons olive oil
2 cups chopped onions
1/2 pound carrots, peel and roughly chop
1/2 pound celeriac peel and roughly chop
2 cups vegetable stock (see p. 289)
1/2 cup whipping cream
1 tablespoon apple cider
Salt and pepper
2 tablespoons of your favorite pesto

Directions

Preheat oven to 350 F. Arrange onions, carrots and celeriac on a large cookie sheet. Drizzle with olive oil and liberally season with salt and black pepper. Roast for 45 to 60 minutes until vegetables are soft and well browned. Remove from oven and place vegetables in the bowl of a food processor. Add vegetable stock and process until pureed. You may have to do this in batches. Transfer soup to a large saucepan and bring to a boil over medium heat. Stir in whipping cream and apple cider. Add salt and pepper if necessary. Bring back to a boil and cook for 3 to 5 minute to marry flavors. Serve soup hot in shallow bowls with a dollop of pesto floating in the center.

. . . .

CHEF'S NOTES

1. Celeriac can be easily roasted. Simply peel and cut into strips or chunks. Drizzle with olive oil and season with salt and pepper. Roast in a 350-degree oven until tender, about 1 hour.

2. Stored in a cool dark place, celery root will remain wholesome throughout the winter.

3. Celeriac can be grated and dried with a home food dehydrator for use as a celery seasoning.

4. Once peeled, celeriac will darken when exposed to air, similar to potatoes or apples. Sprinkle with a little lemon juice or vinegar to keep this from happening.

5. Peeling celeriac is rugged work. The best method is to square off the ends, set the flat end down on a cutting board and hold firmly while peeling vertical strips with a heavy knife. Rotate celeriac and repeat until peel is removed.

6. Mashed or pureed celeriac is tremendous. Cut the root into chunks and boil or steam until very soft. Hand mash or blend in a food processor, season with a little butter, salt and pepper. This is very good alone or combined with mashed potatoes, turnips or rutabagas.

Down on the Farm

September 30

For those of you who might be interested in the kind of stubborn perseverance that goes into my effort here, I will share a fact that many might not believe. Until this last Sunday afternoon, I had not taken as much as two hours off from my duties here during daylight hours on any day since May 15. A friend that I see far too little these days stopped in and suggested that we walk a while in the beauty of the fall. I accepted, and we did, so the work that I could have done had to wait. It has gotten done as I was told that it would, but this newsletter will be very short. Part of the reason for its brevity is the fact that you have 20 things in your box this week, and that is a lot of harvesting, cleaning, sorting, weighing and packaging. Next week you will get a double delivery, so that I can concentrate on garlic planting in the days beyond.

October is here, and I predict that tomorrow the geese will begin to fly.

— David Peterson, Maplewood Gardens

CELERY

We take celery for granted and it's a shame. Few vegetables deliver as much flavor as celery. It is the starting point for most soups and stews and is found on nearly every raw vegetables platter. We walk by it at the farmers market or the supermarket and never give it a thought until we don't have it for a recipe. Celery can be so much more than that. That familiar and pleasing sharpness and that happy crunch are all elements that let celery stand alone as the star of the show. The following recipes should allow you to give celery the love it deserves. It is available locally from late summer on.

Celery with Béchamel

This is a variation of braised celery that eats like a casserole. To make this a main dish you could add bits of ham or chicken.

Serves: 6

Ingredients
1 recipe braised celery (see p. 80)
1 cup béchamel sauce (see p. 277)
1/4 cup grated Parmesan cheese

Directions
Preheat oven to 350 F. Prepare celery as described in the braised celery recipe or use leftover braised celery. Remove from braising pan and un-bundle celery. Arrange in a separate ovenproof baking dish and pour in warm béchamel. Top with cheese and bake for 15 to 20 minutes until bubbly and cheese is brown.

Celery Victor

Named after Chef Victor Hertzler at the Hotel St. Francis in San Francisco, this is another simple braised celery dish.

Serves: 4

Ingredients
1 recipe braised celery (see p. 80), prepared without bacon and chilled completely
3 tablespoons Dijon mustard
1 teaspoon sugar
1-1/2 tablespoons salad oil
Salt and pepper
1 tablespoon chopped fresh chives

Directions
In a small mixing bowl, whisk together mustard, sugar, and 3 tablespoons of the celery cooking broth. Slowly drizzle in oil while whisking vigorously. Season with salt and pepper; stir in the chives. Arrange celery on small plates or large serving platter and drizzle vinaigrettes over top.

Bacon Braised Celery

Here's a little chef's secret: If you add bacon to anything, it will taste better. Try this with pan-fried chicken breast.

Serves: 4

Ingredients

2 cups celery, cut into 1/4-inch sticks; blanch and shock (see p. 287)
2 cups fresh fennel, core and cut into 1/4-slices; blanch and shock (see p. 287)
1/4 cup chopped fresh celery leaves
1/4 cup chopped fresh fennel fronds
2 tablespoons fresh chopped parsley
1/2 cup chopped shallots
1/4 cup vegetable stock (see p. 289)
3 strips of bacon, cut crosswise into 1/2-inch ribbons
Salt and pepper

Directions

Heat a large skillet over medium heat. Add bacon and cook, stirring occasionally, until bacon is fully cooked and crisp. Remove bacon from pan with tongs or a slotted spoon. Set aside on a paper towel to drain. Add the shallots to the bacon drippings and cook for 2 to 3 minutes until soft. Add celery and fennel. Cook the vegetables, stirring frequently, until brown, about 10 to 15 minutes. Add stock and bring to a boil. Reduce heat and simmer, uncovered, until vegetables are tender, about 5 minutes. Remove from heat and season to taste with salt and pepper. Stir in bacon, celery leaves, fennel fronds and parsley. Serve immediately.

Braised Celery

This is a starting point for many recipes. It produces stalks of celery that are tender and rich. They are great by themselves, with the pan gravy, or with a rich velvety sauce like hollandaise or cheese sauce.

Serves: 6

Ingredients

1 stalk of celery, cut into 6-inch sticks
3 slices bacon, diced
1/4 cup diced carrot
1/4 cup diced onion
Vegetable or chicken stock (see p. 289)
Black pepper

Directions

Preheat oven to 350 F. Tie celery into bundles of 2 or 3 sticks with a length of string. Spread carrots, onions and bacon in an ovenproof pan. Lay celery bundles in a single layer in pan. Cover celery completely with stock. Add pepper. Cover pan and cook for 2 hours.

To serve, un-bundle celery and place in a serving dish and sprinkle with chopped parsley.

Note: You could also make a simple pan sauce by removing the celery (keep warm), skimming off as much of the bacon grease as possible, pouring pan juice in a saucepan and cooking down by half over medium-high heat. Remove from heat and vigorously whisk in 3 tablespoons of cold butter. Spoon the sauce over warm celery.

Chilled Celery Salad With Dill

A unique picnic salad or first course.

Serves: 6

Ingredients

2 pounds celery, cut into 1/2-inch slices
1 clove garlic, mince
1 tablespoon lemon juice
2 tablespoons olive oil
2 tablespoons chopped fresh dill
2 tablespoons capers
Black pepper

Directions

In a small mixing bowl, whisk together mustard, sugar, and 3 tablespoons of the celery cooking broth. Slowly drizzle in oil while whisking vigorously. Season with salt and pepper; stir in the chives. Arrange celery on small plates or large serving platter and drizzle vinaigrettes over top.

CHEF'S NOTES

1. To make quick work of dicing celery, cut the stalks in thin ribbons down the long axis with the very tip of your knife. Do not cut all the way through to the end; the celery will stack better when you chop it. Hold the cut celery firmly while chopping across the short axis. This will give you a fine dice without too much fuss.

2. Celery has lot of naturally occurring sodium. It is a great natural way to add salt to a dish.

3. Celery, along with carrots and onions, is the classic start of most soups and stews called mirepoix.

4. Most people have encountered "ants on a log" — celery sticks stuffed with peanut butter and raisins. But you can stuff celery sticks with anything your imagination comes up with. I didn't put any suggestions in the book because they seem kind of "potlucky." Yet, if you have a date with a church basement in your future, feel free to experiment with things like cream cheese spread, egg, tuna and chicken salad or any soft cheese seasoned with fresh herbs.

5. Fresh or dried, celery leaves make a great seasoning herb. To dry celery leaves use a food dehydrator or hang them, leaf side down, in a clean dry place free of sunlight.

6. You can freeze celery but it will lose its crunch, which is perfectly fine for cooked dishes.

CHARD

Reportedly, chard (or Swiss chard) was one of Hemingway's favorite vegetables. One doesn't think of Hemingway eating many vegetables, particularly kinda' wimpy lettuce-like vegetables. However, if a guy as macho as Hemingway can enjoy chard, then I'm sure it's adequate for mere mortals. When I was a youngster, I craved chard, preferring it to all other vegetables. I mostly craved it because it wasn't spinach, which in loyalty to children's tastes I refused to eat, along with liver and canned beets. But I could eat chard in good conscience and often did because it was the one vegetable my parents were able to consistently grow in the patch of dirt behind the garage.

While spinach is a boring vegetable you're "supposed" to eat, chard is a sexy and exciting adventure. It has more flavor and the crisp, crinkly leaves are kind of psychedelic when you look at them really close up. Chard is a close relative of the beet and is also known as "Silverbeet" or "Leaf Beet." Chard should be thoroughly rinsed because the wrinkled leaves tend to trap dirt. Shaking the leaves in a sink full of cold water is the best method. It has a sharp earthy flavor that stands up to other strong flavors and can be steamed, poached or wilted in hot oil. It makes a terrific soup or stuffing. In most areas, you can enjoy chard all summer long and into the autumn.

Swiss Chard Polonaise

Vegetables prepared "Polonaise" are garnished with chopped hard-cooked eggs, fresh chopped parsley and bread crumbs cooked in butter. Many other vegetables can be prepared with this savory topping.

Serves: 4

Ingredients

8 ounces fresh Swiss chard
1 quart vegetable stock (see p. 289)
Salt and pepper to taste
2 hard-cooked eggs
2 tablespoons chopped fresh parsley
1 cup bread crumbs
2 tablespoons butter

Directions

Bring stock or lightly salted water to a boil in a saucepan over medium-high heat.

Trim leaves from ribs of Swiss chard. Slice ribs crosswise and place in boiling stock. Reduce heat and simmer for 30 minutes. Add leaves and cook 15 more minutes. Drain completely in a colander.

While chard is cooking, slice eggs and roughly chop with a knife, set aside. Melt butter in a skillet over medium high heat. Add bread crumbs, salt and pepper. Fry for 5 minutes in butter, add chopped eggs and toss together.

Place cooked Swiss chard in a serving dish. Top with bread crumb mixture and sprinkle with chopped parsley.

. . . .

Swiss Chard With Hot and Sour Broth

Hot and sour soup is a favorite of mine. The broth is a nice partner to the strong flavor of the chard. This eats as a side vegetable or main course and not a soup. The broth should be simply a garnishing sauce in a deep bowl of Swiss chard. This dish is delightfully low in fat and calories.

Serves: 4

Ingredients

3 large bunches (approx. 2 pounds)
    fresh Swiss chard
2 cups vegetable or chicken stock (see p. 289)
1 tablespoon soy sauce
1 tablespoon rice wine vinegar
1 teaspoon fresh ground black pepper
1 teaspoon sesame oil
1 dried red chili
1/2 cup tofu, cut into 1/4-inch cubes

Directions

In a saucepan, combine stock, soy, rice wine vinegar, black pepper, sesame oil, and tofu. Break the chili in half and drop into pan. Bring mixture to a simmer over medium heat. Simmer for 5 minutes, remove from heat and set aside.

Bring 3 quarts of salted water to a boil over high heat. Cut the stems from the Swiss chard and chop the chard into 1-inch strips. Boil the leaves for 5 minutes until tender, drain chard in a colander. Scoop chard into 4 deep soup cups, ladle 1/2 cup of hot and sour broth into each cup. Serve immediately.

. . . .

Swiss Chard and Tomato Dip

An interesting bread dip or sauce for meatballs.

Yields: Approx. 2 cups

Ingredients
3 tablespoons tahini (sesame seed paste)
1 clove minced garlic
Salt to taste
1/3 cup lemon juice
1-1/2 pounds chopped Swiss chard
3 tomatoes, peel and remove seeds (see p. 288)
1/2 teaspoon crushed red pepper
1/4 cup chopped fresh parsley
1/4 cup chopped green onions
1/4 cup chopped walnuts

Directions
Bring 2 quarts of water to a boil over high heat. Add Swiss chard and boil for 5 minutes until tender. Drain in a colander and rinse with cold water to cool. Using your hands, squeeze the chard to wring out as much liquid as possible and set aside.

In a mixing bowl, whisk together tahini, garlic and lemon juice. Blend in the Swiss chard, tomatoes, crushed red pepper, parsley, onions, and walnuts. Stir in just enough water to make the consistency of a dip.

. . . .

Dolmas

Dolma is a Turkish word that refers to stuffed vegetables. In America, a dolma nearly always is a grape leaf stuffed with rice, minced meat, and pine nuts. In my backyard, fresh grape leaves are scarce, but chard is available most of the summer. The leaves are sturdy enough to hold up to the long cooking and there are countless goodies to stuff them with. They can be served room temperature as a snack-type finger food or served warm with an herbed yogurt dressing as an entree. Following the directions, I've listed a sampling of stuffing recipes.

Directions
Cut the ribs (long sinewy piece in center of chard leaf) out of the chard. Cut pieces into roughly 3-inch by 3-inch squares. Boil in lightly salted water for 1 minute to soften and rinse under cold water.

Arrange pieces on a flat surface. Place a small spoonful of stuffing in the center of each leaf. Fold in sides and roll up to form cylindrical envelopes. You may tie them to keep sealed but it is usually unnecessary. Arrange tightly packed in an oven-proof baking dish and drizzle with a little olive oil. Splash with lemon juice, pour on just enough vegetable stock, water, or tomato juice to cover pieces and season with coriander seed and/or cumin. Cover with foil and bake in a 350 F oven for 30 minutes. Remove from pan and serve immediately or cool to room temperature. Dolmas will keep 3 days in the refrigerator.

Note: An alternative to chard is purple orach leaves. The cooked leaves are a beautiful purple color. You may have to boil them a little longer to soften the leaves.

. . . .

Traditional Eastern Mediterranean Stuffing

This stuffing is filled with common Eastern Mediterranean spices and flavors.

Serves: 4

Ingredients

1 cup cooked rice
1 cup cooked ground beef or lamb
1/4 cup olive oil
1 cup diced onion
3 scallions, chopped
1/4 cup chopped fresh parsley
2 tablespoons chopped fresh mint
1/2 cup pine nuts or chopped walnuts
1/2 cup dried cranberries
1 teaspoon cinnamon
1/2 teaspoon allspice
Salt and black pepper to taste

Directions

Heat 2 tablespoons of olive oil in a large skillet. Add yellow and green onions. Cook onions, stirring occasionally, until brown. Add remainder of oil, and ground beef or lamb. Stir together until warm and well coated with oil. Remove from heat and transfer to the bowl of a food processor. Add the remaining ingredients and pulse until ingredients are finely chopped, but not minced. Transfer to mixing bowl, add rice and mix thoroughly. Stuff and cook as directed in introduction to dolmas.

Basic Dolma Stuffing Recipe

Yields: 25 small dolmas

Ingredients

1 cup cooked rice (preferably
    short or medium grain)
1 cup cooked ground lamb or beef
1 cup onion diced large
2 tablespoons chopped fresh mint
Salt and pepper to taste

Directions

Run onion through fine grating blade of your food processor. Remove blade and add lamb or beef and fresh mint to bowl of processor. Pulse a few times to mix ingredients. Transfer processed ingredients to a mixing bowl and fold in cooked rice, salt and pepper with spatula or hands. Stuff and cook as directed in introduction to dolmas.

Tomato and Bulgur Stuffing

Yields: 24 dolmas

Ingredients

1/4 cup bulgur
1 cup fresh diced tomato
1 cup finely diced onion
6-ounce can tomato paste
1/4 cup grated Parmesan cheese
2 tablespoons chopped fresh basil
Salt and pepper to taste

Directions

Soak bulgur in water for 30 minutes. Drain and place in a large mixing bowl with the remaining ingredients. Mix thoroughly with hands. Stuff and cook as directed in introduction to dolmas.

Note: bulgur is a type of whole wheat available in most large supermarkets.

Wild Mushroom Stuffing

Any type of mushroom can be used for this and it is a great way to use any leftover stems you may have from another recipe. The mushrooms, shallots and onions should be finely diced to a consistent size.

Serves: 4

Ingredients

3 cups finely diced mushrooms
1 large or 2 small shallots, dice fine
1 onion, dice fine
3 tablespoons butter
Salt and pepper to taste
Pinch of grated nutmeg
2 eggs

Directions

Melt butter in a large skillet over medium high heat. Add mushrooms, shallots and onions. Cook, stirring occasionally, until vegetables are browned and mushroom liquid has mostly evaporated (this varies based on the type of mushroom). Add salt, pepper and nutmeg to taste. Remove from heat and cool slightly. Mix mushrooms together with 2 beaten eggs. Stuff and cook as directed in introduction to dolmas.

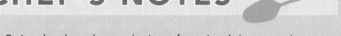

CHEF'S NOTES

1. Swiss chard can be a substitute for spinach in any recipe.

2. Look for baby chard bundles at your farmers market. Gently torn and simply dressed with oil and lemon juice, it makes a wonderful simple salad.

3. Chard freezes well. Simply blanch and shock (see p. 287) chopped Swiss chard. Drain completely and freeze in plastic freezer bags.

4. Swiss chard stems are full of flavor. They take twice as long to cook, so start them first and add the leaves later.

5. Chard can be found in a mild green variety and a stunning red variety with a pronounced earthy flavor.

6. Try cooking Swiss chard in red wine and onions. The pungency of the chard is perfect with the red wine.

CHERRIES

One of the beauties of cherries is that they are adamantly seasonal. They still are very difficult to get fresh outside of late summer and early fall. Perhaps they are a small reminder that we can't have anything we want — anytime we want. There are many varieties but they can be categorized simply as sweet or sour cherries. Sour cherries are better in preserves or recipes. Sweet cherries are terrific hand fruit and can be used in recipes if there are any left. Even in the supermarket, most cherries are reasonably local and the season is short. Enjoy them fresh like a bowl of candy and freeze or preserve a few while you can.

Tart Cherry Clafoutis

Clafoutis, typically, is made with sweet cherries, but the tart cherries available in markets of the upper Midwest can also be used in this comfy little dessert. This recipe calls for a little more sugar to compensate for the tartness. Serve warm straight from the oven with a dollop of whipped cream flavored with orange zest. This dish works well and looks sexy in a 9-inch cast-iron skillet, but any heavy ovenproof pan roughly 9 inches in diameter will do.

Serves: 4 to 6

Ingredients
1/2 cup flour
1/4 teaspoon salt
2 large eggs
1/3 cup sugar (divided)
3/4 cup milk
1/2 teaspoon vanilla extract
1 pound fresh tart cherries, remove pits and stems
1 tablespoon butter

Directions
Place flour, salt, eggs, 2 tablespoons of the sugar, milk and vanilla extract in a mixing bowl. Mix thoroughly with a hand mixer while scraping the sides of the bowl until batter is smooth and free of lumps. Let batter rest for a few minutes.

Melt butter over medium heat in baking pan. Heat until butter is bubbly. Add cherries and cook, stirring occasionally, for 1 minute in pan. Sprinkle cherries with the rest of the sugar and cook until sugar forms into syrup. Remove from heat. Pour batter over the cherries and bake for about 20 minutes until golden around the edges. Resist the urge to peak in oven midway through baking as cake may fall. Remove from oven, dust with a little powdered sugar and serve immediately.

CHEF'S NOTES

1. Cherries freeze well. Lay them in a single layer on a cookie sheet for a few hours and transfer them to airtight containers or freezer bags.

2. Most cherry recipes call for sugar. The amount of sugar will be determined by the type and ripeness of the cherry. Don't be slavish to a recipe; adjust the amount according to taste.

3. Sour cherries pair well with venison and duck.

4. Sour cherries are interchangeable with cranberries in most recipes.

5. There are countless fantastic recipes for cherry jam and preserves. They are easy to make and easier to eat.

6. The absolute best way to eat cherries is to pop them in your mouth and spit out the pits while lazing about on a hot summer day.

Spiced Cherries

Spiced cherries can be canned. Follow the technique outlined in Chapter 7.

Yields: 4 cups

Ingredients
1-1/2 cups red wine
1-1/2 cups sugar
1 lemon
1 bay leaf
1 tablespoon fresh grated ginger
1/2 cinnamon stick
1 teaspoon mustard seeds
2 whole cloves
1 cardamom pod, broken open
  and seeds lightly crushed
12 whole black peppercorns
Salt
2 pounds cherries, pitted

Directions
Enclose mustard seeds, cloves, cinnamon, cardamom and peppercorn in an envelope made of cheesecloth and tie the ends together. Place in a large saucepan. Zest lemon peel from entire lemon into the saucepan with a zester or grater. Cut lemon in half and squeeze juice from the lemon into the saucepan. Add red wine, sugar, bay leaf, ginger and salt. Bring to a boil over medium heat. Boil for 15 minutes.

Add the cherries and return to a boil. Reduce heat and simmer 10 minutes, stirring occasionally. Remove from heat and cool. Remove spice packet and bay leaf. Transfer to a container and cool completely. Serve chilled as a relish with poultry or game.

Sour Cherry Grunt

A grunt simply is compote simmered with tender steamed dumplings. A nice late summer dessert, but its real value comes in the opportunity to insert the word "grunt" into casual conversation.

Serves: 8

Compote Ingredients

1 cup sugar
2 tablespoons cornstarch
1/2 cup orange juice
1 teaspoon lemon juice
4 cups pitted sour cherries
1 cup frozen raspberries
3/4 cup frozen cranberries

Dumpling Ingredients

1 cup flour
1/3 cup pastry, chickpea or sorghum flour
1-1/2 tablespoons sugar
1-1/4 teaspoons baking powder
1/2 teaspoons salt
1/4 teaspoon baking soda
2 -1/2 tablespoons cold butter,
    cut into1/4-inch chunks
2 tablespoons salad oil
3/4 cup buttermilk

Directions

Combine sugar, cornstarch, cinnamon, orange juice, lemon juice, cherries, raspberries and cranberries in a large deep skillet. Mix together completely and bring to a boil over medium heat. You must stir constantly while this mixture cooks. Boil for about 2 minutes until thickened and shiny. Remove from heat, taste and add sugar if you want it sweeter.

To make the dumplings, whisk together both flours, sugar, baking powder, salt and baking soda in a mixing bowl. Add pieces of butter and oil. Cut the butter into the flour mixture with a pastry knife or the back of a fork. Press and cut butter into smaller and smaller pieces until dough looks like fine gravel. Add the buttermilk and mix with a fork until just mixed. Don't overmix. Let dough rest for a few minutes.

Drop spoonfuls of the dumpling mixture, evenly spaced, over the surface of the fruit mixture. Place pan over medium heat and bring back to a simmer. Reduce heat to very low, cover, and simmer until dumplings are fluffy and cooked through, about 20 minutes. Cool on a wire rack for 30 minutes. Top with a sprinkling of sugar and cinnamon. Best served a little warm.

· · · · · · · · · · · · · · · ·

Cherries in Brandy

This is an old European preservation method for cherries. The tart Midwestern Montmorency cherry is the preferred fruit for this preparation. Where I come from this is called "cherry bounce." If you eat enough of them, there will be a noticeable bounce in your spirits. Pull out a jar of these to give you a taste of late summer in mid-winter.

Yields: 12 pints

Ingredients

12 pints fresh tart cherries with stem intact
1 liter brandy
1 cup honey

Directions

Sterilize 12 pint canning jars in a boiling water bath. Whisk together brandy and honey in a mixing bowl. Set aside. Prick each cherry with a needle and firmly pack the cherries into the jars. Pour in brandy to within 1/2 inch of the top of jar. Cover, seal and process 25 minutes as outlined in Chapter 7. Store 3 months before serving.

· · · · · · · · · · · · · · · ·

CHILI PEPPERS

I love spicy food. Most people who love food, love spicy food. One of the joys of eating seasonally is that prodigious cool amounts of chilies are available to sample the entire growing season. The heat from a chili raises a cooling sweat on the brow and cools rather than heats the body. But the chief attraction for me is the sense of excitement and adventure that the chili pepper brings to any dish. Some chilies are mild and smooth, others are blazing and smoky, and yet others are rich and oily. Chilies range from the relatively mild poblano to the searingly hot habanero with scores of varieties available in between.

When working with chilies, you should always wear gloves. The oils, called capsaicin, from chilies will burn sensitive areas and is not easily removed with water. If you ingest an uncomfortable amount of chilies, milk is the answer. It will cool and coat your tongue, throat and stomach. The heat of chilies is measured in Scoville units and the relative heat of any given chili can be found with a simple online search. Chilies can be stuffed, roasted, crushed, boiled and pureed, dried and pickled. Smaller types are available very early in the season and some type of chili will be available at your market the entire season.

Caramelized Chili Jam

Spicy and sweet, this condiment is a great accompaniment to fried foods and is very nice as a relish with artisanal cheese.

Yields: 2 cups

Ingredients

1/4 cup olive oil
3 large onions, diced
3 large garlic cloves, roughly chopped
2 red chilies (Thai or cayenne), seeded and roughly chopped
2 tablespoons dark brown sugar

Directions

Heat olive oil in a large skillet over medium-high heat. Add onions and garlic. Reduce heat to low and cook, stirring frequently, for 20 minutes until onions are very soft. Remove the skillet from the heat and cool slightly. Transfer onions to a food processor. Add peppers and brown sugar. Process the mixture until very smooth. Return mixture to pan and cook over medium heat until most of the liquid evaporates and mixture is the consistency of jam.

Down on the Farm

September 9

You will find three kinds of hot peppers ready this week. Everyone knows jalapenos and last week we delivered Hungarian wax, but the little red ones are HOT!!!! They are Ring-o-fires, a central Mexican cayenne that is three times as hot as a regular cayenne. My chef friend, Randall, author of this book, tells me that he bruises them severely with a slap from the side of a heavy knife and puts one in a pot of soup. When the soup is done he fishes it out because it has done its job. He says that he never eats the pepper, but really enjoys what it has done for the soup.

— David Peterson, Maplewood Gardens

Couscous and Spicy Chili Salad

Served on a bed of butter lettuce or Napa cabbage this is visually appealing as well as sharp and alive with flavor.

Serves: 4

Ingredients

3 tablespoons olive oil
5 scallions, chopped (both green and white parts)
1 clove garlic, minced
1 teaspoon ground cumin
1-1/2 cups vegetable stock (see p. 289)
1 cup couscous
2 tomatoes, diced
1/4 cup chopped fresh parsley
1/4 cup chopped fresh mint
1 jalapeno or other hot chili, seeded and finely chopped
1 lemon
Butter lettuce or Napa cabbage (edible decoration)

Directions

Zest lemon and reserve in a small dish. Wrap the dish with plastic and place in the refrigerator. Heat olive oil in a large saucepan over medium-high heat and then add scallions and garlic. Stir in the cumin and cook, while stirring, 2 minutes. Add the vegetable stock; bring to a boil. Remove the pan from the heat and stir in the couscous. Cover the pan tightly and let sit for 10 minutes. All the liquid should be absorbed. Transfer couscous to a mixing bowl. Add parsley, mint and chopped jalapeno. Cut the zested lemon in half and squeeze the juice into the bowl. Mix all ingredients thoroughly. Let stand for 1 hour to allow flavors to marry. Line a platter with lettuce leaves and place salad on top. Sprinkle reserved lemon zest on the salad.

Cheese Stuffed Chilies

You can use any melting cheese for this recipe which calls for cheddar cheese, but Swiss or bleu cheese would be very good. Large mild poblanos or Anaheim chilies are perfect for stuffing.

Serves: 6

Ingredients

6 poblano or Anaheim chilies
1 pound potatoes
1 cup cream cheese
1-3/4 cups grated sharp cheddar
2 eggs, separated
1 cup flour
Salt and white pepper
Oil for deep frying

Directions

Cut a slit down the long axis of each chili. Place a large skillet over medium-high heat and place peppers in pan. Turn the peppers frequently until skin blisters on all sides. Place in a plastic bag and seal the bag to retain the steam. Let sit for 20 minutes and then remove them from the bag. Gently peel off as much skin as you can. Remove as many seeds through the slit as possible.

While peppers are sweating, peel and cut the potatoes into 1/2-inch chunks. Place in a pot of boiling salted water. Allow the water to return to a boil, reduce the heat and simmer for 5 to 8 minutes until the potatoes are tender. Drain potatoes in a colander. In a large mixing bowl, place cream cheese, cheddar cheese, potatoes, salt and white pepper. Gently stir this mixture until combined. Spoon the mixture evenly into the 6 chilies. Place on a plate and cover with wrap. Chill for an hour.

Preheat a deep fryer to 375 F. Separate eggs, placing egg whites in one mixing bowl and yolks in another. Whip the whites with a hand mixer until they form stiff peaks (peaks are formed as you remove the beaters from the mixture). Whisk the egg yolks rapidly until they turn a pale yellow. Add the whites to the yolks and gently combine with a wooden spoon. Pour flour onto a shallow plate and season with salt and white pepper. Roll peppers, two at a time, in flour. Dip into egg mixture and immediately drop in fryer. Fry until golden brown, about 3 to 5 minutes. Remove from fryer and drain on a paper towel. Fry the remaining peppers and serve immediately.

. . . .

Nuoc Cham

This goes well with any type of Asian fried goodie — spring rolls, egg rolls, won tons, etc. You can find Thai fish sauce at most well-stocked grocery stores.

Yields: 1 cup

Ingredients

2 fresh red chilies
2 garlic cloves, minced
1 tablespoon sugar
3 tablespoon Thai fish sauce
Juice of 1 lime

Directions

Slice the chilies lengthwise and discard the stem. Scrape out the seeds and discard. Grind the peppers to a smooth paste with a mortar and pestle. Transfer paste to a mixing bowl. Add the garlic, sugar, fish sauce and lime juice. Mix completely and store until ready to use.

. . . .

CHEF'S NOTES

1. Sambals are sassy little condiments popular in Indonesia and other Asian countries. They can be brutally hot and should be used carefully, like hot sauce. If your CSA brings you a basket full of hot chilies, you might like to prepare one of these little beauties.

2. The type of chili used largely will determine the heat. They tend to look and taste most appropriate with de arbol, cayenne, or bird's eye chilies. Don't be afraid to make a big batch. They will keep for an extended time in the refrigerator

Basic Sambal
Yields: 2-1/2 cups

Ingredients
- 1 pound fresh red chilies
- 2 teaspoons salt

Directions
Slice the chilies lengthwise and discard the stem. Scrape out the seeds and discard. Grind the peppers to a smooth paste with a mortar and pestle. Transfer paste to a mixing bowl. Add the garlic, sugar, fish sauce and lime juice. Mix completely and store until ready to use.

. . . .

Ginger Sambal

This will wake up a simple grilled chicken breast.

Yields: 1 cup

Ingredients
- 4 red chilies
- 1 small onion, diced
- 2 cloves garlic, minced
- 1 tablespoon fresh grated ginger
- 2 tablespoons sugar
- 3 tablespoons white wine or cider vinegar
- Salt

Directions
Slice the chilies lengthwise and discard the stems. Scrape out the seeds and discard. Place chilies in a food processor along with all of the other ingredients and process until smooth. Store sambal until ready to use.

. . . .

Peri-Peri

Peri-peri is a very simple barbecue marinade. It is particularly good with seafood.

Yields: 1 cup

Ingredients
3 red chilies
1 teaspoon paprika
1 teaspoon ground coriander
1 garlic clove, minced
Juice of 2 limes
1/4 cup olive oil
Salt and black pepper

Directions
Slice the chili lengthwise and discard the stem. Scrape out the seeds and discard. Chop chilies very fine and place in a mixing bowl. Add the paprika, coriander, garlic and lime juice. Drizzle in olive oil while stirring.

Peri-Peri Shrimp

Serve this with rice or a simple green salad.

Serves: 6

Ingredients
2 pounds large shrimp, peeled
2 recipes (2 cups) prepared peri-peri
(see Peri-Peri recipe above)

Directions
Make a shallow slit down the back of each shrimp with a sharp paring knife and carefully remove the mud vein. Rinse the shrimp under running water and pat dry. Place shrimp in a bowl with the peri-peri and mix well until shrimp is well coated. Marinate shrimp for 1 hour.

While the shrimp is marinating, prepare a charcoal or gas grill. Grill should be hot enough that it is uncomfortable to hold your hand over coals for more than 2 seconds. Place the shrimp on the grate in a single layer and cook for 2 to 3 minutes on each side. Be careful not to overcook. They should still be plump and a little translucent in the center. Brush or spoon a little of the marinade on each shrimp before you turn them. Remove them from the grill and serve immediately.

Chili Pepper Mayo

This is a simple spicy sandwich dressing or use in place of tartar sauce.

Yields: 1 cup

Ingredients
1 cup real mayonnaise
1 jalapeno pepper, seeded and finely minced
1 tablespoon lime juice

Directions
Whisk together all ingredients in a mixing bowl. Chill for 1 hour to marry flavors.

Canned Roasted Chilies

Roasted chilies develop a very rich smokiness after extended storage. Use these as an ingredient, a garnish for sandwiches, a simple relish or on a crostini.

Yields: 2 pints

Ingredients

2 pounds of chili peppers (approximately), enough to completely fill 2 pint jars (you may have to eyeball it a little)

1 cup olive or vegetable oil

3/4 cup cider vinegar

3 cloves of garlic, roughly chopped

1/2 teaspoon pickling salt

2 sprigs of fresh thyme or 6 basil leaves

Directions

Roast and skin peppers as outlined in Appendix. Slice roasted peppers into strips and pack tightly into 2 pint canning jars. Incorporate 1 sprig of thyme or 3 basil leaves into each jar. Set aside. Bring oil, vinegar, garlic and salt to a boil over medium-high heat in a skillet, reduce heat and simmer for 5 minutes. Pour hot oil mixture into jars leaving 1/2-inch space between oil and the bottom of the lid. Cover jar, seal and process for 20 minutes, as outlined in Chapter 7 on preserving.

. . . .

Chili Caper Salsa Verde

Green cayenne or jalapeno chilies provide the fire in this savory version of a classic taco sauce.

Yields: 2 cups

Ingredients

4 green cayenne or jalapeno chilies

8 green onions

2 garlic cloves

1/2 cup capers

1 large tarragon sprig

2 tablespoons fresh parsley

1/3 cup extra virgin olive oil

1 lime

1 lemon

1 tablespoon hot sauce

Black pepper

Directions

Cut the chilies in half and scrape out the seeds. Discard the furry ends of the green onions and roughly chop them. Lightly smash the garlic with the flat of a knife. Place chilies, onions and garlic in a food processor and process until well chopped. Rinse the capers under cold water to remove some of the vinegar. Add to the food processor. Add the tarragon and parsley. Pulse the mixture until well blended and chopped.

Pour mixture into a mixing bowl. Zest the peel of the lime into the bowl. Cut the lime and squeeze in the juice. Cut the lemon and squeeze in the juice. Add the olive oil and toss together until well mixed. Add pepper sauce and black pepper to taste. Serve with tortilla chips or as a relish on tacos.

. . . .

Chili Raita

Raita is a typical Indian topping for spicy bean dishes. Try this with pea soup or black bean soup.

Yields: 1-1/2 cups

Ingredients

- 1 teaspoon cumin seeds
- 1 red onion
- 1 garlic clove
- 1 fresh jalapeno chili, remove seeds
- 3/4 cup yogurt
- 3 tablespoons chopped fresh cilantro
- 1/2 teaspoon sugar
- Salt

Directions

Heat a small skillet over medium heat. Add the cumin seeds to the pan and heat, tossing and stirring until they start to pop and release their aroma. Remove the pan from the heat. Transfer the seeds to a mortar and pestle. Crush to a coarse dust. Alternatively you may crush the seeds with the flat of a knife on a cutting board.

Dice the onion. Mince the garlic. Mince the chili as finely as you can with a knife. Combine the cumin, onion, garlic, chili, yogurt, cilantro, sugar and salt to taste in a mixing bowl. Mix all ingredients thoroughly. This will keep several days in the refrigerator.

. . . .

Roast Peppers in Cream

This is a traditional Mexican dish. It is typically made with poblano chilies, which are fairly mild, but can be made with any roasted chili. The cream tames the heat and makes this a welcome side dish or main course at any meal.

Serves: 6 to 8

Ingredients

- 2 pounds roasted chili peppers, cut into ½-inch wide strips (see p. 288)
- 3 tablespoons corn or vegetable oil
- 1 onion, cut into thin slices
- 1/4 cup whipping cream
- 2 tablespoons sour cream
- Salt
- 2 tablespoons chopped fresh cilantro

Directions

Heat oil in a large skillet over medium-low heat. Add onions and cook, stirring frequently, until the onions are soft, about 5 minutes. Add chilies and salt to taste. Continue to cook and stir for 5 more minutes. Whisk together whipping cream and sour cream in a small bowl. Pour into pan with peppers, bring to a boil and cook for 2 minutes. Serve immediately with a sprinkle of cilantro.

. . . .

Chili Herb Salsa

This is more of a spicy pesto. It is great on broiled fish.

Yields: 3 cups

Ingredients

1-1/2 cups chopped fresh cilantro
1/4 cup chopped fresh parsley
2 fresh red chilies, preferably cayenne
1 garlic clove, minced
1/2 cup shelled pistachios
1/2 cup grated Parmesan cheese
1/3 cup olive oil
2 limes
Salt and black pepper

Directions

Slice the chilies, scrape and discard the seeds. Place in the bowl of a food processor along with the cilantro, parsley, garlic and pistachios. Pulse in the processor until chopped but not pulverized. Transfer to a mixing bowl and add the cheese, oil, and the juice of the limes. Salt and pepper to taste and mix ingredients thoroughly. Chill until ready to serve.

CHEF'S NOTES

1. Most of the heat in chili peppers resides in the seeds and fleshy ribs. If you remove these, you will tone down the heat considerably.

2. In most recipes, including the ones I offer, a generic "chili pepper" is called for. While most hot chilies are interchangeable in recipes (allowing for size) there are distinct differences, both bold and subtle, between the different types. The scope of this book doesn't allow a detailed description of the different chilies that may cross your path. My advice is to have some fun and experiment.

3. Chili peppers are the perfect dried food. Dry them according to your food dehydrator's directions. They can then be ground for a seasoning or simply bruised a little and dropped whole into soups and stews.

4. It bears repeating. The capsaicin in very hot chilies (jalapeno, cayenne, birdseye, habanero) is a strong chemical. Wear gloves, do not rub your eyes or go the bathroom. If cooking large quantities, do not breathe in the perfume.

5. Chili peppers are best frozen after roasting (see p. 288). Roast and peel chilies, cut into desired shape and freeze in airtight containers or freezer bags.

6. To remove seeds from a chili pepper and still keep the chili whole for stuffing or display, simply cut off the top and scrape out the inside with a vegetable peeler. This should remove most of the seeds and flesh.

CORN

As a kid I awaited the first cobs of corn to appear in the grocery store as though it were Christmas. I don't remember getting that excited about any vegetable and I knew it would only be around for a short period of time. I loved the sweetness, I loved the butter that you slathered all over the corn and I particularly loved the little skewers that you thrust into the ends — the ones that look like little plastic cobs of corn. The whole experience meant summer and fun and family. We would sit around the table arguing about the relative merits of the cobs with the little white kernels or the cobs with the plump golden kernels. To my mind they were both pretty good and gone way too soon. I still get that charge over a freshly picked ear of sweet corn — I'm still waitin' for summer...

Corn Fritters

A great side to fried fish and chicken.

Serves: 6 as a side

Ingredients

2 ears of shucked corn
2 eggs separated
1/4 cup whipping cream
1/2 teaspoon salt
1/2 teaspoon sugar
1/4 cup cornmeal
1/4 cup flour
Black pepper

Directions

Preheat deep fryer to 350 F. Cut the kernels form the ears of corn by standing the cobs on a cutting board and running a sturdy knife down between the cob and kernels and rotating the ear until it is clean. Place the kernels in a large mixing bowl. Whisk in egg yolks, cream, salt, sugar and black pepper. Stir in cornmeal and flour and mix until smooth. Let batter rest for 30 minutes.

While batter is resting whip egg whites with a hand mixer until they form peaks. Fold egg whites gently into the corn batter. Drop batter, 1 tablespoon at a time, into hot oil. Fry batter 3 to 5 minutes until they are caramel-brown and crusty. You may have to turn fritters with a wooden spoon to brown both sides as they float. You will have to make these in batches. Keep fritters warm in a low oven until you finish. Serve with fine local honey, maple syrup, or maple herb sauce (see p. 157).

Oven-Roasted Sweet Corn

If you can roast corn the day it is picked, it will yield an almost magical sweetness!

Serves: 4

Ingredients

4 ears shucked sweet corn
3 tablespoons chopped fresh cilantro
3 tablespoon fresh lime juice
2 tablespoons olive oil
1 tablespoon water

Directions

Preheat oven to 400 F. In a large shallow pan, combine cilantro, lime juice, olive oil, and water. Mix well. Roll each cob in the olive oil mixture and place on a shallow baking sheet. Roast in the oven, turning occasionally and basting with the remaining oil cilantro mixture until corn is tender, 20 to 30 minutes. Serve immediately.

Corn and Zucchini Salsa

Enjoy this salsa over grilled chicken or fish, as a salad garnish or with tortilla chips. A perfect late summer treat.

Yields: 2 cups

Ingredients

2 zucchini about the size of a bratwurst
1 ear of sweet corn
2 tablespoons olive oil
1 large tomato, remove seeds
   and chop (see p. 288)
1/2 cup lime juice (about 4 fresh limes)
1/4 cup cider vinegar
1 jalapeno or other spicy pepper,
   remove seeds and chop fine
2 tablespoons chopped scallions
2 cloves garlic, mince
Black pepper
Salt

Directions

Preheat oven to 400 F. Rub the corn with 1 teaspoon of olive oil and roast for 30 to 40 minutes until kernels are golden and a little crispy. Remove from the oven, cool long enough to allow handling and cut the kernels off the cob with a large knife. Simply stand the corn on end and run the blade of the knife down between the cob and kernels.

While corn is roasting, trim ends of zucchini, cut in half lengthwise, scoop out seeds and dice into 1/4-inch pieces. Place zucchini in a colander, sprinkle with 1 teaspoon salt and toss well. Let zucchini sit for 5 minutes to draw out some moisture. This will improve the texture of the salsa. Rinse under cold running water, shake dry and pat with paper towels. Combine the corn, zucchini, remaining olive oil, tomatoes, lime juice, vinegar, and peppers in a large skillet over medium-high heat. Bring mixture to a boil, reduce heat and simmer uncovered, stirring occasionally, for 2 minutes. Remove from heat and transfer to a serving bowl or storage container and chill completely.

Tip: This salsa can also be canned. While still hot ladle into a hot sterilized canning jar and process in a hot water bath for 15 minutes (see Chapter 7).

CHEF'S NOTES

1. Sweet corn is best eaten as soon as possible after it is picked. The sugars in the corn very quickly turn to starch.

2. Sweet corn roasted over an open fire is a special treat. Remove as much of the silk as possible without removing the husk, recover the corn with the husk and roast for 20 to 30 minutes.

3. Sweet corn can be frozen whole or cut from the cob. Either way, you should blanch the corn whole for 8 to 10 minutes in boiling salted water. Place whole ears in large freezer bags or cut the corn from the cob with a sturdy knife. Place in airtight containers or freezer bags.

4. In Central and South America, the practice is to eat sweet corn with a little salt and a squeeze of lime. Save an ear or two and try this.

Brown Butter Corn With Basil

This is a great way to reclaim leftover corn. The butter and basil bring it back to life.

Serves: 4

Ingredients
3 cups cooked corn kernels
2 tablespoons butter
1 cup chopped fresh basil
Salt and pepper

Directions
Heat butter in a large skillet over medium-high heat. Continue to heat as butter boils and foams. When the foam subsides, the butter solids on the bottom of the pan should have turned golden brown. Add corn, salt, and pepper. Cook, stirring, for 2 minutes until corn is warm. Remove from heat and stir in basil. Serve immediately.

From *The Everyday Cookbook*
· circa 1890 ·

Boiled Green Corn

"Choose young sugar-corn, full grown, but not hard; test with the nail. When the grain is pierced, the milk should escape in a jet, and not be thick. Clean by stripping off the outer leaves, turn back the innermost covering carefully, pick off every thread of silk, and re-cover the ear with the thin husk that grew nearest it. Tie at the top with a bit of thread, put in boiling water salted, and cook fast from twenty minutes to half an hour, in proportion to size and age. Cut off the stalks close to the cob, and send whole to the table wrapped in a napkin.

Or you can cut from the cob while hot and season with butter, pepper, and salt. Send to table in a vegetable dish."

Picnic Corn Relish

A classic barbecue side.

Serves: 6

Ingredients

1/2 teaspoon ground cumin
1/4 cup white wine vinegar
2 teaspoons sugar
1 teaspoon celery seeds
3 ears just cooked corn
1 large tomato, peel, core, remove
    seeds and dice (see p. 288)
1/2 red onion, finely chopped
1/4 cup chopped sweet pickle
Salt
Splash of Tabasco

Directions

Cut the kernels from the corn by standing corn up vertically. With even forceful downward sweeps of the knife, cut the kernels from the cob circling around cob until all kernels are removed. Place corn in a mixing bowl. Add tomatoes, onion, and pickles.

Heat a small skillet over medium heat. Add the cumin and toast in a dry pan for 30 seconds until fragrant. Add the sugar, vinegar, and celery seed. Stir while heating until sugar just dissolves. Remove from heat. Pour vinegar mixture over corn mixture. Salt to taste and shake on a little Tabasco. Toss all ingredients. Cover bowl and chill for 1 hour.

CRANBERRIES

In late September and early October, if you find yourself in central Wisconsin, take a drive along the rural roads and gaze upon the truly beautiful site of the cranberries floating on the bogs ready to be harvested. The air is chilly, the sun is high and the explosion of crimson is breathtaking. It is one last gift of color before the starker beauty of winter soon to come. The fresh season for cranberries is short, but don't fret, they freeze well.

Autumn Cranberry Pudding

This is a version of an English summer pudding using the cranberries that typically appear in October. If you still can get local fresh cranberries at Thanksgiving, consider this in place of the traditional cranberry sauce.

Serves: 6 to 8

Ingredients

1 pound fresh cranberries
1 apple, peel and dice
1/2 cup raisins
3/4 cup brown sugar
2 cups cranberry juice cocktail
1/4 teaspoon vanilla extract
1 lemon
1 cinnamon stick
10 slices bread from a square loaf, remove crust
1 cup heavy cream
2 tablespoons sugar

Directions

Combine the cranberries, apple, raisins, brown sugar, vanilla, cinnamon stick and cranberry juice cocktail in a saucepan over medium high heat. Bring the mixture to a boil, reduce heat and simmer for 10 to 15 minutes. Remove from heat. Using a lemon zester or hand grater, add the zest from the lemon to the cranberry mixture. Cut the lemon in half and squeeze in the juice. Mix well and pick out cinnamon stick. Set aside.

Line a 1-1/2-quart bowl with plastic film. The film should hang 1 or 2 inches over the lip of the bowl. Line the bottom of the bowl with slices of the bread, cutting and trimming to fully cover the bottom of the bowl. Pour in the cranberry mixture. Cut and arrange the remaining bread to cover the top of the bowl. Place a sheet of film over everything and put a plate on top of the pudding that is smaller than the diameter of the bowl. Set bowl in a pan to collect over flow juice and place at least a 3-pound weight on top of plate. Chill the pudding for at least 12 hours.

Place very cold cream in a mixing bowl. Add 2 tablespoons of sugar and beat with a hand mixer, starting at medium speed and slowly increasing speed as cream thickens. Blend until very stiff. Keep cold in refrigerator.

Remove weight, plate and film from top of bowl. Turn bowl over on to a serving platter and unmold. Remove wrap. Serve in wedges with whipped cream.

Roast Pork Loin With Cranberry Jus

This is a wonderful autumn supper — Sweet, tart and savory.

Serves: 4

Roast Ingredients
2 pounds pork loin
1/4 cup poppy seed
1 tablespoon dried thyme
Salt
Black pepper

Directions
Preheat oven to 350 F. Mix spies and rub onto the outside of the pork loin. Roast in the oven until the internal temperature reaches 140 F. Remove roast from pan and set aside to rest.

Cranberry Jus Ingredients
1/2 cup cranberry juice cocktail
1/2 cup prepared beef gravy
2 tablespoons butter
1/2 cup fresh cranberries
1/4 cup chopped green onions
1 tablespoon chopped parsley

Directions
Place pork roasting pan on top of stove and turn heat up to medium. Add cranberry juice cocktail and let sizzle to raise little browned bits up from bottom of pan; reduce by half. Add gravy and cranberries. Bring to a boil. Remove from the heat and vigorously stir in butter with wire whisk until sauce looks a little creamy. Stir in green onions and chopped parsley. Slice pork and arrange in serving dish. Cover with cranberry jus and serve immediately.

. . . .

Spiced Cranberry and Apple Juice

This juice is very good served warm.

Yields: 2 cups

Ingredients
3 cups fresh cranberries
4 red apples, core and cut into wedges
3 tablespoons honey
1/2 teaspoon ground cinnamon
1/4 teaspoon ground nutmeg

Directions
Process cranberries and apples through juicer until juice is extracted. Stir in honey, cinnamon, and nutmeg. Serve in 2 glasses garnished with apple slices.

. . . .

Cranberry Vinaigrette

Try this on a salad of fresh spinach leaves and chopped nuts.

Yields: 5 cups

Ingredients

2 cups fresh cranberries
1/2 cup sugar
1 teaspoon of fresh thyme
1 cup red wine vinegar
1/2 cup salad oil
1/2 cup maple syrup

Directions

Place the cranberries, sugar and thyme into a food processor and rough chop. Add vinegar and, while processor is running, slowly add oil then add maple syrup.

. . . .

Three Berry and Grapefruit Preserves

If you haven't eaten all of your summer berries and have frozen a few, this spread is outstanding and will reward your foresight and discipline.

Yields: 4 pints

Ingredients

12 ounces fresh cranberries
3 cups blackberries, if frozen use the juice as well
3 cups raspberries, if frozen use the juice as well
1-1/2 cups sugar
Juice from 2 grapefruit, about 1 cup

Directions

In a stainless steel or enamel saucepan (avoid aluminum), combine the cranberries, 2 cups blackberries, 2 cups raspberries, sugar and grapefruit juice. Bring to a boil over medium heat. Once boiling, reduce heat and simmer, stirring frequently, for 25 to 30 minutes. Add the remaining berries after 20 minutes. Preserves are done cooking when the liquid coats the back of a spoon (about the consistency of warm pancake syrup). Ladle into 4 pint canning jars leaving a 1/4-inch space between the preserves and the top of the jar. Cover and seal jars. Process jars in a boiling water bath for 15 minutes, as outlined in Chapter 7.

. . . .

Cranberry Vodka Sorbet

This is easiest with an ice cream maker but you can make it by simply freezing in a shallow pan and stirring every hour or so. It will be chunkier but delicious nonetheless. Serve in stemware and splash with a little Vodka.

Serves: 4

Ingredients

2 cups sugar
2 cups water
1 cup fresh or frozen cranberries, process into a fine paste
1/4 cup lemon juice
Splash of vodka
Orange zest

Directions

Bring sugar and water to a boil and let boil for 5 minutes to form a simple syrup. Let cool completely in the refrigerator. Once cool, pour into an ice cream maker along with the remaining ingredients and prepare according to the directions. Once sorbet has thickened, scoop into a covered container and cure in the freezer for a few hours.

CHEF'S NOTES

1. Cranberries are a great addition to stews and braises. The acidity goes particularly well with wild game.

2. In most recipes, cranberries will have to be sweetened. Always adjust the sugar based on the tartness of the berry.

3. Cranberries freeze well. Simply freeze whole fruit in airtight containers or freezer bags. You may also make cranberry sauce or cranberry puree and freeze that.

CUCUMBERS

Cucumbers are one of those vegetables that have lost all its personality due to its year-round cultivation. We've become used to seeing beautiful uniform displays of shiny perfect cucumbers on display in supermarket aisles. They look beautiful and invite you to bring them home but, once you eat them, you realize that they are just a tasteless crunch. This is not how it has to be. Heirloom varieties of cucumbers that you find at farmers markets are loaded with forgotten flavors. Some varieties are slightly bitter, others sweet, and still others tart. They have funny shapes and their skins aren't shiny, but they taste like a vegetable and not a cup full of water with seeds.

Fresh cucumbers are available from mid-summer on and they are available in large quantities. If you are a CSA member, it might be wise to get comfortable with pickling because cucumbers do not freeze well and you are likely to be flooded with them at some point.

Cucumber Ginger Salad

When cucumbers are abundant, this salad makes a great light side. The taste is clean and the flavors are sharp.

Serves: 4 to 6

Ingredients
4 large cucumbers, peel and remove seeds
Salt
1/4 cup white wine vinegar
1/4 cup cider vinegar
1/2 cup sugar
2 tablespoons fresh grated ginger
2 tablespoons fresh chopped parsley

Directions
Slice the cucumbers as thin as possible (1/8-inch thick). Place cucumbers in a colander set over a bowl. Sprinkle with about 1 teaspoon of salt and toss well. Refrigerate for 2 hours. This will allow the salt to draw some moisture out of the cucumbers. In the meantime, combine vinegars, ginger and sugar in a large mixing bowl. Whisk vigorously until sugar dissolves. When cucumbers are ready, wash your hands and manually squeeze all the moisture you can out of the cucumbers. Place cucumbers in bowl with vinegar mixture, add parsley and toss well. This salad is best served immediately but can be prepared a day in advance.

From *The Everyday Cookbook*
· circa 1890 ·

Pickled Cucumbers

Wash and wipe six hundred small cucumbers and two quarts of peppers. Put them in a tub with one and half cupfuls of salt and a piece of alum as large as an egg. Heat to the boiling point three gallons of cider vinegar and three pints of water. Add a quarter of a pound each of whole cloves, whole allspice and stick cinnamon, and two ounces of white mustard seed, and pour over the pickles.

Cucumber Salad With Toasted Spices

Toasting whole seed spices is a wonderful way to add a little smokiness to a recipe. This is a distinctive buffet salad. It is best served the day you make it.

Serves: 4

Ingredients
1 teaspoon cumin seeds*
1 teaspoon black mustard seeds*
1/2 cup cottage cheese
1/2 cup plain yogurt
Salt
2 medium cucumbers, unpeeled
    with the seeds scooped out
1 onion, diced
1 tomato, diced
2 tablespoons chopped fresh cilantro
*Whole seed spices can be found at gourmet
    shops, coffee shops or by mail order.

Directions
Heat a small skillet over medium-high heat. Add seeds to pan and toast while shaking the pan. Seeds will sputter and pop and you may want some type of cover to keep them in the pan. When most of the seeds are popped and brown, remove pan from heat and set aside.

Place yogurt and cottage cheese into a food processor or blender and whip smooth while adding toasted spices and salt to taste.

Dice cucumbers into ¼-inch pieces; combine in a mixing bowl with diced onions and tomatoes. Stir in yogurt mixture. Refrigerate 30 minutes before serving to allow flavors to marry.

Cucumber Pistachio Relish

A nice change of pace from plain pickle relish.

Yields: 1/2 cup

Ingredients
1 large cucumber
1/4 cup finely chopped pistachio nuts
1/4 cup extra virgin olive oil
Salt and pepper to taste

Directions
Slice cucumber in half from end to end. Scoop out all the seeds with a teaspoon leaving only firm flesh and peel. Dice cucumber. Toss with remaining ingredients.

CHEF'S NOTES

1. Refrigerator pickles can be made with all types of brine. I've included one recipe here and samples of spicy and sweet pickle brine can be found in the seasonal combo section.

2. The variations of cucumber salads are endless. Slice cucumbers very thin or seed and chop. Mix with yogurt and herbs, mayonnaise mixed with sour cream and garlic, any vinaigrette, or any creamy salad dressing are great salad bases.

3. Much of the moisture in cucumbers is in the seeds. If you want less moisture in a salad scrape the seeds out with a spoon.

4. The Romans used cucumbers to scare away scorpions and mice. It might be best to always have one handy.

Cucumber Finger Sandwiches

Make these sandwiches with a variety of late summer vegetables and serve with a chilled soup and fresh fruit for a mid-summer patio picnic.

Yields: Approx. 40

Ingredients
20 slices white or wheat bread (frozen)
1 large cucumber, slice very thin
3/4 cups butter or cream cheese, room temperature
2 teaspoons minced fresh garlic
1 tablespoon lemon juice
1 tablespoon extra virgin olive oil
Salt and pepper

Directions
Toss cucumber slices with a little salt and place in a colander for 1-1/2 to 2 hours to draw out some moisture.

In a separate bowl mix together oil, lemon juice and fresh ground black pepper. Add the cucumber slices and toss until well coated.

Thoroughly mix garlic with cream cheese or butter. Spread one side of all the bread slices with a thin layer of the garlic mixture. Arrange cucumber slices in a single layer on 10 of the bread slices. Top with the remaining slices to form sandwiches. Cut sandwiches while the bread is still frozen with a very sharp knife. This will allow you to have very precise and attractive corners on the sandwiches. Trim crusts from sandwiches to form consistently sized squares. Cut sandwiches in squares, triangles or fingers.

Refrigerator Dills

In my opinion, refrigerator pickles are crisper and more flavorful than the canned variety. However, they must be kept refrigerated and that limits how many jars you can make and store. This is my favorite recipe.

Yields: 2 quarts

Ingredients
About 2 dozen small (approx. 2 inches long) pickling cucumbers (they should pack tightly in the jars.)
6 sprigs fresh dill
4 cloves garlic
1 cup rice wine vinegar

Directions
Tightly pack about a dozen cucumbers, 3 sprigs of dill and a garlic clove in each sterilized 1-quart jar. Pour 1/2 cup of vinegar in each jar. Fill the jars with cold water to within 1/4-inch of the top. Cover and seal the jars. Place in the refrigerator and let flavors marry for at least 1 week. Pickles will keep for at least 2 months in the refrigerator.

· · · · · · · · · · · · · · ·

Tzatziki

This is the famous gyro dip but it also makes a very good spread for crusty bread or pita.

Yields: 5 cups

Ingredients
6 cups yogurt, drain to yield 3 to 4 cups yogurt cheese (see p. 289)
2 large cucumbers, peel, remove seeds and dice very fine
5 garlic cloves, mince
2 tablespoons olive oil
1 tablespoon chopped fresh dill

1 tablespoon chopped fresh mint
1 tablespoon champagne or white wine vinegar
Salt and black pepper

Directions
Stir together all ingredients until thoroughly mixed. Refrigerate for at least 4 hours to allow flavors to marry.

· · · · · · · · · · · · · · ·

Cucumber Cooler

This juice is a meal. Fortified with yogurt and pecans, it will sate your hunger.

Serves: 2

Ingredients
3 cucumbers, quarter lengthwise and cut into 2-inch strips
1 jalapeno chili, remove seeds and stem and cut in half
1/2 cup packed cilantro
1/2 cup yogurt
1/2 cup chopped pecans or walnuts
Salt and pepper to taste

Directions
Feed cucumbers, jalapeno and cilantro through your juicer until juice is fully extracted. Pour juice into a blender or processor. Add yogurt and nuts. Blend until smooth and foamy. Add salt and pepper to taste. Serve in 2 glasses.

· · · · · · · · · · · · · · ·

Cucumber Salad With Yogurt

At some point each summer you will find this salad on my table.

Serves: 4

Ingredients

- 2 large cucumbers
- 3/4 cup plain yogurt
- 1/2 teaspoon paprika
- 1/2 teaspoon lemon juice
- 1 teaspoon chopped fresh chives
- Salt and pepper

Directions

Peel the cucumbers and slice lengthwise. Scoop the seeds out and discard. Sprinkle a little salt on the cucumbers and place in a colander poised over a bowl. Leave for 30 minutes to allow some of the liquid to leach out of the cucumbers. Rinse the cucumbers and dice into 1/4-inch pieces. Place in a mixing bowl.

In a small bowl, combine the yogurt, paprika, lemon juice and chives. Mix thoroughly. Salt and pepper to taste. Combine yogurt with cucumbers and mix well. Serve well chilled.

Cold Cucumber Soup

If you are at a loss for what to do with all the large cucumbers that have found their way into your vegetable drawer, try a lunch of cold cucumber soup and a platter of cucumber finger sandwiches (see recipe p. 108).

Serves: 4

Ingredients

- 3 cups seeded and diced fresh cucumber
- 1 cup chopped scallion (greens included)
- 2 cups cottage cheese
- Salt and black pepper
- 2 tablespoons fresh chopped parsley

Directions

Place cucumber, scallions, and cottage cheese in a food processor; process until a smooth puree. Liberally season with salt and pepper. Chill for at least one hour. When ready to serve, add just enough cold water to make the consistency of a thick soup. Serve in shallow bowls. Garnish with sliced cucumbers and chopped parsley.

Simple Cucumber Radish Slaw

A very simple slaw to use as a counterpoint to spicy grilled meat or as a light side salad.

Serves: 4

Ingredients

- 1 cucumber, remove seeds
- 3 radishes
- 1 tablespoon sesame oil
- 1 tablespoon sesame seeds
- 2 teaspoons salt

Directions

Grate cucumber and radish, then transfer to a colander set over a bowl. Sprinkle with salt and toss. Let set for 30 minutes to draw the moisture out of the salad. Rinse cucumber and radishes with cold running water, shake and pat dry. Place in a mixing bowl. Toss with sesame seeds and oil.

Warm Cucumber Dishes

Yes, cucumber can be cooked. They make a very good side dish with chicken breast or whitefish. They are best cut large and slowly simmered, but if you are short on time dice the cucumber small and cook quickly.

Buttered Cucumber

Serves: 4

Ingredients

1 pound of cucumbers, remove seeds and
   soft flesh and cut into 3/4-inch chunks
1/2 cup diced onions
3 tablespoons butter, divided
2 tablespoons water
Salt and pepper to taste
2 tablespoons chopped fresh herbs

Directions

Heat 2 tablespoons butter over medium-high heat in a large skillet. Add onions and cook until soft. Add cucumbers, salt and pepper and water. Reduce heat to very low, cover and cook gently for 20 minutes. Add remaining tablespoon of butter and chopped herbs to pan. Toss together until well mixed. Serve immediately.

Cucumber and Tomato Sauté

Serves: 4

Ingredients

1 pound of cucumbers, remove seeds
   and dice into 1/4-inch pieces
2 tablespoons olive oil
1/2 cup fresh tomatoes, remove seeds
   and dice into 1/4-inch pieces
2 cloves garlic, minced
Salt and pepper to taste
1/4 cup chopped fresh basil

Directions

Heat olive oil in a large skillet over medium-high heat. Add cucumbers and garlic. Cook cucumbers and garlic, stirring constantly, until garlic just browns. Reduce heat to low, add tomatoes, salt and pepper. Stir cucumbers and tomatoes together and cook for an additional 2 to 3 minutes. Add basil and toss together. Serve immediately.

Cucumbers With Cream

Serves: 4

Ingredients

1 pound of cucumbers, removed seeds and
   soft flesh and cut into 3/4-inch chunks
1/4 cup chopped shallots
1/4 cup heavy cream
Pinch of grated nutmeg
Salt and pepper to taste
2 tablespoons chopped fresh chives

Directions

Heat heavy cream and shallots over medium high heat until boiling. Add cucumbers, salt, pepper and nutmeg. Reduce heat to very low and simmer uncovered until cream thickens to a sauce, about 15 minutes. Pour into serving dish and sprinkle with chives.

DANDELION

It may seem odd to put a chapter about dandelions in this book, but we occasionally see the greens offered at farmers markets and in CSA boxes. I'm sure that the neighbor's of any farmer growing dandelions for greens are pretty irritated. Still, that doesn't change the fact that the greens are really tasty. Traditionally, dandelion greens are cooked with bacon and a little vinaigrette, but you can use them as you would use any leafy salad green. The greens are best from immature plants.

Dandelion and Bacon Salad

This is the traditional method of serving dandelion greens. For this salad you should find small leaves from plants that have not flowered yet. If you prefer a vegetarian salad, simply replace the bacon with some grated or shredded Parmesan cheese.

Serves: 4

Ingredients

9 ounces fresh young dandelion greens
4 to 5 slices good bacon, diced
    in very small pieces
2 tablespoons extra virgin olive oil
1 tablespoon dry white wine
Salt and pepper to taste
1 tablespoon white wine, cider or rice vinegar
Optional: 2 hard-cooked eggs

Directions

In a large salad bowl, prepare simple vinaigrette by whisking together olive oil, white wine, salt and pepper. Add dandelion greens and toss with dressing. Arrange quartered cooked eggs in a decorative pattern on top of the salad.

Cook bacon in a large skillet over medium heat until thoroughly browned. Pour off half the grease. Return bacon to heat and add vinegar to bacon pan. Scrape the yummy bits of cooked bacon off the bottom of the pan while the vinegar boils and sputters. Pour entire contents of skillet over top of salad. Serve immediately.

Fettuccine With Garlic Scapes and Dandelion

This could be the first plate of fresh food you eat each season. Not only will you have a fantastic lunch, you also will get some yard work done. Garlic scapes are the pencil-thin shoots from a fresh garlic plant. You will find them at many farmers markets and in some CSA boxes.

Serves: 4

Ingredients

12 ounces fettuccine
1/2 cup dried tomatoes (see p. 292)
1/2 cup garlic scapes, thinly chopped
    into little nuggets
2 tablespoons olive oil
8 ounces young dandelion greens,
    roughly chopped
1/2 cup shredded Parmesan cheese
Salt and pepper to taste

Directions

Cook the paste according to package directions. Drain and set aside while still warm. Heat oil over low heat in a large skillet. Add garlic scapes and tomatoes. Cook for 3 to 5 minutes until garlic softens. Add 1/4 cup of water, increase heat to medium and cover. Cook for several minutes until tomatoes are tender. Add chopped greens and recover. Cook 1 minute longer until greens are wilted. Add cooked pasta and cheese to skillet and toss until well mixed. Season with salt and pepper and serve immediately.

. . . .

Dandelion Greens Wilted in Shallot Butter

With any wilted green, you should be careful not to overcook. Cook quickly and serve immediately.

Serves: 4

Ingredients

1 pound dandelion greens cut from
    young plants, rinse well
1/2 shallot butter, half the recipe (see p. 281)
1 tablespoon fresh chopped chives

Directions

Melt shallot butter in a large skillet over medium-low heat. Add dandelion greens and cook, stirring frequently, until leaves are just wilted, 2 to 3 minutes. Transfer to a serving dish and sprinkle with chives. Serve hot.

. . . .

CHEF'S NOTES

1. If you are using dandelion greens for a salad, you should only use very young and tender leaves. Larger mature leaves can be braised until tender.

2. The sticky "goo" inside dandelion stems is said to be effective in removing corns and warts.

3. The flowers make a nice wine and the roots, when roasted and dried, make a very good coffee substitute. Neither of these recipes is within the scope of this book but are available with a little research.

Dandelion Salad With Warm Balsamic Dressing

Dandelion greens hold up well with a warm dressing. This dressing is rich and sweet with pecans.

Serves: 6

Ingredients
2 pounds young dandelion greens
3 tablespoons olive oil
3 cloves garlic, minced
1/4 cup chopped pecans
2 tablespoons balsamic vinegar
Salt and pepper to taste

Directions
Cut tough stems from dandelion greens and place in a large decorative serving bowl. Heat olive oil in a small skillet over medium heat. Add garlic and nuts and cook 3 to 5 minutes until garlic is light brown. Stir in vinegar. Season with salt and pepper and allow mixture to warm through. Whisk dressing in pan to fully combine and pour over greens. Serve immediately.

EGGPLANT

For a very long time I could not figure out any use for eggplant. To me, nothing looked so cool, yet delivered so little — big globes of bright purple that looked like they might deliver a life-changing experience only to give us a kind of bland and mushy tedium. I had to learn to coax the personality out of eggplant and to appreciate its subtle kind of intrigue. It can be cooked in a variety of ways and carries flavors extremely well. When it is well cooked, it has a delicious creamy consistency that is addicting when pureed or chopped into dips or spreads. It fries very well and is the main ingredient in myriad layered casseroles.

There are countless varieties of eggplant you might find at a farmers market, from the huge purple ones we are used to seeing in the supermarket to the narrow white ones that are particularly mild to the contorted pastel lavender ones that are especially mysterious. Nothing says summer like a row of market stands overloaded with a nest of shiny and variegated eggplant. Any of these recipes will allow you to deliver on the promise that this colorful display promises.

Broiled Eggplant With Fresh Mozzarella

This is a simple side for well-seasoned meats. Fresh mozzarella is sometimes called Buffalo mozzarella for reasons that are a mystery to me. It is a fresh soft cheese with a light clean taste and it can be found in most supermarkets.

Serves: 4

Ingredients

4 small long eggplants the size of a
    bratwurst sliced lengthwise
1 clove garlic minced
1 tablespoon chopped fresh oregano or basil
Salt and black pepper to taste
1/4 cup bread crumbs
1/4 cup olive oil
1 cup fresh mozzarella sliced into strips

Directions

Preheat the oven to 350 F. Lay eggplants, flesh-side up, in a shallow baking dish. Cut shallow slits into the flesh of the eggplant and set aside. Combine garlic, herbs, bread crumbs, salt, pepper and olive oil in a mixing bowl. Press this mixture in equal parts on the eggplant. Place in oven and broil until tender and well browned, about 20 minutes. Remove from oven and lay strips of mozzarella across the top of the eggplant. Return to oven for 5 minutes until cheese melts. Serve immediately.

Fried Eggs a la Catalane

In classic French cooking, a dish garnished with tomatoes, eggplant and especially garlic is considered to be in the Catalonian style. Whatever the style, this is a great breakfast.

Serves: 4

Ingredients

8 small or 4 large round slices of eggplant, peel and slice 1/2-inch thick
8 small or 4 large round slices of fresh tomato
Salt and pepper to taste
4 large eggs
2 cloves garlic, mice
Olive oil for cooking
2 tablespoons chopped fresh parsley

Directions

Heat 2 tablespoons of olive oil in 2 separate skillets over medium heat. Salt and pepper eggplant and tomato slices. Gently pan fry tomatoes in one pan and eggplant in the other until lightly browned. Remove to a serving platter and arrange tomato slices with eggplant slices in a decorative shingle pattern. Keep warm.

Clean out one of the skillets and heat an additional 2 tablespoons of olive oil over medium heat. Fry eggs to desired doneness. Halfway through frying, season with salt and pepper and add minced garlic. Allow garlic to brown slightly in the pan while eggs finish. Lay fried eggs over tomatoes and eggplants. Pour olive oil and garlic in pan over eggs and sprinkle with parsley.

. . . .

Eggplant, Tomato and Basil Dip

In midsummer, serve this dip with warm flatbread and chilled white wine to people you like.

Yields: 3-1/2 cups

Ingredients

1 pound eggplant
1 tomato
1/4 cup olive oil
1/2 cup fresh basil leaves
1 glove garlic
1 tablespoon lemon juice
Salt and pepper to taste
1/4 cup feta cheese

Directions

Preheat broiler. Remove the stem from the eggplant and the core from the tomato. Slice both into 1/2-inch slices and lay in a single layer on a shallow baking sheet. Broil about 5 to10 minutes on each side until eggplant is well browned and tomatoes are softened. While the tomato and eggplant are cooking, place the basil and garlic in a food processor and process until finely chopped. Once the eggplant is well browned, transfer to the food processor along with the tomatoes and any accumulated juices. Process in short bursts until the mixture is roughly chopped. Remove processed ingredients and transfer to a mixing bowl. Toss with lemon juice, salt and pepper. Chill in refrigerator and garnish with crumbled feta cheese.

. . . .

Baba Ghanoush

The best- known of the roasted eggplant dips. You will find many recipes for baba ghanoush and most are very good, but this one is rich and garlicky.

Yields: 4 cups

Ingredients

2 pounds eggplant (any type)
3 garlic cloves, minced
1 tablespoon (approx.) lemon juice
1 tablespoon tahini* or peanut butter
1/2 cup (approx.) olive oil
Salt and pepper to taste
1/3 cup fresh diced tomatoes
* Tahini is a Middle Eastern sesame puree. It has a rich distinctive taste and is widely available at larger supermarkets.

Directions

Preheat the oven to 500 F. Roast eggplants in the oven until skin is black and wrinkled. Allow the eggplant to cool to the touch. Scoop the pulp from inside the skin and place in a food processor. Process until smooth while adding the olive oil — it should be the consistency of sour cream. While food processor is running, add garlic and tahini or peanut butter. Add salt and pepper to taste. Add lemon juice to taste (be careful). Remove to serving bowl and fold in fresh, diced tomatoes. Serve with crackers, fresh crusty bread, vegetables, pita crisps, croutons, tortillas.

Imam Biyaldi

This is a famous Turkish stuffed eggplant dish. The name refers to a legendary imam who fainted with joy from its breathtaking fragrance. You would have to really like eggplant to faint over this recipe. However, at the very least, it should raise a smile on the faces of you and your guests.

Yields: 8 cups

Ingredients

6 long narrow eggplants
1-1/2 cups thinly sliced onions
3/4 cup olive oil
3 large cloves garlic, crush and roughly chop
1/2 cup loosely packed flat leaf parsley
2 cups peeled, seeded and chopped fresh tomatoes (see p. 288)
Salt to taste
1 cup water
1 tablespoon sugar
1 lemon, zest and juice

Directions

Preheat oven to 350 F. Slice eggplants in half lengthwise. Scoop out the inside of the eggplants to form hollow vessels. Salt the inside of the eggplants and invert over paper towels for 1 hour. Rinse the eggplants and pat dry.

Heat 1/4 cup of olive oil over medium heat in a large skillet. Add onions and cook slowly until soft. Stir in garlic and cook until fragrance is released. Remove from heat and stir in tomatoes, parsley and zest from one lemon. Add salt to taste.

Fill the cavities of the eggplants with heaping portions of the tomato mixture and place in a deep baking dish or Dutch oven. Pour the remaining olive oil in equal amounts over the stuffed eggplants.

Mix together water, sugar, and the lemon juice and pour into the bottom of the pan. Cover the pan and bake for 1 hour until eggplant is very soft. This may be served warm but I think it is much better cold with pita chips or warm flatbread.

Caponata

Caponata and Eggplant Parmesan consume more eggplant in America than all other dishes combined. All of the ingredients should be available at your farmers market or in your garden or CSA box around midsummer. The flavors are friendly, familiar and satisfying. You can roast instead of fry the eggplant, but the result is a little mushier. This can be a great vegetarian main course, a sauce for pasta, or a side to grilled meats.

Serves: 6 to 8

Ingredients

1-1/2 pounds eggplant, cut into 3/4-inch cubes
Salt and pepper to taste
1 cup olive oil
3 cups diced onions
1-1/2 pounds fresh tomatoes, roughly chop
1 cup stuffed green olives, roughly chop
1/2 cup ripe olives
3 tablespoons capers
1 cup diced celery
1/3 cup red wine vinegar
2 teaspoons sugar

Directions

Lay eggplant on a pan lined with paper towels and sprinkle liberally with salt. Lay a second pan over the eggplant and weigh down with a sack of potatoes, or a bowling ball, or a very large relative. Let the eggplant sit for at least 30 minutes. Remove weight, rinse off eggplant in a colander and pat dry with a towel. This removes some bitterness and gives a better cooked texture to the eggplant.

Heat 1/2 cup of olive oil over medium-high heat in a large skillet. Add eggplant and fry, turning occasionally, until browned on all sides. Remove from oil, salt and pepper lightly, and set aside.

Heat 1/2 cup of olive oil over medium heat in a large saucepan or pot. Add the onions and sauté until translucent. Add the tomatoes, olives, celery and capers to the pot. Reduce heat, cover, and simmer for 10 minutes. Add eggplant, vinegar and sugar to the pot. Cook uncovered for a few minutes, stirring occasionally, until sugar dissolves and eggplant is warmed through.

. . . .

Ginger Broiled Eggplant

This simple dish can be served as a relish or a small salad.

Serves: 4

Ingredients

1 large eggplant
Salt to taste
1/2 cup soy sauce or tamari
1/4 cup Mirin*
1 teaspoon grated ginger
*Mirin is a sweetened rice wine. It is available in most wine shops or liquor stores.

Tip: Fresh ginger root can be kept in the freezer and grated unpeeled as needed with a hand grater.

Directions

Peel the eggplant and cut into 1/4-inch thick circles. Cut slices into 1/4-inch thick strips like French fries. Arrange strips on a clean towel and sprinkle with salt. Let stand for 30 minutes to draw out moisture. Pat eggplant dry and place in a mixing bowl. Add soy sauce, Mirin, and ginger to the bowl. Toss until well mixed. Set aside to marinate for at least 3 hours. Preheat the broiler. Pour eggplant and marinade in a single layer on a shallow baking pan. Broil, turning once, until cooked but still a little firm, 6 to 7 minutes. Serve at room temperature in a side dish or on a bed of greens.

. . . .

Moussaka

This is a hefty Eastern Mediterranean dish of layered lamb and eggplant. You can substitute ground beef or soy crumbles for the lamb if you like, but the lamb makes this authentic and it's worth doing a little extra legwork to find ground lamb. In any event, even people who don't like eggplant will enjoy this dish, it's a very macho plate of food.

Serves: 8

Ingredients

1 large onion, diced
2 cloves garlic, minced
1 bay leaf
Salt and pepper to taste
1 pound ground lamb
1 teaspoon dried oregano
1 teaspoon ground cinnamon
2 cups diced tomatoes
1 cup vegetable or meat stock (see p. 289)
2 large eggplants, peeled and sliced
    no thicker than ¼-inch
Olive oil for frying
Sauce
2 eggs
2 tablespoons flour
Salt and pepper to taste
1/2 tablespoon grated nutmeg
2-1/2 cups yogurt

Directions

Preheat oven to 350 F. Heat 1 tablespoon of olive oil in a large skillet over medium heat. Add onions, garlic and bay leaf. Cook gently until onions are soft but not browned. Add ground lamb and cook, stirring regularly, until lamb has browned. Pour off and discard most of the fat. Add tomatoes, oregano, cinnamon, stock, salt and pepper. Reduce heat, cover pan and simmer for 30 minutes.

While the lamb mixture is cooking, heat 2 tablespoons of olive oil over medium-high heat in another large skillet. Salt and pepper the eggplant slices and lightly brown on both sides. You will have to do this in batches and may have to add oil to the pan. Set aside slices on a towel-lined plate as they finish.

Layer eggplant and lamb mixture, as you would for a lasagna, in a smallish ovenproof casserole dish being careful to end with a layer of eggplant. In a small bowl, beat 2 eggs with 2 tablespoons of flour, salt, pepper and nutmeg. Add yogurt and mix well. Pour this mixture over the top of the moussaka and spread evenly. Bake uncovered for about an hour until the sauce has thickened and is well browned. Allow to rest for 15 to 20 minutes before cutting and serving.

. . . .

CHEF'S NOTES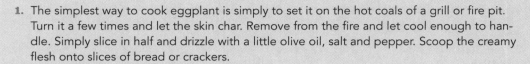

1. The simplest way to cook eggplant is simply to set it on the hot coals of a grill or fire pit. Turn it a few times and let the skin char. Remove from the fire and let cool enough to handle. Simply slice in half and drizzle with a little olive oil, salt and pepper. Scoop the creamy flesh onto slices of bread or crackers.

2. Most recipes require that you salt egg plant and weep out some of the moisture before cooking. This is supposed to make the eggplant less bitter. I'm not convinced it does this, but it does dry the eggplant out a little and allows it to brown better.

3. The only way you can freeze eggplant is to roast and puree it before you freeze it. Baba Ghanoush or Eggplant, Tomato and Basil Dip are delicious dips that can be frozen for a mid winter treat.

4. Eggplant fries very well. This is one technique that is improved by weeping the moisture out with salt. Cut eggplant into French fry-size strips, sprinkle with salt and let sit on top of paper towel for at least an hour. Rinse off salt with cold water and shake dry. Dust with flour, salt and pepper, dip in prepared tempura batter (see p. 286) and fry until golden. Sprinkle with Parmesan cheese and serve with marinara sauce.

5. The bitterest part of eggplant is the seeds and soft flesh surrounding the seeds. This is most pronounced in large eggplant. If you prefer a milder eggplant, look for the smaller varieties.

6. Eggplant should always be cooked to remove the mildly toxic substance solanine.

FENNEL

As a young man, my only experience of fennel was the mysterious licorice seeds that got caught in my teeth when I ate summer sausage. In those days, I had no idea that those seeds could actually grow into something and I was puzzled why any sane person would put seeds in summer sausage. Thank God one grows up. I would surely miss the seeds in my summer sausage and I have been introduced to fresh fennel bulb. It has a truly distinctive flavor and is one ingredient that I rarely have any trouble finding a home for. I'll add it to almost anything. It is fantastic as the main event in a dish, yet pairs with nearly anything. It's great with roasted meats, poached fish and shellfish, nearly any fruit, in entrees, salads, or desserts.

When using fennel bulb cold, it is important to shave the fennel as thin as possible to maximize the sweetness and minimize the bitterness. When cooking, particularly slow cooking, the fennel should be cut into slightly larger pieces in order to keep them from disintegrating. In the northern climates, where I reside, fennel bulbs rarely get much larger than a tennis ball. However, with longer growing seasons, they can get much larger. It is usually available from mid-summer on.

Tomato Fennel Salad

You will be disappointed with this salad unless you can find beautifully ripe heirloom tomatoes. This tasty orange vinaigrette dressing works very well with the fennel. However, you may want to experiment with other vinaigrettes. The technique is outlined on page 278.

Serves: 4

Ingredients

1-1/2 pounds fresh tomatoes, cut into wedges small enough to fit on a fork
1 small fennel
2 tablespoons extra virgin olive oil
1 tablespoon cider vinegar
2 oranges
Salt and pepper to taste

Directions

Zest both oranges into mixing bowl. Cut oranges in half and squeeze juice in bowl with zest being careful to remove any seeds. Add vinegar, salt and pepper to orange juice. Slowly drizzle in olive oil while vigorously stirring with wire whisk. Set aside.

Cut fennel fronds from bulb and set aside. Cut off and discard core end of bulb. Shave fennel bulb as thin as your knife skills will allow. Add fennel and tomatoes to dressing and toss gently to coat with dressing. Serve in a decorative salad bowl with a sprinkling of chopped fennel fronds and garnished with one or two whole fronds placed vertically in salad.

Chermoula Marinated Salmon With Braised Fennel

All the flavors going on in this dish may confuse your tongue. Take a deep breath and enjoy the ride.

Serves: 6

Ingredients

6 ounces fresh salmon filets
1 recipe (1 cup) chermoula (see p. 146)
Salt and black pepper
4 fennel bulbs, save some of the fronds
2 tablespoons butter

Directions

Preheat oven to 350 F. Arrange salmon in a shallow baking dish and coat completely with the chermoula. Cover with plastic wrap and refrigerate for 1 hour 15 minutes. Halve each fennel bulb and carve out the tough core. Slice the bulbs into 1/4-inch wide strips. Heat butter and 1/2 cup water in a large skillet over medium-high heat. Bring to a boil and add fennel. Cover and cook for 10 minutes, stirring occasionally. Uncover, reduce heat, and simmer until fennel is tender, salt and pepper to taste. While fennel is cooking, bake salmon, uncovered, until just cooked through, 15 to 20 minutes.

Spoon equal amounts of the fennel on six plates or shallow bowls, set a salmon filet on top of fennel and garnish fish with a few fennel fronds. Serve warm.

. . . .

Roast Salmon a la Nage

"A la Nage" literally means "swimming" and the salmon in this dish swims in a light soup of red wine and fresh vegetables. I only include it in the fennel chapter because fennel is the most distinctive flavor in the broth. This is a simple and healthy way to prepare any fish.

Serves: 4

Ingredients

1-1/2 pounds fresh salmon filets,
    cut into 6-ounce portions
1 bottle dry red wine
3 garlic cloves, smash and roughly chopped
2 shallots, finely dice
1 clove
1/2 stick cinnamon
1 bouquet garni
1 cup 1/4-inch diced carrots
1 cup 1/4-inch diced celery
1 cup sliced leeks
1 fennel, slice thin 6 ounces fresh salmon filets
1 recipe (1 cup) chermoula (see Appendix)
Salt and black pepper
4 fennel bulbs, save some of the fronds
2 tablespoons butter
1 tablespoon sugar
Salt and pepper to taste
2 tablespoons olive oil
2 tablespoons fresh chopped parsley

. . . .

Pork Braise With Fennel and Apples

You can use any cut of pork in this recipe, but pork hocks are a fantastic choice for braises. The connective tissues in this very tough cut of meat and the marrow in the bone combine to make a rich, yummy pan gravy that tenderizes the meat and carries the flavor of the fennel well. Make this on a chilly fall day with the last of your storage fennel and apples.

Serves: 4

Ingredients

4 medium pork hocks
1 large or 2 small fennel, cut into 1/4-inch strips
1 cup apple cider
1/4 cup cider vinegar
2 apples or pears, sliced
1 bay leaf
Cracked black pepper to taste
Salt to taste
2 tablespoons olive oil
1 onion, diced
2 tablespoons red wine
2 tablespoons brandy
2 tablespoons chopped parsley

Directions

Preheat oven to 350 F. The technique for meat braises is simple. Rub hocks liberally with salt and pepper. Heat oil and brown the meat thoroughly in the same pot that you are going to roast in. A thick-bottomed Dutch oven or pot is the best vessel. The goal is to sear and flavor the meat and also to scorch and burn bits of the meat on the bottom of the pot. This will give the juices a rich, savory flavor and color. Once the meat is browned on all sides and the bottom covered with scorched bits, add the onions and cook until translucent. While pot is still hot, add cider and vinegar and let it sputter and boil all the bits off of the bottom of the pot. Add bay leaf and fennel to the pot. Cover tightly with a lid or foil and roast in the oven for 2 hours. After 2 hours, remove the pot from the oven, add the apples and the brandy, cover the pot again, and roast an additional 30 minutes to 1 hour. The pork hock braise is done when the meat pulls easily away from the bone. Sprinkle with chopped parsley. Serve with dumplings, spaetzle, or boiled potatoes.

. . . .

Carrot and Fennel Juice

A bracing breakfast juice.

Serves: 2

Ingredients

6 medium carrots
2 celery stalks
1 fennel bulb
Black pepper to taste

Directions

Cut carrots and celery into chunks that will fit into your juicer. Trim the woody stem end from the fennel and remove any green fronds. Cut the fennel into pieces that will fit into your juicer. Run all pieces through the juicer. Stir in black pepper to taste. Enjoy!

. . . .

Bouquet Garni

The bouquet garni can have any selection of fresh herbs. This is a very simple version.
Bundle these together with string or wrap in a small piece of cheesecloth.

Ingredients
    2 sprigs fresh parsley
    1 sprig thyme
    1 bay leaf

Directions
Preheat oven to 350 F. Place wine, garlic, shallots, bouquet garni, cloves and cinnamon in a saucepan and bring to a boil over medium-high heat. To marry flavors, cook for 2 minutes and then add carrots, celery, leeks, fennel and sugar. Bring back to a boil and cook a further 2 minutes; salt and pepper to taste. Remove from heat and fish out bouquet garni, cinnamon stick, and clove. Set aside.

Arrange salmon filets in a shallow casserole. Drizzle a little olive oil on them and season with salt and pepper. Pour vegetables over salmon, cover and bake in oven. Serve filets in shallow bowls and ladle vegetables and broth over the top. Sprinkle with chopped fresh parsley.

. . . .

Fennel, Garlic and Navy Bean Soup

A light, vibrant summer soup.

Serves: 8

Ingredients
    1 large fennel bulb
    1 onion, chopped
    18 garlic cloves
    1 quart vegetable stock
    1 bouquet garni (see above)
    4 fresh tomatoes, core and remove seeds
    2 cups cooked navy beans (any beans
        will do either canned or cooked
        as outlined on p. 287)
    1/4 cup chopped chervil or parsley

Directions
Cut the green stems from the fennel bulb and pick off the frilly green fronds. Chop the fronds finely and set aside. Cut the core end of the fennel and discard. Quarter and chop the fennel in chunks like you might celery. Place fennel, onion, garlic, stock, and bouquet garni in a large pot and bring to a boil over high heat. Reduce the heat and simmer for 15 minutes. Add the tomatoes and simmer 5 minutes more. Add beans, parsley or chervil and chopped fennel fronds. Simmer 5 more minutes.

. . . .

Mashed Potatoes With Fennel

Try this with duck or pork chops.

Serves: 4

Ingredients

1 pound potatoes, peeled
1 fennel bulb
1 tablespoon olive oil
1 tablespoon sesame oil
Salt and pepper to taste
2 tablespoon chopped fresh cilantro

Directions

Cut potatoes into large chunks. Place in a pot full of water and bring to a boil over high heat. Once water is boiling, reduce heat and simmer for about 20 minutes until potatoes are soft.

While potatoes are cooking, cut the core from the fennel and carve into 4 to 6 wedges. Place in a separate pan of salted water and bring to a boil over high heat. Reduce heat and simmer for 20 minutes until very tender. Drain water from pan and transfer fennel to a food processor and process, scraping the bowl occasionally, until smooth.

Drain the water from the potatoes and return to pot. Add the fennel puree, olive oil, sesame oil, cilantro, salt and pepper. Mash potatoes thoroughly with a potato masher. Serve hot.

CHEF'S NOTES

1. The wispy fronds that usually come with fresh fennel are very delicate and tasty. Chop them fine and sprinkle as a garnish. They also make a fine plate garnish.

2. Bulbs will keep for two weeks refrigerated, but they don't freeze well.

3. Fennel is believed to ease discomfort from flatulence, urinary disorders and constipation. Now that's a jackpot!

4. Fennel can be chewed as a breath freshener or to quiet hunger pangs.

5. Allow the green stalks to dry and burn them on a grill fire to flavor salmon or tuna with a distinctive smoke.

6. Fennel is delicious battered and deep fried. Prepare with the tempura batter found on p. 286 and sprinkle with lemon juice.

7. Wild fennel is found in many parts of the country. It doesn't develop the large bulb but the fronds make a delicious herb.

FIDDLEHEADS

If one looks at a fiddlehead in the right frame of mind, one imagines the beginning of an Escher print or maybe tiny forest-green ping-pong paddles. Visually, fiddleheads are one of the coolest looking goodies ever to turn up in a market basket. They are the tiny undeveloped shoots of an ostrich fern picked just before they open. They are not typically cultivated, but many people forage for them in the early spring and offer them at farmers markets.

If you've never tried fiddleheads, they are worth a little legwork and are usually available in the north from late April to mid-May. If you're fortunate enough to find fiddleheads, you will discover an exciting celery-like crunch and a mild flavor that suggests asparagus.

You should look for the smallest, tightest spirals; these are the freshest. Prepare them simply. You can gently cook them in steam or boiling water but in my opinion, and you bought this book for my opinion, they are best lightly sautéed with a little garlic. You will never have a lot of these, so it is unlikely that you will have to store them for long. A few simple recipes and you will have had your fiddlehead experience for the year.

Sautéed Fiddleheads With Garlic

Serve this dish with grilled fish or shrimp.

Serves: 4

Ingredients
1 pound fiddlehead ferns, trim and wash well
2 tablespoons olive oil
2 cloves garlic, minced
2 slices bacon, dice into 1/4-inch pieces
Salt and pepper to taste

Directions
Heat the oil in a large skillet over medium high heat. Add bacon and cook, stirring occasionally, until lightly browned. Add fiddleheads and garlic and stir to mix. Cover pan and cook 3 to 4 minutes. Uncover and cook an additional 3 minutes, stirring occasionally. Season with salt and pepper and serve immediately.

CHEF'S NOTES

1. To prepare fiddleheads, first trim a bit off the thick stem end and rinse the fuzz off the outside.

2. You can buy canned fiddleheads, but they are nasty. When you make that nasty food face, just remember I told you so.

Fiddleheads With Dijon Yogurt

Like asparagus, fiddleheads pair well with Dijon mustard.

Serves: 6 as a side

Ingredients

1 pound fresh fiddleheads
1/4 cup plain yogurt
1/4 cup mayonnaise
1 lemon
2 teaspoons Dijon mustard
2 scallions (green onions), chop both
    green and white parts
Salt and pepper to taste
2 quarts of salted water

Directions

Bring salted water to a boil over high heat. Add the fiddleheads and allow water to come back to a boil. Reduce heat and simmer for 6 to 8 minutes until fiddleheads are just tender. Drain well and place in a serving dish.

While fiddleheads are cooking, zest the lemon with a zester or hand grater and place in a mixing bowl. Cut lemon in half and squeeze juice into the same bowl being careful to remove seeds. Add yogurt, mayonnaise, mustard, scallions, salt and pepper to taste to fiddleheads and mix well. Top the fiddleheads with lemon mixture while piping hot.

Fiddleheads With Brown Butter

Brown butter is fantastic on green vegetables. This is a perfect pairing.

Serves: 6 as a side

Ingredients

1 pound fiddleheads
2 quarts salted water
1 stick (1/4 pound) of brown butter (see p. 282)

Directions

Bring salted water to a boil. Add fiddleheads and allow water to come back to a boil. Reduce heat and simmer, uncovered, for 6 to 8 minutes until fiddle-heads are just tender. Transfer to a serving bowl, top with the brown butter and serve immediately.

GARLIC

People have been saying magical things about garlic for 7,000 years. Originating in Western Asia, garlic has been esteemed as a diuretic, laxative, insurance against the plague, cure for the common cold, antiviral, antifungal, and protection against gremlins, demons and vampires. I'm sure some of that stuff is true, but who the hell cares? It tastes good and this is a cookbook. No scent is more welcome to dinner guests than the fragrance of garlic wafting about the house as they arrive. It hints at the promise of good things to come.

Garlic is used in every major cuisine and one variety or other is grown in all corners of the globe. You will find garlic as an ingredient in more recipes than any other single item. It can be sharp and pungent when used raw or lightly cooked or smooth and surprisingly sweet after roasting or long cooking. In fact, garlic has as much natural sugar as cantaloupe, which explains the incredible stickiness of a fresh clove of garlic. Garlic can be kept in a cool, dry, place for months, but there is something special about a bulb of garlic recently snatched from a farmers' market. The cloves are plump and fragrant, perfect for roasting whole and spreading on crusty bread. The recipes in this section all use garlic as the main ingredient and are a nice sampling of both the lightly cooked and long-cooked techniques.

Aigo Boulido

The Provencal name for boiled garlic soup. It is more of a tea, but poured over good crusty bread and served with hunks of cheese and fruit it becomes a soulful meal. In Provence there is a saying, "l'aigo boulido suavo lo vito" (garlic soup saves one's life).

Yields: 2 quarts

Ingredients
2 quarts water
12 garlic cloves, roughly chop
1 teaspoon kosher salt
Sprig of sage
Sprig of thyme
1 bay leaf
8 slices of French bread
Olive oil for drizzle

Directions
Tie the herbs and bay leaf in a bundle with string or in an envelope of cheesecloth. Set aside. Bring water to a boil. Add the garlic and salt to the water and simmer for 15 minutes. Remove from heat and drop in the herb packet. Let steep for a few minutes. Remove herbs from soup. Arrange slices of good crusty bread in the bottom of shallow soup bowls. Drizzle bread with extra virgin olive oil. Ladle hot soup over bread and serve immediately.

Aigo Boulido With Poached Eggs

If I had to eat the same breakfast every morning for the rest of my life, this would be it.

Serves: 4

Ingredients
1 quart Aigo Boulido (see recipe on p. 128)
4 large eggs
4 slices crusty French bread
Fresh chopped parsley

Directions
Place bread in bottom of shallow soup bowls and drizzle with olive oil. Poach eggs to desired doneness in Aigo Boulido. Place egg on top of bread. Ladle soup over eggs and bread. Salt and pepper to taste. Sprinkle with fresh parsley.

Garlic Scape Pesto

A scape is the curly flowering part that sprouts from a garlic plant. They are abundant at farmers markets in spring and early summer. This pesto packs a garlicky punch.

Yields: 4 cups

Ingredients
1 pound garlic scapes, roughly chop
1-1/4 cups grated Asiago cheese
1 cup olive oil
1 tablespoon lemon juice
Salt and pepper to taste

Directions
Place all items in the bowl of a food processor and process until smooth while drizzling in the olive oil. This will keep for several weeks in the refrigerator or you can freeze it indefinitely.

Roast Garlic

Roast garlic is now served in many fine restaurants in place of table butter for bread. Once roasted, garlic loses its sharpness and becomes sweet, rich and tender. It is very simple and makes an elegant statement at a formal dinner or a leaner alternative to butter on your bread every day.

Yields: 1/2 cup

Ingredients
1 large head of garlic
Olive oil

Directions
Preheat oven to 400 F. Remove any loose papery skin from head of garlic. Brush with olive oil and wrap in a small piece of foil. Roast in the oven for 30 to 40 minutes. Remove from oven and slice horizontally across the cloves with a very sharp knife.

Serve warm with bread or rolls on side plates with a drizzle of olive oil and a sprinkling of kosher salt. Garlic can be squeezed out of the heads or scooped out with a knife. They will keep 1 week in the refrigerator.

Garlic Refrigerator Pickle

Enjoy this great snack right out of the jar, in a cocktail or on an antipasto tray.

Yields: 1 pint

Ingredients

3/4 cup white wine vinegar
1/2 cup water
2 teaspoons coarse salt
1/8 teaspoon Old Bay seasoning
6 large heads of garlic, separate into
    cloves and remove skins
1 lemon
1 large top of fresh dill
1 red chili, cayenne or Thai
1 quart of water

Directions

Bring 1 quart of water to a boil over medium-high heat. Add garlic and allow water to return to a boil. Reduce heat and simmer for 5 to 10 minutes until garlic becomes tender but not mushy. Drain in colander and pour into a bowl of ice water to stop the cooking. Drain ice water and set aside. In the same pot, combine water, vinegar, salt and Old Bay seasoning. Bring to a boil over medium-high heat. Add the cooked garlic, reduce heat to very low and allow garlic to steep in liquid for 10 minutes.

    With a vegetable peeler, peel the lemon in a spiral from top to bottom. Try to cut as little of the white pith as possible. If you can't keep it in one piece don't fret, just shave as much of the shiny outer peel as you can. Place peel in a clean 1-pint canning jar. Cut the lemon in half and squeeze the juice into the pan with the garlic. Gently bruise the chili with the back of a knife and place in jar. Place dill in the jar. Ladle in the garlic and pour in enough liquid to fill jar to within ½ inch of the top. Cover and seal jar. Cool at room temperature and store in refrigerator. Will keep for at least 1 month.

Gremolata

This is a classic Italian condiment. It typically is used as a finishing touch on top of roasted or braised meat.

Yields: 1/3 cup

Ingredients

1 lemon
1/4 cup parsley, finely chop
3 cloves garlic, mince
Salt and coarse black pepper to taste

Directions

Zest lemon onto a large sturdy cutting board being careful not to dig too deeply into the peel. The soft, white inside peel is unpleasantly bitter. Mix together in a small pile with the minced garlic. Sprinkle a little salt on this and mash and scrape it with the flat of a large knife. Continue to scrape with a sliding motion using the salt as an abrasive until garlic is the consistency of toothpaste. Scrape lemon and garlic off cutting board and into a small mixing bowl. Cut remainder of lemon in half and squeeze juice into bowl. Mix together with parsley and coarse pepper to taste.

CHEF'S NOTES

The basic Gremolata recipe can easily be modified with different mixtures of citrus and herbs:

1. Replace the lemon and parsley with lime and cilantro and use as a condiment on fish tacos or grilled corn on the cob.

2. Mix with a little olive oil and use as a light pasta sauce.

3. Replace the lemon with orange for a sweeter taste that pairs well with salmon.

4. Replace the parsley with finely chopped basil to garnish grilled zucchini or tomatoes.

CHEF'S NOTES

1. Unless you want your cloves to be whole, the best way to peel garlic is to give each clove a light tap with the flat of a knife. This should loosen the papery skin from the clove.

2. Garlic is sharpest and most pungent raw. Once garlic is cooked the sugars are developed and it becomes very sweet.

3. Never burn garlic. Be mindful of the heat in your pan and turn it down if your garlic starts to char. Lightly browned garlic is sweet and wonderful. Burnt garlic is bitter and nasty.

4. Garlic can be frozen whole, unpeeled, or pureed with olive oil and frozen in containers.

5. Garlic skins are mandatory ingredients in a vegetable stock (see p. 289). Save them in a small baggy in the refrigerator until you make stock.

6. The easiest way to crush garlic is to use a mortar and pestle and they can be very expensive. The cheapest way is to lay the cloves on a cutting board and sprinkle them with a little salt. Press down on the cloves with the flat of a knife and rub back and forth while pushing down very hard. The salt will abrade the garlic and leave you a delicious, pungent garlic paste.

Down on the Farm

September 1

Much of our energy here this past week has been given to the processing of the summer's garlic crop. The last of it has been cut off from the stalks in the garlic barn and transferred to screens in my machine shed where it has been peeled and sorted into seed garlic and eating garlic. Yesterday we shipped 330 pounds of it to Colorado, where it will be sold to garlic lovers who wish to plant some of their own. Back here at the gardens, we have been sorting both red and golden shallots for shipping next week to the Twin Cities. Sometime between now and Wednesday next, I must take time out from the garden crops to jug up 30 gallons of maple syrup that will accompany the garlic and shallots to Minneapolis. Oh yeah, and there are the six restaurants and two stores that I supply weekly in addition to the CSA. Did I mention that the weeds are getting out of control?

— David Peterson, Maplewood Gardens

HEAD LETTUCE

To many people lettuce is iceberg lettuce — pale green flavorless heads of water — really just an excuse to eat heavy creamy dressings. These heads are trucked all over the country from fields in Salinas and Yuma. I'm going to assume that if you've picked up this book you are poised to turn the corner on an iceberg lettuce salad. I offer a handful of head-lettuce dishes that requires nary a leaf of iceberg. Your market or CSA will deliver delicious romaine, butterhead, red oak, raddichio and crisphead varieties. They are available from early summer on.

Pan-Grilled Radicchio With White Wine Butter

The tartness of the sauce goes well with the bitterness of the radicchio — A unique side vegetable.

Serves: 6 to 8 as a side

Ingredients

1 large or 2 small heads of
    radicchio, core and clean
3 cups chopped or shredded
    romaine or butter lettuce
2 tablespoons chopped fresh chives
1/4 cup fresh chopped parsley
1 cup mayonnaise
1/2 cup plain yogurt
1/4 cup buttermilk
1 clove garlic, crush and roughly chop
1 tablespoon Worcestershire sauce
2 tablespoons white wine vinegar
1/2 teaspoon sugar
Salt and pepper
Dash of chili sauce
1/2 cup crumbled blue cheese

Directions

Cut off the core of the radicchio and carefully cut the head into 6 to 8 wedges. Heat the olive oil in a large skillet over medium heat. Arrange the wedges, cut-side down, in the hot pan, salt and pepper to taste and cook for about 5 minutes. Turn the wedge to the second cut side and fry 5 more minutes. Remove from pan and arrange on a serving platter.

    Add shallots, wine and vinegar to the pan that the radicchio was cooked in. Bring to a boil and allow liquid to cook down to nearly dry. Remove the pan from the heat and briskly mix in the butter, a chunk at a time, until it is fully melted and the sauce is smooth and frothy. Pour butter sauce over radicchio and sprinkle with chopped parsley.

Garlic Roasted Radicchio

The rugged texture of radicchio holds up very well to roasting.
This makes a fantastic side to roast chicken.

Serves: 8

Ingredients

8 garlic cloves, mince
1/4 cup olive oil
1 tablespoon fresh thyme
1/4 cup balsamic vinegar
Salt and pepper
4 heads raddichio, cut in half
1/4 cup Parmesan cheese

Directions

Combine garlic, olive oil, thyme, vinegar, salt and pepper in a large mixing bowl. Whisk until foamy. Add radicchio, toss well, cover and let soak at room temperature for at least one hour. Preheat oven to 425 F. Arrange the radicchio on a baking sheet and pour remaining dressing over the heads. Roast for 20 to 25 minutes until radicchio starts to get crisp. Serve immediately with grated Parmesan cheese.

. . . .

Braised Romaine Lettuce

You often find an insurmountable pile of romaine heads in you CSA box.
This tasty braise is a break from non-stop Caesar salads.

Serves: 4

Ingredients

4 to 5 heads romaine lettuce
1/2 cup diced raw bacon
1 carrot, dice
1 red onion, slice into strips
1 cup vegetable stock (see p. 289)
2 tablespoons chopped fresh thyme
1 tablespoon butter
2 tablespoons chopped fresh parsley
Salt and black pepper

Directions

Preheat oven to 350 F. Trim the stem end of the lettuce 1 inch from bottom. Bring a large pot of salted water to a boil over medium-high heat. Add the lettuce, allow water to come back to a boil, reduce heat and simmer for 5 minutes. Drain lettuce and rinse thoroughly under cold running water. Drain again and pat away as much water as possible.

Grease a large baking dish with pan spray, butter or shortening. Spread the onions, bacon, carrots and thyme on the bottom of the pan. Arrange the lettuce in the pan in an even layer. Pour on the stock and season with salt and pepper. Cover with a piece of wax paper or parchment rubbed with butter. Braise in oven for 30 to 40 minutes. Remove lettuce to a serving platter add chopped parsley to the remaining pan juices. Whisk in the butter and pour over the lettuce.

. . . .

Nicoise Salad

With a little digging, you will find an easy thousand Nicoise salad recipes. I think its popularity is partly due to the mildly pretentious thrill Americans might get from saying the word "nee-suaz" at cocktail parties. Nonetheless, it is a beautifully simple and satisfying plateful of cooked and raw vegetables with some eggs and tuna thrown in for machismo. The Nicoise Salad requires a little more labor than your average salad, about the same amount of time and effort as a meatloaf, but the results are dazzling and the salad will stand alone as the centerpiece of a mid-summer dinner.

Serves: 6

Ingredients

2 6-ounce grilled tuna steaks or 12 ounces canned white tuna

Olive oil for frying

6 hard-cooked eggs, peel and quarter

1 pound small waxy potatoes, fingerling or any new potato

Salt and pepper

2 heads butter lettuce, clean, dry and tear

3 tomatoes, slice in wedges

1 onion, dice fine

1/2 pound green beans, preferably the small "haricot vert"

1/4 cup incise or kalamata olives (any olive will do in a pinch)

2 tablespoons capers

1-1/2 cups Dijon vinaigrette (see p. 279)

Optional: 6 small anchovy filets

Directions

Sear tuna (skip if using canned tuna) using 2 tablespoons olive oil in a large skillet over medium-high heat. Season tuna steaks with salt and pepper and sear in hot pan for 2 to 3 minutes on both sides until cooked through. Remove from pan and set aside.

Cut potatoes into bite-size pieces and blanch and shock them (see p. 287). Drain completely, toss with 1/4 cup of vinaigrette and set aside.

If you are using large beans, cut them in half, and blanch and shock them (see p. 287). Drain completely, toss with 2 tablespoons of vinaigrette and set aside. Toss the lettuce with 1/4 cup of the vinaigrette in a mixing bowl until well dressed. Arrange in a layer on a large serving platter. Crumble tuna by hand into large chunks and dress with 2 tablespoons of the vinaigrette. Mound tuna in the center of the platter.

Place tomatoes and onions in a mixing bowl with 3 tablespoons of vinaigrette and toss gently. Arrange in a circle around the mound of tuna. Place beans and potatoes at opposite ends of the platter. Place olives and eggs in mounds around the outside of platter. Place anchovies in a small pile on top of tune and scatter capers over the whole mix. Drizzle remaining dressing over the salad and serve immediately.

. . . .

Butter Lettuce With Candied Walnuts

*This recipe calls for a Dijon vinaigrette. Feel free to experiment
with other vinaigrettes (see Chapter 5).*

Serves: 8

Ingredients

4 to 5 heads romaine lettuce
1/2 cup diced raw bacon
1 carrot, dice
1 red onion, slice into strips
1 cup vegetable stock (see p. 289)
2 tablespoons chopped fresh thyme
1 tablespoon butter
2 tablespoons chopped fresh parsley
Salt and black pepper

Directions

Preheat oven to 350 F. Trim the stem end of the lettuce 1 inch from bottom. Bring a large pot of salted water to a boil over medium-high heat. Add the lettuce, allow water to come back to a boil, reduce heat and simmer for 5 minutes. Drain lettuce and rinse thoroughly under cold running water. Drain again and pat away as much water as possible.

Grease a large baking dish with pan spray, butter or shortening. Spread the onions, bacon, carrots and thyme on the bottom of the pan. Arrange the lettuce in the pan in an even layer. Pour on the stock and season with salt and pepper. Cover with a piece of wax paper or parchment rubbed with butter. Braise in oven for 30 to 40 minutes. Remove lettuce to a serving platter add chopped parsley to the remaining pan juices. Whisk in the butter and pour over the lettuce.

CHEF'S NOTES

1. Fresh head lettuce is fantastic grilled. Rub with a little olive oil, salt and pepper and cook until just charred. Dress with grilled vegetables and any vinaigrette.

2. Lettuce needs to be rinsed of sand and soil. The lettuce must be dry for the dressing to coat properly. Use a salad spinner or place leaves in a big piece of cheesecloth and twirl overhead to force water out.

3. We are regularly told to tear lettuce rather than cut with a knife. We do this because the lettuce will brown along the knife cut. The browning will take several hours, so it should not be a problem if you are eating your salad right away.

Simple Herb Salad

If you love a vegan, prepare this salad for them. You couldn't eat any lower on the food chain without becoming a single-celled organism.

Serves: 2 as a main course

Ingredients

2 cups lettuce leaves, any variety (baby romaine, butter or red butter, red coral, lolla rosso, red romaine, chicory or even iceberg)
2 cups mizuna, arugula, cress or mache
2 tablespoons basil leaves pulled from stems
1/2 cup celery leaves or fennel fronds
1/2 cup parsley leaves pulled whole from sprig
1/2 cup bite-size pieces of sorrel
Salt and black pepper
A very good extra virgin olive oil
Fresh lemon or lime

Directions

Rinse all lettuce and tear into bite-size pieces. Dry in a salad spinner or by making a pouch of cheesecloth and twirling it over your head until all loose moisture is removed. (It's probably best to do that outside.) Place the lettuce in a mixing bowl. Add basil, celery or fennel, parsley, sorrel, salt and pepper. Drizzle in just enough olive oil to coat the lettuce — 1 to 2 tablespoons. Zest lemon or lime with zester or hand grater and add to lettuce. Cut the lemon or lime in half and squeeze in the juice being careful to remove seeds. Give the salad a final toss and serve immediately with hunks of warm crusty bread.

Make Your Own Salad

Try these combinations or make up your own. Fresh greens and herbs are so naturally diverse and flavorful that you can hardly build a bad salad:

1. Oregano, marjoram, chives, orange.

2. Mint, cilantro, tarragon, rice wine vinegar.

3. Chives, shaved garlic scapes, chive blossoms, white wine vinegar.

4. Lemon thyme, dill, sorrel, lemon thyme blossoms, vermouth

Radicchio Risotto

Radicchio holds up very well to the cooking and stirring that goes on with a risotto. The color is fun and the mild bitterness is a nice accent in this rice dish.

Ingredients

2 cups short- or medium-grain
    rice, preferably arborio
2 large heads of radicchio (about 12 ounces)
1 onion, dice
1/4 cup butter
1/4 cup olive oil
1 quart vegetable stock (see p. 289)
Salt and pepper to taste
1/2 cup grated Romano or Parmesan cheese

Directions

Cut off the core end of the radicchio and slice crosswise into very thin ribbons. Set aside.

Melt butter over medium heat in a large pot. Add olive oil and onions and cook for 5 minutes until onions just start to brown. Add to the pot with onions and cook them until they have wilted. Add 2 cups of the stock, increase heat to medium-high and bring to a boil. Add the rice and stir continuously until all the liquid is absorbed. Add remaining stock, 1/2 cup at a time, stirring until liquid is absorbed. Cook until rice is tender but not soft. Stir in cheese, cover, and let rest for 2 minutes.

· · · · · · · · · · · · · · · ·

Carved Radicchio With Bleu Cheese

Some of the best salads are simply lettuce and dressing. The color contrast between the lettuces accented with a creamy dressing is simple, attractive, and delicious.

Serves: 6

Ingredients

1 large or 2 small heads of
    radicchio, core and clean
3 cups chopped or shredded
    romaine or butter lettuce
2 tablespoons chopped fresh chives
1/4 cup fresh chopped parsley
1 cup mayonnaise
1/2 cup plain yogurt
1/4 cup buttermilk
1 clove garlic, crush and roughly chop
1 tablespoon Worcestershire sauce
2 tablespoons white wine vinegar
1/2 teaspoon sugar
Salt and pepper
Dash of chili sauce
1/2 cup crumbled blue cheese

Directions

In medium bowl combine mayonnaise, yogurt, buttermilk, chives, garlic, Worcestershire sauce, vinegar, sugar, chili sauce, salt and pepper. Mix well to combine. Gently stir in cheese. Nest 1/2 cup romaine or butter lettuce onto each of 6 individual salad plates. Cut radicchio into 6 wedges, place wedges, cut-side up on green lettuce. Garnish with parsley.

· · · · · · · · · · · · · · · ·

HERBS

Nothing brings freshness and brightness to cooking like fresh herbs. I've collected them in one section because, while they have different characters and preferred uses, they get used in similar ways and many times are interchangeable in recipes. There is seasonality to herbs, but herbs grown indoors can be available locally year-round. To prepare them, simply pick the leaves from the stems and chop with a knife. Use the stems in your vegetable stock.

One mistake that home cooks make with fresh herbs, a mistake I often see repeated in recipes, is to use them in place of dried herbs. They are two different things. Fresh herbs do not stand up well to long cooking. The flavorful oils and aroma disappear when cooked too long. Fresh herbs should always be added to a dish at the end of cooking. Long cooking releases the flavor of dried herbs and these should be used in a simmering sauce, stew or braise.

MIXED HERB RECIPES

At various times of the year farmers markets, CSAs and backyard gardens are overflowing with fresh herbs and greens. Many times there is a short window of time where these herbs are at their best and we are persuaded to save that quality when we can.

Pestos are the perfect way to take advantage of the quantities of basil, thyme, chives, mint, parsley, oregano, cilantro, and garden greens that can surprise us with their fecundity throughout the season. And pestos can be used for almost anything — as a pasta sauce, a seasoning, an ingredient, a marinade, and as a spread on sandwiches, crusty bread, or crackers. They will keep for two weeks in the refrigerator and indefinitely if frozen so make large batches and freeze them for a taste of the summer in the middle of February.

The technique for creating pesto is straightforward. They usually contain greens or herbs, a dry Italian cheese like Parmesan or Romano, nuts (this is optional if you are allergic, but you should add more cheese or a little bread crumbs), and oil. I've given you a sampling of pesto recipes, but the possibilities are endless and you should experiment with any of the elements. The result, nearly always, will be good.

Thyme Pesto

Mix this with a little red wine and baste steaks with it. No herb goes better with grilled red meat than thyme.

Yields: 1-1/2 cups

Ingredients

1/2 cup fresh thyme leaves
1 cup fresh parsley
1/4 cup Asiago cheese
3 cloves garlic
1/3 cup extra virgin olive oil
1/3 cup toasted pine nuts
Salt and pepper to taste

Directions

Pulse all ingredients in a food processor until minced and pasty and slowly add olive oil while blade is spinning. The pesto can be made tight for a spread or looser for a pasta sauce by adding more oil.

. . . .

Sage Pesto

Thinned with white wine or water; this pesto is a great marinade and baste for oven-roasted chicken

Yields: 5 cups

Ingredients

1 cup fresh sage leaves
2 cups fresh parsley
3 cloves garlic
3/4 cup pecans
3/4 cup Parmesan cheese
2/3 cup extra virgin olive oil
Salt and pepper to taste

Directions

Pulse everything in a food processor until minced and pasty and slowly add olive oil while blade is spinning. It can be made tight for a spread or looser for a pasta sauce by adding more oil.

. . . .

Classic Basil Pesto

Pesto can be made tight for a spread or looser for a pasta sauce by adding more oil.

Yields: 1-1/2 cups

Ingredients

2 cups fresh basil leaves
1 cup olive oil
1 cup grated Parmesan cheese
1/2 cup roasted pine nuts
2 cloves garlic
Salt and pepper to taste

Directions

Pulse everything in a food processor until minced and pasty and slowly add olive oil while blade is spinning.

. . . .

Mixed Herb Pesto

This pesto is a useful all- purpose seasoning.

Yields: 7 cups

Ingredients
2 garlic cloves
1 cup fresh basil
1 cup fresh parsley
1 cup fresh spinach
1/2 cup fresh oregano
1/2 cup pistachio nuts
3/4 cup olive oil
Salt and pepper to taste

Directions
Pulse everything in a food processor until minced and pasty and slowly add olive oil while blade is spinning. It can be made tight for a spread or looser for a pasta sauce by adding more oil.

Zesty Fresh Herb Marinade

Soak chicken, fish or vegetables one hour in this flavorful marinade. This is an all-purpose go-to marinade.

Yields: 1/2 cup

Ingredients
2 tablespoon Dijon mustard
2 tablespoon chopped fresh thyme
2 teaspoons chopped fresh rosemary
2 teaspoon chopped fresh chives
1 tablespoon water
2 teaspoons red wine vinegar
1 finely chopped shallot
2 cloves minced garlic

Directions
Whisk together all ingredients in a mixing bowl. Use or store up to 1 week in the refrigerator.

Herb Flavored Vinegars

Vinegar adds a flavor splash to anything. They look nice on a shelf and make great gifts.

Yields: 1 quart

Ingredients
- 1 quart white vinegar
- 1 orange
- 10 whole black peppercorns
- 1 cinnamon stick
- Flavorings (choose one group)
- 3/4 cup fresh basil leaves
- 24 sprigs fresh tarragon
- 24 sprigs fresh thyme

Or
- 1/4 cup fresh basil leaves
- 8 sprigs fresh thyme
- 8 sprigs fresh rosemary

Directions
Remove orange peel with a vegetable peeler and cut 3 strips, each strip 3 inches long. Sterilize a quart jar in a water bath. Using a large stainless steel saucepan, combine vinegar, orange peel, peppercorns, cinnamon and your chosen herb combination. Bring to a boil and cook 1 minute. Remove jar form water bath and fill with vinegar. Cover and store at room temperature.

. . . .

Sage Cakes

Good honest food to serve with roast meat or sausages, this is a simple rustic savory pancake.

Serves: 4 to 6

Ingredients
- 1 cup flour
- 1 teaspoon sugar
- 1/2 teaspoon salt
- 2 eggs, separated
- 1 cup buttermilk
- 1/4 cup finely chopped fresh sage leaves
- Equal amounts butter and vegetable oil for frying
- 2 tablespoons butter
- 1/4 cup grated Parmesan cheese

Directions
In a mixing bowl combine flour, sugar, and salt. Stir in egg yolks, buttermilk and sage. Mix until smooth but do not overmix. Let batter rest for 30 minutes. Beat the egg whites in a separate bowl with a hand mixer until they are stiff and gently fold into the batter. Heat 1/2 tablespoon each of butter and vegetable oil in a large skillet over medium-high heat. Drop spoonfuls of the batter onto hot pan and cook 3 to 5 minutes until golden on the bottoms. Flip pancakes and brown the other side. Transfer pancakes to a plate and keep warm in a low oven. Fry pancakes in batches until batter is used up. Add butter and oil to the pan as needed for frying. Spread the pancakes with butter just before serving and sprinkle with Parmesan cheese.

. . . .

Herb Dumplings

Drop these little beauties in a soup or stew or fry in butter and toss with fresh vegetables.

Yields: 3 dozen

Ingredients
- 1 large baking potato, peel and cut into chunks
- 2 large beaten eggs
- 1 cup fresh chopped herbs (parsley, tarragon, oregano, chives, basil, thyme; a mixture or all one type)
- 1 cup flour
- Salt and pepper to taste

Directions
Place potatoes in a pot of lightly salted water and bring to a boil over medium-high heat. Cook until tender, 15 to 20 minutes. Drain in a colander, return to the pan and mash completely. Stir in the eggs with a wooden spoon. Add chopped herbs, salt, pepper and flour. Gently mix all ingredients being careful not to overmix. Dough should be somewhat sticky. Turn dough out onto a work counter and cover with plastic wrap. Let rest for 30 to 40 minutes. Separate dough into 3 piles. Break off 12 equal-size nuggets from each pile and roll into an irregular ball. Continue until all dumplings are formed. Add flour to make them easier to work with, if needed. Bring a deep skillet full of water to a boil over medium-high heat. Reduce heat to a simmer and add 12 to 15 dumplings at a time. Simmer 7 to 8 minutes until they float. Remove with a slotted spoon. Continue with remainder of dough.

. . . .

Mint-Cilantro Relish

I love unusual steak sauces. This light sauce shines on a New York strip or rib-eye steak.

Yields: 3 cups

Ingredients
- 1/4 cup lime juice
- 2 whole green onions, white and green parts
- 1 Serrano or Anaheim chili, remove stems and seeds
- 1 clove garlic
- 2 tablespoons fresh grated ginger
- 1 teaspoon sugar
- 1 cup tightly packed cilantro
- 1 cup tightly packed mint
- 2 tablespoons water

Directions
Place all ingredients in a blender or the small bowl of a food processor and puree. You may have to scrape down the sides from time to time to make sure it gets well mixed. Spoon relish over roasted or grilled meats just before serving.

. . . .

Fresh Mint Chutney

Serve this simple relish with fried vegetables or crisp flatbreads. Make a big batch; it freezes well.

Yields: 2 cups

Ingredients
2 tablespoons lime juice
2 tablespoons honey
3 tablespoons water
1-1/2 cups tightly packed fresh mint leaves
2 jalapeno chilies, remove seeds and finely chop
1/4 cup dried coconut
Salt

Directions
Combine all ingredients in a food processor and process until very smooth. It will keep several days in the refrigerator or up to one year in the freezer.

. . . .

Mint Yogurt Sauce

A classic Eastern Mediterranean condiment.

Yields: 2 cups

Ingredients
1 cup plain yogurt
1/2 cup finely chopped fresh mint
1/2 cup finally chopped cilantro

Directions
Combine all ingredients in a bowl and mix well. Serve with spicy meatballs or cooked beans.

. . . .

Fried Parsley Sauce

A great alternative to tarter sauce on fried fish.

Yields: 1/2 cup

Ingredients
1/4 cup olive oil
1/4 cup chopped fresh parsley
2 tablespoons lemon juice
1/4 teaspoon salt

Directions
Heat oil in a small skillet over medium-high heat. When oil is hot, but not smoking, add parsley. Fry parsley in oil, stirring constantly (mixture may splatter a bit, be careful) for 1 minute until it darkens slightly. Remove from heat and stir in the lemon juice and salt. Spoon the sauce over fried fish or seafood.

. . . .

Tabbouleh

Tabbouleh is a Middle Eastern salad of bulgur wheat, fresh tomatoes and herbs, usually parsley and mint. Bulgur wheat can be found in most well-stocked supermarkets or co-ops.

Yields: 8 cups

Ingredients

2-1/2 cups bulgur wheat
3 cups fresh, diced tomatoes (save
    as much juice as possible)
1-1/2 cups finely chopped onions
2 tablespoons chopped fresh mint
2 tablespoons chopped fresh parsley
Salt and pepper
1/2 cup olive oil or sesame oil
2 tablespoons lemon juice
8 green onions, chop both white and green parts
2 heads romaine lettuce leaves, clean

Directions

Place bulgur in a bowl and cover with enough water to allow for swelling. Let soak for at least 20 minutes. Drain thoroughly in a colander and place in a large mixing bowl. Add tomatoes and their juice, onions, parsley, mint, salt and pepper. Pour over olive oil and lemon juice. Toss completely with your hands or a pair of wooden spoons. Chill for 3 hours.

Traditionally this is served with romaine lettuce leaves. The leaves can be used to scoop the tabbouleh from a decorative serving bowl or you may form individual lettuce cups. In either case, garnish the salad with the chopped green onions.

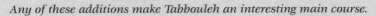

CHEF'S NOTES

Any of these additions make Tabbouleh an interesting main course.

1. Add 2 pounds of small cooked shrimp and toss well.

2. Boil 2 pounds of chicken in salted water until chicken is cooked through. Chill completely and dice. Toss with salad.

3. Add 1 pound of smoked salmon to salad and toss together.

Chermoula

Chermoula is an intensely flavored Middle Eastern herb and spice blend. It is traditionally served with lamb but is also very good with chicken or any mild fish.

Yields: 1 cup

Ingredients

1 teaspoon ground cumin
1 teaspoon ground coriander
16 black peppercorns
1/4 teaspoon red pepper flakes
1/2 teaspoon kosher salt
1 teaspoon paprika
1/2 cup finely chopped parsley
1/4 cup finely chopped cilantro
3 tablespoons olive oil
3 tablespoons lemon juice
1 tablespoon minced garlic

Directions

Crush fine cumin, coriander, peppercorns, red pepper flakes and salt with a mortar and pestle. Transfer to a small mixing bowl and stir in all other ingredients. Let set for 20 minutes to marry flavors. Use as a marinade or a topping just before serving.

. . . .

Persillade

Persillade is a savory French seasoning mixture made up of varying amounts of chopped parsley and raw garlic. It is always added at the end of cooking so as not to mute the impact of both the parsley and the fresh garlic. Spoon over slices of baked ham or grilled steaks or mix into mashed potatoes.

Yields: 1/2 cup

Ingredients

6 tablespoons finely chopped parsley
3 large cloves garlic, mince
Salt

Directions

Combine parsley and garlic in a small bowl. Sprinkle with a little salt and let rest for 20 minutes. Add to recipe just before serving.

. . . .

Cilantro Chutney

The toasted spices in this relish bring an authentic Indian flavor.
I love this chutney with fried or steamed spring rolls.

Yields: 1 cup

Ingredients

1 teaspoon cumin seeds
3 tablespoons sesame seeds
1/4 cup chopped pecans
1 packed cup of picked cilantro leaves
2 jalapeno chilies, remove seeds
    and roughly chop
1 tablespoon fresh grated ginger
2 tablespoons water
1 tablespoon brown sugar

Directions

Heat a skillet over low heat. Add cumin seeds, sesame seeds and pecans. Roast ingredients in pan, stirring frequently, until nuts and seeds are brown and fragrant. Transfer seed mixture to the bowl of a food processor. Add the cilantro, jalapenos, ginger, water and brown sugar; process until smooth. Chutney should be the consistency of a thin paste. Add a little water if you need to. You may also add 1/4 cup of sour cream to turn this into a dip. Both versions freeze well so make a big batch.

. . . .

Fried Shrimp and Cilantro Canapes

Though these are fried, they eat very light. They could be a cocktail party snack or a main course.

Makes 12 pieces

Ingredients

12 raw jumbo shrimp, peel and leave tails on
2 beaten eggs
4 tablespoons cornstarch
2 tablespoons chopped cilantro
1 tablespoon chopped fresh chives
6 slices white bread, remove crusts and
    cut into 2-inch by 3-inch rectangles
Oil for deep-frying

Directions

Preheat fryer to 350 F. Cut a slit down the back of each shrimp and remove the dirt vein. Cut a little deeper and gently flatten the shrimp.

   Mix the eggs, 2 tablespoons of cornstarch, cilantro, and chives. Whisk together completely. Place remaining cornstarch in a small dish and dust each shrimp with cornstarch. Dip each piece of bread in the egg mixture and allow excess to drain off. Set these on a plate. Dip each shrimp in the egg mixture and gently press one shrimp, cut-side down, on each piece of bread. Drop pieces 3 or 4 at a time into hot oil and fry for 1 minute. Drain in a pan lined with paper towel. When all are fried, serve immediately with chili cilantro dip below.

. . . .

Cilantro Jalapeno Pesto

*Leave out the jalapeno if you want a more sedate flavor. Mix this with
a little soy and Thai fish sauce for a yummy spring roll dip*

Yields: 3 cups

Ingredients
2 cups fresh cilantro (a few stems are okay)
2-1/2 tablespoons toasted pine nuts
1/4 cup extra virgin olive oil
5 cloves garlic
1 tablespoon fresh lime juice
1/3 seeded jalapeno pepper
1/4 cup grated Parmesan cheese

Directions
Place all ingredients except the oil in the bowl of
a food processor. Process until smooth and while
mixing slowly drizzle in oil.

Chili Cilantro Dip

This is very good with spring rolls or egg rolls.

Yields: 1 cup

Ingredients
1/4 cup soy sauce or tamari
1/2 teaspoon chili paste (found in Asian
groceries and better supermarkets)
2 tablespoons chopped fresh cilantro

Directions
Whisk all ingredients together in a mixing bowl.

CHEF'S NOTES

1. Curly parsley sprigs can be deep fried and used as a garnish for fried foods.

2. For a simple fruit dressing mix 2 parts olive oil, 1 part vinegar, 1 part honey and 1 part chopped fresh mint. Add a pinch of cumin and drizzle over melons or apples.

3. All herbs freeze best when blended into pestos. You may dry them in a food dehydrator or simply air-dry.

4. Most herbs have very short shelf lives and should be used immediately.

5. Cilantro is great against an acidic background. Combine in recipes with lime, lemon or any vinegar.

KOHLRABI

While celeriac is the ugliest vegetable at the market, kohlrabi is the funniest looking. They look like green tennis balls with arms and if I unfocus my eyes I can imagine the "Great Gazoo" from the Flintstones. Kohlrabi needs to be peeled and it cooks much like turnips and rutabagas.

Pan-Grilled Kohlrabi

You can make this with any oil, but if you eat at my, house you'll get it cooked in butter.

Ingredients
- 2 large kohlrabi
- 1/4 cup butter
- Salt and pepper
- 1 tablespoon fresh chopped basil

Directions
Peel kohlrabi with a sharp paring knife. Chop kohlrabi into 3/4-inch chunks. Place into a saucepan full of lightly salted water. Place over medium-high heat and bring to a boil, reduce heat, and simmer for 20 to 30 minutes until chunks are tender. Drain in a colander and shake dry. Melt butter in a large skillet over medium heat. Add kohlrabi, season with salt and pepper, and cook until chunks are brown on one side, about 5 minutes. Stir and continue to cook for 5 more minutes. Serve immediately with a sprinkling of basil.

. . . .

Scalloped Kohlrabi With Ham

The kohlrabi version of classic comfort food.

Serves: 6

Ingredients
- 3 pounds kohlrabi, (5 to 6) peel and
  slice into 1/8-inch slices
- 1 cup roughly chopped ham
- 2 cups (1/2 recipe) bechamel sauce (see p. 277)
- 1/4 cup shredded Swiss cheese
- 1/3 cup bread crumbs

Directions
Bring lightly salted water to a boil in a large saucepan. Add sliced kohlrabi to water, allow to come back to a boil, reduce heat and simmer until tender, 25 minutes. Drain in a colander and shake dry. Place the kohlrabi in a shallow baking dish.

Prepare the bechamel and keep warm.

Stir in the ham and cheese until cheese melts. Pour sauce over kohlrabi and spread evenly. Sprinkle with bread crumbs. Bake until brown and bubbling, 30 to 40 minutes. Serve warm.

. . . .

Kohlrabi Cakes

Make this early in the season when the kohlrabi and garlic scapes are plentiful.
A garlic scape is the green shoot from a garlic plant (see Garlic section).

Serves: 4 to 6

Ingredients

4 kohlrabi, peel and hand grate or
    shred in a food processor
1/4 cup very thinly sliced garlic scapes
2 beaten eggs
2 tablespoons bread crumbs (see p. 284)
Pinch of red pepper flakes
Salt and pepper
Cooking spray

Directions

Place grated kohlrabi in a colander set atop a bowl. Sprinkle with 1 teaspoon salt and rest for 30 minutes to draw out moisture. Rinse kohlrabi under running water and shake dry. Using your hands squeeze handfuls of the kohlrabi to wring out as much moisture as possible and place kohlrabi in a large mixing bowl. Add garlic scapes, eggs, bread crumbs, black pepper and red pepper flakes. Mix thoroughly to form a stiff batter. Heat a large skillet over medium heat and spray pan with a generous amount of cooking spray. Drop large teaspoonfuls of batter on the hot pan and flatten into cakes. Fry until golden brown, about 4 minutes. While cakes are frying, spray the uncooked sides of the cakes with the cooking spray. Turn the cakes and brown the other side. Transfer kohlrabi cakes to a low oven to keep warm. Repeat until all the batter is used. Serve the cakes warm with Mint Yogurt Sauce (p. 144), Chili Raita (p. 96), or Sambal (p. 92).

. . . .

Mashed Kohlrabi With Orange

A very good side with baked ham or a stuffing for grilled chili peppers.

Serves: 6

Ingredients

2 pounds peeled kohlrabi, cut
    into 1/2-inch chunks
1 orange
1 tablespoon orange juice concentrate
1 tablespoon butter
Salt and pepper

Directions

Bring a saucepan full of water to a boil over medium-high heat. Add the kohlrabi and a teaspoon of salt and bring back to a boil. Reduce heat, and simmer for 30 minutes until kohlrabi is very soft. Drain in a colander and shake dry.

While kohlrabi is cooking, remove the zest from the orange with a zester or hand grater, place in a small bowl and set aside. Transfer the cooked kohlrabi to the bowl of a food processor. Cut the orange in half and squeeze in the juice being careful to extract seeds. Add the orange juice concentrate, butter, salt and pepper to taste. Process until just smooth. Do not overmix. Place mashed kohlrabi in a serving bowl and gently fold in orange zest. Serve warm or store in refrigerator for up to 3 days.

. . . .

LEEKS

"Aren't leeks those really big green onions?" I believe if I ever have a conversation about leeks with anyone, it invariably starts this way. While leeks are interchangeable with onions in most recipes, they express a singular personality. Green onions are sharp and acidic while leeks are rich and earthy. They can steal the show in a cream soup or roasted whole. They shine in salads and sides and can be poached, fried or steamed. In many parts of the world, leeks are revered. In ancient Egypt, they were worshiped. So please, give a little respect and don't call it a big onion.

The large leeks that most of us are familiar with emerge in CSAs and markets in late summer or fall. Baby leeks appear earlier in the season and are wonderfully tender. The desirable part of the leek is the white part of the leek from the root end to about 1 inch into the green part. Peel off the tough outer leaves and trim off the hairy roots and about 1/8-inch of the end. If buying leeks at a farmers market, look for leeks that are bright green with no yellowing and that stand up stiff and straight. Smell them, if they make you salivate they are likely fit to buy.

Creamed Leeks

This is a unique garnish for grilled steak or salmon.

Serves: 4

Ingredients
1/2 pound leeks, washed and
   cut into 4-inch strips
2 tablespoons butter
1 cup heavy cream
Salt and pepper to taste

Directions
Heat the butter in a large skillet over medium-low heat. Add the leeks and season with salt and pepper. Cook slowly in butter for 15 minutes, stirring occasionally. Add cream to the skillet and raise heat to bring to a boil. Boil briefly, cover, and reduce heat to a simmer. Cook for a further 15 minutes. Remove cover and allow cream to cook down to a thick sauce coating the leeks. Adjust the seasoning and serve immediately.

Braised Leeks

Try this as a side dish topped with grated cheese or chopped fresh herbs.

Serves: 6 to 8

Ingredients

1 pound leeks, wash and cut into rings or quarters
2 tablespoons butter
1 cup vegetable stock (see p. 289)
Salt and pepper to taste

Directions

Preheat oven to 350 F. Spread leeks in a medium-size casserole dish. Salt and pepper liberally and dot with small pieces of butter. Pour stock over the leeks. Bake leeks, uncovered, for 40 minutes.

. . . .

Leek, Potato and Coriander Bake

Rich late-season comfort food.

Serves: 4

Ingredients

2 tablespoons olive oil
2 tablespoons butter
1 pound of leeks, clean well and
    cut into 1/2-inch rings
2 pounds waxy potatoes (red, Yukon, or
    fingerlings), cut into 1/2-inch slices
1 teaspoon whole black peppercorns
2 teaspoons coriander seeds
Salt

Directions

Preheat oven to 400 F. Place butter and oil in a large shallow roasting pan. Place in the oven to melt the butter. Stir in the leeks and potatoes to coat with the butter and oil. Shake pan to level ingredients. Crush the peppercorns and coriander in a mortar and pestle or with the bottom of a heavy skillet. Sprinkle this mixture on potatoes. Add 1 teaspoon salt. Stir ingredients to combine. Cook for 40 to 50 minutes until potatoes are golden and tender.

. . . .

Potato-Leek Soup

For many, this soup is the only time they ever eat leeks. This is a fairly light version. If you like a creamier soup you may replace 2 cups of the stock with 2 cups of heavy cream.

Serves: 6

Ingredients

3 large leeks, rinse well and chop crosswise
1 tablespoon butter
4 cups vegetable stock (see p. 289) or water
2 pounds potatoes, peel, roughly dice and
    store in water to prevent browning
1/4 cup chopped fresh herbs (any)
1/8 teaspoon cayenne pepper
    or a dash of Tabasco
Salt and pepper to taste

Directions

Melt butter over medium-low heat in a soup kettle. Add leeks to the kettle, cover, and cook for 8 to 12 minutes, stirring occasionally. Add stock and potatoes to the leeks. Liberally season with salt and pepper (potatoes absorb a lot of salt). Increase heat to medium high and bring to a boil. Reduce heat and simmer, uncovered, for 20 to 25 minutes until the potatoes are very soft.

Remove the pan from the heat and place one half of the soup into the bowl of a food processor. Process until very smooth and return to the pan. Reheat soup and stir in herbs and cayenne pepper. Taste and adjust seasoning. Serve in shallow bowls with crusty bread.

. . . .

Down on the Farm

September 2

You might have noticed that there have been no leeks in the boxes. I seem to remember reporting earlier in the season, after we had a downpour, that the force of the rain had separated the leaves slightly from the stalks, and at the time, I wasn't sure of the effect that it would have in the future. It seems that the heavy dews resulting from the consistent high humidity levels of the summer seeped down between stalk and leaf and caused the intersection to rot. Eventually, many of the leaves have rotted altogether, and the crop is pretty much ruined. It is counter-intuitive that things should rot in such a dry year, but it has happened. We have had some trouble with the onions, too, but it is much less of a problem.

— David Peterson, Maplewood Gardens

CHEF'S NOTES

1. Every cookbook will tell you that no matter how clean a leek seems on the outside it hides sand and dirt between the inner layers of the root end — This one is no different. The best way to remove the soil is to slice the leek in half lengthwise and hold leeks vertically under running water to rinse out the dirt.

2. If you have an abundance of leeks, try making a minced leek flavor base. A spoonful of this will give a rich earthy flavor to any recipe and can be mixed with water or cream for a quick soup. Clean and chop the leeks, sauté in oil or butter until soft and puree in a food processor. Use or freeze within 2 weeks.

3. Blanch and shock sliced strips or rings and toss with your favorite vinaigrette (see Chaper 5) for a simple salad.

4. Leeks pair well with mustard and bacon.

5. Leeks can be frozen whole. Cut the green tops and trim the root end, rinse thoroughly and freeze well wrapped or in containers.

6. The dark green part should not be discarded. It gives a tremendous flavor to stocks and broths (see soup stock on p. 289). You can also use them as a bed for roasted meats; it will season the drippings for richer gravy.

MACHE

Mache is another of the greens we see turning up in commercial spring mixes or mesclun. I'm reluctant to treat them as a group because they all have very distinctive flavors and the curious cook will find more pleasure in playing with them in isolation. Mache has a nutty flavor that even shines through very strong vinaigrettes. It is also known as "corn salad" because it tends to grow wild in abundance near cornfields. It is very hardy and should be available in farmers markets and CSAs throughout the season.

Mache with Panir Cheese and Butter Dressing

The lettuce in this salad should be room temperature so the butter does not set on the leaves when it is tossed. If served immediately while the dressing is a little warm, this salad is a beauty. If you let it sit too long, it becomes a gritty mess.

Serves: 4

Ingredients
6 cups mache
4 tablespoons butter
1 cup diced panir cheese (see p. 285)
4 teaspoons lemon juice
Salt and pepper

Directions
Place the mache in a large mixing bowl. Heat butter in a skillet over medium heat. Add cheese and cook, stirring occasionally until cheese browns slightly, 5 to 10 minutes. Remove from heat. Add lemon juice, salt and pepper. Swirl pan to mix well. Pour over lettuce and toss well. Serve and eat immediately.

Mache, Beet and Apple Salad

Enjoy a fine early autumn salad.

Serves: 4

Ingredients
1 cup cooked beets, peel and slice into wedges
1 pound mache, wash and remove thick stems
1 apple, slice into thin wedges
1/2 cup Dijon vinaigrette (see p. 279)
2 tablespoons chopped walnuts
2 tablespoons crumbled bleu cheese

Directions
Combine beets, mache, apple and vinaigrette in a large salad bowl. Mix well and place in serving bowl. Sprinkle with walnuts and bleu cheese. Serve immediately.

CHEF'S NOTES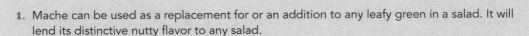

1. Mache can be used as a replacement for or an addition to any leafy green in a salad. It will lend its distinctive nutty flavor to any salad.

2. Like most greens, mache will not keep long and should be eaten within a few days. If you have a glut of "corn salad" try quickly braising with a little sesame oil and a splash of soy sauce. It will wilt down to a delicious warm salad.

Mache Salad With Asparagus and Pine Nuts

This salad uses a technique that is not often seen. The asparagus is served raw sliced very thin. This does away with the woodiness and leaves a sweet crunch.

Serves: 4

Ingredients
- 2 tablespoons pine nuts
- 1/4 cup extra virgin olive oil
- 2 tablespoons white wine vinegar
- Salt and pepper
- 6 large asparagus
- 6 cups mache
- 1/2 cup shredded Parmesan cheese

Directions
Preheat oven to 350 F. Place pine nuts in a single layer on a cookie sheet. Roast pine nuts for 3 to 5 minutes, until lightly browned. Remove from oven and let cool. Whisk together oil, vinegar and salt and pepper to taste in a large mixing bowl. Cut off the woody ends of the asparagus and discard. Cut off the tips of the asparagus and place in the bowl with dressing. Slice the spears on a diagonal into 1/8-inch slices. Place sliced asparagus in bowl with dressing. Add mache and pine nuts to mixing bowl and gently toss the salad until all is well coated with dressing. Serve in a large salad bowl or on individual plates. Top with the shredded Parmesan cheese.

MAPLE SYRUP

Sap running from the sugar maples is a sure crier of spring in northern climates. It signals the genesis of a new season of growth and of green and plenty, or it would if we still paid attention to the rhythm of the seasons. Maple syrup on the table once was and could be so much more significant than a dressing for our pancakes. Eating seasonally is about connecting to natural rhythms, and the hint of spring, the gush of sap and the promise of rebirth are all connected to a wonderful mythic hopefulness.

Go ahead, pour it on your pancakes, but please try to invest that first golden taste with some of the magic it deserves. You will find fine maple syrup at farmers markets and some CSAs year-round.

Maple Syrup Tart

So sweet and so good!

Serves: 8

Directions

Preheat oven to 350 F. Prepare the pie dough and line a 9-inch pie pan. Fold a piece of aluminum foil around the outer lip of crust to prevent burning while baking. Bake empty shell until bottom crust is brown. Remove from oven and cool completely.

Combine syrup and heavy cream in a saucepan over medium-high heat. While mixture is heating, combine cornstarch and water in a small bowl and mix together until smooth. When syrup mixture just begins to boil, slowly pour in cornstarch while constantly stirring. Bring back to a boil and cook for 2 minutes until thickened. Remove from heat and pour into baked pie shell. Spread nuts evenly over the top of tart. Let tart cool completely before serving.

. . . .

Maple Herb Sauce

Very good on corn bread, pound cake or shortcake.

Yields: 3/4 cup

Ingredients

1/2 cup real maple syrup
2 tablespoons apple cider
2 teaspoons lemon juice
1/4 cup fresh chopped chives or sage

Directions

Combine all ingredients in a mixing bowl and stir until smooth.

. . . .

Pork Chops Glazed With Maple and Mustard

Maple and mustard make a very simple and delicious barbeque sauce. Pair this with grilled fresh asparagus and mashed kohlrabi with orange for an early summer deck party.

Serves: 4 to 6

Ingredients

6 pork chops, 8 ounces each
3 tablespoons Dijon mustard
1-1/2 tablespoons maple syrup
Dash of Tabasco
1 tablespoon chopped fresh chives
Salt and black pepper

Directions

Prepare gas or charcoal grill. Heat should be about medium and coals should be white and glowing with little flame. Whisk together mustard, maple syrup and Tabasco. Arrange pork chops on a platter and sprinkle both sides liberally with salt and pepper. Brush a light coating of the sauce over each side of the pork chops with a pastry brush or the back of a spoon. Place on grate and grill chops until well-browned and liquid starts to rise on the uncooked side, about 5 minutes. Turn chops and baste cooked side with more of the maple mustard sauce. Grill another 5 minutes until pork is cooked through but not dry. Turn and baste second side. Remove from grill and arrange on a serving platter and sprinkle with fresh chives. If you like, make a second batch of the sauce as a dip.

CHEF'S NOTES

1. You can substitute maple syrup for honey in many recipes. Honey loses some of its sweetness when heated and maple syrup may be a better option.

2. Mix maple syrup into plain yogurt for a terrific fresh fruit dip.

2. Mix maple syrup with melted butter and toss with any combination of autumn root vegetables. Roast in a shallow pan until vegetables are soft.

From *The Everyday Cookbook*
· circa 1890 ·

Flannel Cakes

"Beat six eggs very light, stir in them two pounds of flour, one gill of yeast, small spoonful of salt, and sufficient milk to make a thick batter. Make them at night for breakfast, and at ten in the morning for tea. Have your griddle hot, grease it well, and bake as buckwheat. Butter and send them hot to the table, commencing after the family are seated."

Melon Salad With Maple and Cumin

This dressing is a favorite of mine for fruit salads. Try it on apples, pears and berries.

Serves: 4 as a side

Ingredients
- 1 pound of cantaloupe, peel and cut into 1/2-inch chunks
- 2 tablespoons vegetable oil
- 1 tablespoon rice wine vinegar
- 1 tablespoon pure maple syrup
- 1/4 teaspoon ground cumin
- 1 tablespoon fresh chopped mint
- Salt and pepper to taste

Directions
Whisk together oil, vinegar, maple syrup, cumin, mint, salt and pepper in a small mixing bowl. Toss dressing with cantaloupe and serve immediately.

. . . .

Creamy Maple Topping

Use this topping in place of whipped cream on any dessert.

Yields: 1-1/2 cups

Ingredients
- 1/2 cup sour cream
- 1/2 cup cream cheese (room temperature)
- 1/2 cup maple syrup

Directions
Combine all ingredients in a mixing bowl and mix together with a hand blender until smooth.

. . . .

MUSHROOMS

The Pharaohs declared mushrooms royal food and forbade the average Joe from eating them, and for centuries they were thought to have magical properties. I think this may be because they are so mysterious. They grow in shady places where other things can't grow; they pop up out of nowhere; and they seem to be bright and sentient. Some of that mystery is gone now but at least the average Joe can have a plate without going to jail. In the last 20 years we have seen the emergence of cultivated exotic mushrooms. Mushrooms, once foreign to American tastes, have now become common on all kinds of menus and beautiful shiitake, crimini, porcini, chanterelle and morel mushrooms are now available at farmers markets and in some CSAs. They are available year-round.

Baked Porcini Mushrooms

Also called "Ceps," these mushrooms can be found in the CSA boxes of more adventurous farmers and at many farmers markets. Any mushroom with a medium to large cap, including common cultivated white mushrooms, can be substituted in this simple lunch dish.

Serves: 4

Mushroom Ingredients
4 large porcini mushroom caps
2 tablespoons olive oil
2 ounces minced prosciutto ham
Salt and black pepper

Salad Ingredients
2 tablespoons extra virgin olive oil
2 tablespoons sherry, cider or red wine vinegar
Pinch of sugar
2 cups tightly packed fresh greens
    (arugula, sorrel, endive, spinach)
Kosher salt
Fresh ground black pepper

Directions
Preheat oven to 450 F. Cut shallow crosses in the tops of the mushrooms. Arrange on a cookie sheet and drizzle with half of the olive oil and season with salt and pepper. Bake in oven for 5 minutes. Turn mushrooms over, oil and season bottoms and bake a further 3 minutes. Garnish the mushrooms, bottom-side up, with the minced prosciutto.

Prepare salad dressing by whisking together oil, vinegar and sugar. Set mushrooms while still warm in a small nest of fresh greens. Spoon dressing over mushroom and salad and season with salt and pepper.

Morel Mushrooms

At my house we won't eat any other food until all the morels are gone. Whether you find them in your backyard or at your farmers market they are a treat that deserves serious homage. This is the only recipe for morels that I am going to include. Simply sauté them in butter and serve them on warm slices of crusty bread with a grating of the best imported Parmesan cheese. I have eaten an entire basket this way, but still got weepy when they were gone.

Serves: 6 as an appetizer

Ingredients

6 large morel mushrooms, rinse
   and cut in half lengthwise
1 cup flour
Salt and pepper
2 tablespoons butter
6 slices (1/2-inch) crusty French bread
Parmesan cheese for grating

Directions

Combine flour, salt and pepper in a shallow pan. Toss mushrooms with flour to coat lightly. Melt butter in large skillet over medium-high heat. Place mushrooms cut-side down in hot butter and fry for about 2 minutes. Turn mushrooms and fry an additional 1 or 2 minutes.

Place warm mushrooms on slices of bread and grate a good Parmesan cheese over the top. When those are gone, do it all over again.

· · · · · · · · · · · · · · · ·

Chanterelle and Endive Salad

About mid-July these golden beauties begin to appear in farmers markets. Chanterelles should be cooked slowly to remain tender.

Serves: 4

Salad Ingredients

1 head curly endive, rinse well and dry
2 cups chanterelle mushrooms, roughly chop
2 tablespoons butter
2 tablespoons finely chopped shallots
4 tablespoons chopped fresh parsley
4 tablespoons sesame seed
1 small tomato quartered
8 sliced croutons (see p. 283)

Dressing Ingredients

1/4 cup extra virgin olive oil
1 tablespoon sesame oil
2 tablespoons rice wine vinegar
Salt and pepper

Directions

Melt butter in a large skillet over medium-low heat. Sauté mushrooms for 2 minutes and then season with salt and pepper. Add shallots and chopped parsley and cook a further 2 minutes. Vigorously whisk together all dressing ingredients.

Toss endive with half of the dressing and arrange on 4 plates. Toss the other half with the warm chanterelles. Arrange the endive on 4 salad plates. Spoon a small mound of the mushrooms in the center of the endive. Sprinkle with sesame seeds. Garnish plates with tomato wedge and crouton.

· · · · · · · · · · · · · · · ·

Mushroom Stuffing or Duxelle

Duxelle can bring instant mushroom flavor to any dish. Use it to stuff or garnish chicken breasts, steaks or pork chops. It also adds an elegant richness to any cream soup. This stuffing freezes well and is a great way to preserve an abundance of mushrooms. You can make it with any type of mushroom as well as the leftover stems you might otherwise throw out.

Yields: 4 cups

Ingredients

3 cups finely chopped mushrooms
1 onion, mince
1 large shallot, mince
1 tablespoon butter
Salt and pepper
1/2 cup bread crumbs (see p. 284)

Directions

Melt butter in a large skillet over medium high heat. Add mushrooms, onions, shallots, salt and pepper. Cook, stirring occasionally, until vegetables are browned and all the water from the mushrooms has evaporated. Add bread crumbs and mix thoroughly.

. . . .

Hot and Sour Mushroom Broth

A staple of Chinese restaurants, this soup is simple and bold. This is a vegetarian version but any combination of cooked meat or seafood works very well.

Serves: 4

Ingredients

1 cup dried shiitake mushrooms or 1-1/2
    cups fresh sliced shiitake mushrooms
4 cups vegetable stock (see p. 289)
1 cup tightly packed spinach leaves
1/2 red bell pepper, slice into thin strips
4 slices ginger root
7 ounces tofu, cut into 1/2-inch cubes
4 chopped scallions
2 dried red chilies, seed and finely chop or
    1 tablespoon crushed red pepper
2 tablespoons fish sauce (available
    in Asian markets)
3 tablespoons lime juice

Directions

Soak dried mushrooms in 1 cup of warm water for 30 minutes. Combine vegetable stock and ginger in a large saucepan and bring to a boil over medium-high heat. Reduce heat and simmer for 10 minutes. Remove the ginger. Pour the mushroom soaking liquid through a strainer and into the vegetable stock. Rinse the mushrooms under cold water to remove any grit and add to pan. Add spinach, red pepper, tofu, scallions, dried chilies, fish sauce, and lime juice. Bring back to a boil, reduce heat, and simmer for 5 minutes.

. . . .

CHEF'S NOTES

1. If you are not handy with a knife, it is very easy to slice consistent pieces of mushrooms with an egg slicer.

2. Sliced mushrooms will brown, to avoid this, slice them just before service.

2. Shiitake mushroom stems are very tough but they can be used for vegetable stocks or cooked and pureed for stuffing.

4. When cleaning mushrooms never soak them; they will absorb too much water and become bland.

5. Fresh mushrooms should be used in 3 to 5 days depending on the type. Never store in airtight containers, but cover just enough to keep them from drying out.

6. When cooking mushrooms, take the time to cook them completely. The flavors will not develop fully until they are well cooked.

Wild Mushroom Gravy

Yes, it is as good as it sounds. Get rid of your A-1® steak sauce and your Heinz 57®, this is the sauce your steak deserves.

Yields: 5 cups

Ingredients

1/2 pound wild mushrooms (any variety), clean well and remove tough stems
2 tablespoons olive oil
1/4 cup brandy
1 to 5-cup recipe espagnole (see p. 286)

Directions

Chop mushrooms in desired manner. You may chop them fine or into thin slices that are more visible in the sauce. Heat oil in a large saucepan over medium heat. Add chopped mushrooms. Cook, stirring regularly, until mushrooms are soft and well browned, about 10 minutes. Add the brandy and cook for 5 more minutes. Add the espagnole and bring to a boil, reduce heat and simmer for 10 minutes to marry flavors. If you want a thinner sauce, stir in a little water. This may seem like a large batch. Scale it down or freeze it. It freezes well.

ONIONS

The ancient Egyptians used onions as an element in mummification. The next time you see a mummy in a museum somewhere, give some thought to the power of onions. I suspect if they can keep old Tut from turning to dust there might be a small chance that they could keep you young. If they can't do that, my grandpa always claimed they would put hair on your chest! Really?

Some types of onions are available all season long and if stored well you can have local onions all winter long. Sharp and fresh-tasting scallions start arriving in late spring followed by smaller varieties of bulb onions ending with the large storage onions you get late in the season.

Chili Onion Kofte

Kofte are tasty Indian-style fritters. They are easy to make but do require some legwork to find chickpea flour. Also called gram or besan, it can be found in the ethnic aisle of some supermarkets, the flour section of some co-ops and undoubtedly in an Indian grocery store. If you can't find a source near you it is very easy to find and order on-line. You may try this with wheat flour, but the flavor will be a little bland and the texture a little soft.

Serves: 4

Ingredients

1-1/2 pounds onions, peel and
    slice into thin strips
1 teaspoon ground coriander
1 teaspoon ground cumin
1/2 teaspoon turmeric
2 fresh jalapenos, remove seeds
    and chop very fine
3 tablespoons fresh chopped cilantro
3/4 cup chickpea flour
1/2 teaspoon baking powder
Oil for deep frying
4 lemon wedges
Salt

Directions

Heat oil in deep fryer to 375 F. Place onion slices in a colander placed over a bowl. Sprinkle onions with about 1 teaspoon salt and toss well. Let onions sit for 45 minutes, stirring once or twice, to draw moisture out. Rinse onions under running water. Squeeze the onions with your hands to wring out as much moisture as possible. Transfer onions to a mixing bowl and add the coriander, cumin, turmeric, jalapenos and cilantro. Mix well. Add the chickpea flour and the baking powder and mix thoroughly with your hands. Mixture should become a very thick batter, something like cookie dough. Form mixture into golf ball-size nuggets. Batch should make 12 to 15 balls.

Deep fry koftas in batches of 4 or 5 until well browned. You may have to turn them with a wooden spoon when they float to top to brown all sides. Remove from fryer and drain on paper towel. Serve with lemon wedges and minted yogurt (see p. 144).

Lyonnaise Sauce

Why is it called "Lyonnaise" sauce? See the remarks for Lyonnaise Potatoes.
What is it good for? Anything that would be enhanced by rich brown gravy!
Serve it with roasted or grilled meats, potatoes or root vegetables.

Yields: 5 cups

Ingredients
- 1/2 cup diced onions
- 1 tablespoon butter
- 1 cup white wine vinegar
- 1 cup dry white wine
- 2 cups espagnole (see p. 286) or prepared beef gravy

Directions
Melt butter over medium heat in a sauce pan. Add onions and cook, stirring occasionally, until onions are soft and lightly browned. Add vinegar and wine and cook this liquid down until all of it is nearly evaporated. Add the espagnole and stir mixture together. Warm through and adjust the thickness of the sauce with water.

· · · · · · · · · · · · · · · ·

Ginger Soy Dip

A good dip for batter-fried foods.

Yields: 1/2 cup

Ingredients
- 1/4 cup soy sauce
- 1 tablespoon rice wine vinegar
- 1 teaspoon fresh grated ginger
- 1 teaspoon tahini (sesame seed paste)
- 1/4 teaspoon sugar
- 1 teaspoon sesame seeds

Directions
Vigorously whisk together all ingredients.

· · · · · · · · · · · · · · · ·

Ginger Onion Chutney

Best results are realized with very fresh, mild white or yellow onions —
delicious condiment for grilled pork chops, or try it warm on a BLT.

Yields: 2 quarts

Ingredients
- 2 pounds white or yellow onions, slice thin
- 1-1/2 cups brown sugar
- 1 cup raisins
- 3/4 cup white wine
- 3/4 cup white wine vinegar
- 1 garlic clove
- 3/4 cup peeled and chopped fresh ginger
- 3 whole cloves
- Pinch of curry powder

Directions
Place all ingredients in a large saucepan or stock pot. Bring to a boil over medium heat. Reduce heat and simmer for about 2 hours. Will keep indefinitely in the refrigerator.

· · · · · · · · · · · · · · · ·

Onion and Honey Tart

You may think that onion pie is just wrong. This recipe will change your mind.

Serves: 8

Ingredients

- 2-1/4 pounds onions, slice thin
- 2 tablespoons butter
- 4 tablespoons fresh local honey
- 1 teaspoon ground cinnamon
- 1/4 teaspoon salt
- Pinch of black pepper
- 1 homemade pie crust (see
    p. 285) or store-bought

Directions

Bring a large pot of water to boiling. Add onions and cook for 3 minutes. Drain completely in a colander or strainer. Melt butter in a large skillet over medium-low heat. Add onions and cook slowly without browning while stirring. When onions are soft and translucent, add honey, cinnamon, salt and pepper. Stir thoroughly and remove from heat.

Preheat oven to 450 F. Roll out 1 recipe of pie crust (see p. 285) or use a pre-made 9-inch crust. Line a 9-inch greased pan with crust and cut to shape. Fill with the onions and bake for 15 minutes. Cover tart with foil and bake 15 minutes more. Serve warm as a savory or a dessert.

. . . .

Asian Scallion Pancakes With Ginger Soy Dip

A great cocktail party snack.

Serves: 4

Ingredients

- 3 ounces (by weight) all-purpose flour
- 3 ounces (by weight) rice flour
- 1 large beaten egg
- 1 teaspoon toasted sesame oil
- 6 scallions (green and white parts), chop very fine
- 2 tablespoons fresh chopped cilantro
- 1/2 red bell pepper, slice in thin strips
- Peanut or vegetable oil for frying

Directions

In a mixing bowl combine the all-purpose and rice flour. Make a well in the center and add the beaten egg. Whisk the flour and egg together and gradually add 1 cup of cold water until a smooth batter is formed. Stir in sesame oil and let rest for 30 minutes. Heat a thin layer of oil over medium heat in the bottom of a 7- or 8-inch skillet. Pour one quarter of the batter in the pan. Sprinkle one-fourth of the scallions, red pepper strips, and cilantro on the batter. Cook 3 to 4 minutes until the pancake is set and browned. Flip the pancake with a spatula and cook the other side for 3 more minutes. Remove from pan. Make 3 more pancakes with remaining batter, adding oil to the pan, as you need it. Cut the pancakes in small squares or thin wedges. Serve with Ginger Soy Dip (see p. 165).

. . . .

Onion Soup

When the world gives you onions, make onion soup!

Serves: 8

Ingredients

- 2 cups diced or sliced onions
- 2 tablespoons butter
- 1/4 cup flour
- 6 cups rich vegetable or beef stock (see p. 289)
- 1/4 cup port wine or sherry
- 8 thick-sliced croutons
- 8 slices Swiss cheese or 1 cup shredded Parmesan cheese

Directions

Melt butter in a soup kettle over medium heat. Add onions and cook, stirring occasionally, until onions are soft and translucent. Sprinkle with flour and continue cooking for 2 minutes. Pour in stock and port or sherry, increase heat and bring to a boil, stirring constantly. When soup boils, reduce heat and simmer gently for 30 minutes. Taste occasionally and season with salt and pepper.

To serve, ladle soup into bowls and float a crouton on top. Sprinkle with shredded Parmesan cheese or lay a slice of Swiss cheese over the crouton and bake in a 450 F-degree oven until the cheese melts.

Onion and Roast Chili Relish

I put this on any grilled sandwich. It also makes a nice salad on a bed of greens.

Yields: 3 cups

Ingredients

- 1 cup roasted red chili peppers (see p. 288)
- 1 teaspoon whole allspice
- 1/2 teaspoon whole black peppercorns
- 1 teaspoon dried oregano
- 2 white onions
- 2 garlic cloves
- 1/3 cup white wine vinegar
- 1 cup cider vinegar
- Salt

Directions

Place allspice, black peppercorns and oregano in a mortar and pestle. Crush until coarsely ground. Alternatively, you may process in a spice or coffee mill. Lightly smash the garlic with the flat of a knife. Heat a small pan over medium-high heat. Add the garlic and cook for 4 to 5 minutes, stirring frequently, until garlic browns. Remove from pan and set aside.

Peel the onions and slice in half from the core end down. Lay each half flat and slice thin semi-circles of onion. Transfer the sliced onion to a large mixing bowl. Finely chop the roasted chilies and add to the onions. Add the ground spices, both vinegars, garlic and salt. Fully mix all the ingredients. Cover bowl with plastic wrap and let flavors mix in the refrigerator for at least one day.

CHEF'S NOTES

1. Onions should be stored in a dark, cool, dry place. They are sensitive to light. Store in trays or in mesh bags. Do not store them near potatoes.

2. Onion juice is good for coughs and cold but I think I would rather be sick than drink it!

2. Onions are in nearly every savory recipe and if you find a recipe without onions you probably could add them without doing much harm.

4. Red onions are very tasty raw or very quickly cooked, but tend to disappear in long cooking recipes. They will also bleed a little color when cooked, so if you don't want a pink sauce, stick to white or yellow onions.

Baked Onions With Feta

If you store your onions properly, you can enjoy this little treat all winter long. Serve it along with some grilled tomatoes for a very macho steak accompaniment.

Serves: 6

Ingredients
6 tennis ball-size onions of any type
1 quart chicken or vegetable stock (see p. 289)
1 tablespoon olive oil
3/4 cup crumbled feta cheese
1/4 cup bread crumbs
1 tablespoon chopped fresh herbs
Salt and pepper to taste

Directions
Peel onions. Cut off the top fourth of each onion and trim the stem end just enough to allow onion to stand steady. Arrange onions top down in a large pot. Add stock to pot and bring to a boil.

When stock is boiling, reduce heat and simmer for 20 to 30 minutes until onions are soft but not falling apart. Remove from heat. Drain and reserve stock for future use.

Preheat oven to 400 F. Allow onions to cool enough so that you can handle. Arrange onions, top-side up, in a shallow baking dish and season with salt and pepper. Combine cheese, bread crumbs, olive oil and fresh herbs in mixing bowl and toss lightly. Gently press 2 ounces of mixture on top of cooked onions. At this point, onions may be set aside and reheated just prior to serving. Heat onions in oven until tops are browned.

PARSNIPS

My notion of parsnips is forever colored by the image of Elmer Fudd (those of you under 35 may need to Google that) chopping up parsnips and carrots to make a tasty Bugs Bunny stew. Most of us (over the age of 35 anyway) know how that ended. I've intentionally left out any rabbit stew recipe in honor of Fudd's never ending hunger. The good news is that you don't need a smart aleck rabbit to enjoy parsnips. They look like sturdy beige carrots and cook a lot like carrots with the distinction that they have a potato like starchiness that is more satisfying than carrots. They are available locally very late in the season and are terrifically sweet after a frost. They can be stored for several months in a cool dry place.

Citrus Spiked Parsnip Mash

All root vegetables are very good mashed. The sweetness of the parsnips and the hint of tartness from the citrus make this a very distinctive side dish. Serve with broiled fish.

Serves: 6 to 8

Ingredients
- 1 pound parsnips, peel and cut into 1-inch chunks
- 1 pound potatoes, peel and cut into 1-inch chunks
- 1 orange or lime
- 1/4 cup whipping cream
- 2 tablespoons butter
- Salt and pepper
- 1/4 teaspoon grated nutmeg
- 2 tablespoons fresh chopped parsley

Directions
Bring a large pot of lightly salted water to a boil over high heat. Add parsnips and potatoes. Allow water to come back to a boil, reduce heat and simmer uncovered for 20 to 30 minutes until parsnips and potatoes are tender. While vegetables are cooking, zest orange or lime and set zest aside.

When parsnips and potatoes are cooked, drain in a colander. Return to pot and add whipping cream, butter, zest, salt, black pepper and nutmeg. Cut orange or lime in half and squeeze juice into pot. Mash the mixture with a potato masher or process, until smooth in a food processor. Transfer to a serving bowl and sprinkle with parsley. Serve immediately.

From *The Everyday Cookbook*
· circa 1890 ·

Parsnips and Salt Pork

2 pounds salt pork, 6 parsnips

"Cut salt pork into small pieces and partly cover with water and cook until almost done. Then add the parsnips, which have been cut in 1-inch pieces. Cook until both the salt pork and the parsnips are tender."

Curried Parsnip Soup

There is nothing better to warm you up on a chilly December day.

Serves: 6

Ingredients

2 pounds parsnips, peel and roughly chop
1 onion, diced
2 tablespoons butter
2 cloves garlic, mince
1 tablespoon curry powder
2 cups diced tomatoes
4 cups vegetable stock (see p. 289)
1 bay leaf
2 sprigs of thyme
1/4 cup plain yogurt for garnish
2 tablespoon chopped fresh parsley for garnish

Directions

Heat butter over medium heat in a large soup pot. Add the onion and garlic and cook, stirring gently, for 3 minutes until onions and butter are lightly browned. Stir in the curry powder and cook 1 minute more. Add the parsnips and stir until the parsnips are well coated. Add the tomatoes, stock, bay leaf and thyme. Bring to a boil; reduce heat and simmer, covered, until the parsnips are tender. Remove the thyme and bay leaf. Place soup in a food processor and process until smooth. You may need to do this in batches. Return to the pot and reheat soup; season with salt and pepper to taste. Ladle into shallow bowls, top with a dollop of yogurt and a sprinkling of chopped fresh parsley. Serve with hunks of naan bread or focaccia.

Parsnip and Apple Mash

Parsnips and apples are seasonal and flavor companions. Eat a big bowl of this mash topped with a dollop of sour cream or alongside pork or braised short ribs.

Serves: 4

Ingredients

1-1/2 pounds parsnips, peel and roughly chop
2 tablespoons butter
1 cup finely diced onions
2 granny smith apples, peel, remove seeds and roughly chop
1/4 cup sour cream
1/8 teaspoon allspice
Salt and pepper

Directions

Bring a pot of lightly salted water to a boil over medium-high heat. Add parsnips, allow water to come back to a boil, reduce heat and simmer for 20 minutes until parsnips are tender.

While parsnips are cooking, melt butter in a skillet over medium heat. Add onions, apples, salt, and pepper. Cook, stirring occasionally, until apples are tender, about 5 to 8 minutes. Scoop parsnips out of water and place them in a large mixing bowl. Add apple and onion mixture, sour cream, and allspice. Mash completely with a potato masher. Add a little of the parsnip's cooking liquid to thin mixture to the desired consistency. Serve hot.

· · · · · · · · · · · · · · · ·

Parsnip Crisps

A wonderful alternative to potato chips. Try them with a drizzle of tart lemon vinaigrette (see p. 279). Yummy!

Yields : A big bowl

Ingredients

1 pound parsnips
Salt
Oil for deep-frying

Directions

Preheat fryer to 350 F. Peel the parsnips with a vegetable peeler. Continue to peel off shavings the thickness of potato chips. Add the parsnips to the fryer and deep fry in small batches for 1 to 2 minutes until crisp. Place them onto a paper towel to drain. Sprinkle with salt and serve.

· · · · · · · · · · · · · · · ·

Parsnip and Tomato Juice

The start of a great Bloody Mary.

Serves: 2

Ingredients

4 parsnips
4 celery stalks
5 large or 8 small fresh tomatoes (about 1 pound)
1/4 teaspoon ground coriander
1/4 teaspoon ground cumin
1/4 teaspoon ground cardamom
Fresh ground black pepper

Directions

Cut parsnips and celery into pieces that will fit into your juicer. Core the tomatoes and quarter. Run ingredients through juicer as directed by manufacturer. Stir in coriander, cumin, cardamom and black pepper to taste. Serve in a cocktail, over ice, or in small glasses for breakfast.

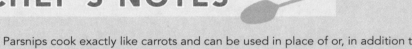

CHEF'S NOTES

1. Parsnips cook exactly like carrots and can be used in place of or, in addition to, carrots in any recipe. They are particularly good in long cooking roasts and stews. They are less colorful than carrots but noticeably sweeter.

2. You occasionally find a parsnip with a large distinct core. These typically are woody and unpleasant; discard these.

2. For a quick side, cook fork-size chunks of parsnips in boiling water for 5 minutes. Drain and toss with butter or olive oil and any chopped fresh herb (I like mint).

4. Freezing parsnips: Cut into the desired shape (circles, lengths, etc.) Blanch and shock (see p. 287). Freeze in airtight containers or freezer bags.

5. Roasted parsnips are among the finest roasted vegetables. Toss pieces with a little butter, sugar, salt and pepper and roast until tender.

6. In Roman times, parsnips were considered a powerful aphrodisiac. I'll say no more.

PEARS

Pears are perhaps the oldest know fruit to be consumed by man. While Eve is said to have eaten an apple, it is just as likely that a fine sweet pear tempted her. They are known to have been consumed in the Caucuses in pre-history and man has been playing around with pears ever since. There currently are over 6,000 known varieties. They are cultivated in every climate and on every continent. Along with apples they are the plentiful treat of autumn. Perhaps a tear-shaped fruit to signify the melancholy parting of summer ...

Broiled Salmon With Pear and Chilies

You also could grill the salmon for this recipe. Sweet and spicy relishes are great with fish.

Serves: 4

Ingredients

- 1 tablespoon salad oil
- 1/2 red onion, diced
- 3 tablespoons orange juice
- 1 lemon
- 2 tablespoons white wine
- 1/3 cup sugar
- 2 cups peeled and diced pears
- 3 tablespoons chopped scallions
- 1 jalapeno or cayenne chili, remove seeds and mince
- 2 tablespoons diced red peppers
- 3 tablespoon chopped fresh mint
- 1-1/2 pounds salmon filet, separate into 4 portions
- 1 tablespoon olive oil
- 1 tablespoon fresh lemon juice
- Salt and pepper
- Paprika

Directions

Remove zest from lemon with a zester into a small bowl. Set aside. Heat oil in a large skillet over medium-high heat. Add onions and cook for 2 minutes until onions soften. Cut the lemon in half and squeeze in the juice being careful to remove seeds. Add orange juice, lemon zest, wine and sugar. Boil ingredients until it evaporates by half. Stir in the pears and cook 5 to 10 minutes until soft, but not mushy. Remove from heat and transfer to a mixing bowl. Stir in scallions, chilies, red pepper and mint.

Place salmon filets in a shallow pan. Brush with olive oil, squeeze over a little fresh lemon, and season with salt, pepper and paprika. Broil until fish is cooked through, 10 to 15 minutes. Remove from broiler, arrange on a serving platter and top with pear and chili relish. Serve immediately.

Pears in Riesling Syrup

Serve this warm with shortcake or ice cream.

Serves: 4

Ingredients

2 pears, peel, core and slice in half
1 stick butter
1-1/3 cups sugar
1 bottle (750 ml) Riesling or other sweet wine

Directions

Heat butter and sugar over medium heat in a large deep skillet, stirring regularly until it forms into light brown syrup. Add the wine and stir to mix. Place pear halves in syrup and bring to a boil. Reduce heat and cook until pears are tender, 20-30 minutes. Serve warm or at room temperature.

. . . .

Basic Pear Sauce

This is a basic applesauce recipe made with pears. Experiment with different seasoning combinations and try stirring in fresh mint or rosemary just before canning.

Yields: 10 cups

Ingredients

4 pounds pears
1 cup water
1/4 cup lemon juice
1/2 cup honey
Optional: 1 teaspoon cinnamon
Optional: 1 teaspoon ground cloves
Optional: 1 teaspoon ground nutmeg

Directions

Sanitize canning jars (your size preference) in a water bath or prepare freezer bags of choice. In a large pot, place all the ingredients but the pears. Core and peel pears. Cut into large chunks and drop immediately into the pot. Bring to a boil over medium-high heat; reduce heat and simmer, uncovered, for 20 to 25 minutes until apples are tender. Mixture can be canned or frozen at this point.

If you would like a smoother sauce, place in a food processor and process to the desired consistency. Remove jars from water bath and fill with sauce to within 1/2-inch of top. Cover jars, seal, and process for 20 minutes in a boiling water bath as outlined in Chapter 7.

. . . .

Pan-Grilled Pears in Minted Honey Butter

A great waffle or pancake topping.

Serves: 4 to 6

Ingredients

4 pears, core and slice into 1/4-inch slices
2 tablespoons butter
1 recipe minted honey butter (see Appendix)

Directions

Melt 2 tablespoons butter in a large skillet over medium-high heat. Add pear slices and cook, stirring occasionally, until pears are soft and lightly browned, about 10 minutes. Add honey butter. Stir and toss until butter is melted and pears are well coated. Serve immediately.

. . . .

Pear Gratin

Amazing comfort food — Perfect for a potluck or served alongside roast chicken or turkey.

Serves: 6

Ingredients
4 large ripe pears
1 tablespoon butter
1/3 cup Dijon mustard
1-1/2 cups whipping cream
1 tablespoon fresh chopped thyme
1/2 teaspoon mace or nutmeg
1 cup bread crumbs (see p. 284)
1/4 cup bleu cheese crumbles
Salt and pepper

Directions
Preheat oven to 325 F. Core the pears and quarter lengthwise. Slice each quarter into ¼-inch slices. Melt butter in a large skillet over medium-high heat. Add the pears and season to taste with salt and pepper. Cook, stirring frequently, until pears are just tender, about 5 minutes.

Whisk together cream, mustard, thyme, and mace or nutmeg.

Layer half of the pears in a baking dish. Pour half of the cream mixture over the pears. Layer second half of pears in pan and pour over remaining cream mixture. Top with bread crumbs. Bake until cream is thick and bubbly and the bread crumbs are brown, about 1 hour. Remove from oven and sprinkle with bleu cheese. Bake an additional 8 minutes. Remove from oven and let rest 10 minutes before serving.

. . . .

Pears in Red Wine Jus

An elegant late summer dessert.

Serves: 6

Ingredients
6 large pears
1 bottle (750 ml) dry red wine, divided
1 tablespoon cornstarch
1/2 cup sugar
1 cinnamon stick
6 whole cloves
1 lemon
1 orange
1/4 cup sour cream

Directions
In a small bowl, stir together cornstarch with 2 tablespoons of red wine until it forms a thin paste. Set aside.

Using a zester or hand grater, prepare zest from the orange and lemon.

Combine the rest of the wine, sugar, cinnamon stick, cloves and the zest in a saucepan over medium heat. Bring to a boil and simmer for 2 minutes until sugar is dissolved. Reduce heat.

Peel the pears, leaving the stem intact. Place pears in pan of wine, cover, and simmer, turning pears occasionally, for 30 minutes. Remove pears and place in a serving dish. Pour wine mixture through a fine sieve and return to the pan. Bring to a boil over medium-high heat and whisk in cornstarch paste. Sauce should thicken within 1 minute.

Pour thickened wine over pears and let cool. Place sour cream in a small bowl. Cut the lemon in half and squeeze the juice from the lemon into the bowl with the sour cream. Mix well and spoon over pears.

. . . .

PEAS

Thomas Jefferson held an annual competition among his friends to see who could grow the first peas of the season. The prize was the honor of hosting the group to dinner where the lucky farmer could gloat about his horticultural skills and present sympathetic toasts to his unlucky brethren. The arrival of the first peas was thus celebrated. If you grow peas and have neighbor's who grow peas, this would be a fine tradition to start. If not, the first fresh peas of the season are worthy of some sort of celebration — Maybe a game of Twister or a big pitcher of daiquiris?

There are three main types of peas available. Shell peas are the familiar peas that we find frozen and in cans. They are horrid in cans, uninteresting frozen, but magical when pulled fresh from the shells and cooked immediately. Sugar snap peas are eaten whole, shells and all, and are crunchy, sweet and delightful. Snow peas are flat with very tiny peas inside. They are the familiar flat pod you find in Asian stir-fries. Peas are an early-season treat and should be enjoyed while available. They will disappear with the high heat of summer.

Basic Boiled and Buttered Peas

Unless you have an abundance of fresh peas, there really is no reason to serve them any other way. Buttered fresh peas are so perfectly sweet that you would have to eat them many days in a row to tire of them.

Serve: 4 as a side

Ingredients

1 pound fresh shelled peas
4 tablespoons butter
Pinch of sugar

Directions

Bring enough lightly salted water to cover the peas to a boil over medium-high heat Add peas and cook until the peas are just tender, but not mushy or discolored, 10 to 20 minutes depending on pea size. Drain off the water through a colander and return to the pan. Place pan back onto medium-high heat and add butter and sugar. Stir gently until butter has melted. Serve piping hot.

Peas With Mint

Fresh peas have a longstanding and venerable relationship with mint. You can replace the mint with tarragon, chervil, lemon thyme, or chives, if you like.

Serves: 4

Ingredients
1 pound fresh shelled peas
5 to 6 fresh whole mint leaves
4 tablespoons butter
Pinch of sugar
3 tablespoons chopped fresh mint

Directions
Bring enough lightly salted water to cover the peas to a boil over medium-high heat. Add peas, whole mint leaves and cook until the peas are just tender, but not mushy or discolored, 10 to 20 minutes depending on the size of the peas. Drain off the water through a colander, pick out the mint leaves and return to the pan. Place pan back onto medium-high heat and add butter and sugar. Stir gently until butter has melted. Add chopped fresh mint and stir gently. Serve immediately.

. . . .

Peas With Bacon and Spring Onions

Peas and spring bulb onions will be available at the same time. Take advantage of this natural pairing.

Serves: 4

Ingredients
1 pound fresh shelled peas
3 strips raw bacon, dice into small pieces
12 spring onions, clean and trim
1 tablespoon chopped fresh parsley
Black pepper

Directions
Bring peas and onions to a boil in lightly salted water and cook until tender but not mushy. Drain off water and remove the onions. Set onions aside. Place the peas in a bowl of ice water to stop cooking. Drain off ice water and set cooked peas aside. Heat bacon in a large skillet over medium heat until some of the fat renders. Add the onions and cook with the bacon until the bacon is fully cooked and the onions are lightly browned. Pour off one-third of the rendered fat. Add the cooked peas and stir gently to combine all ingredients; season with black pepper. Serve immediately with a sprinkling of chopped parsley.

. . . .

From *The Everyday Cookbook*
· circa 1890 ·

Creamed Green Peas

"Cook two cups of shelled green peas quickly in boiling water until tender. Add one teaspoon salt, level, drain off water and add one-half cup of cream. Slowly bring to a boil and serve."

Peas With Prosciutto

Prosciutto is a semi-dry cured Italian-style ham that lends a fantastic richness to the peas. You can find it at any well-stocked market.

Serves: 4

Ingredients
1 pound fresh, shelled peas
1 shallot
1/2 cup finely diced prosciutto ham
2 tablespoons olive oil
Black pepper
1/2 cup vegetable stock

Directions
Peel and cut shallot once lengthwise. Heat olive oil in a skillet over medium heat. Add shallots and prosciutto. Cook for 5-10 minutes, stirring occasionally, until the prosciutto crinkles up a bit. Add the peas and grate in black pepper to taste. Add the stock and simmer, uncovered for 10 to 20 minutes until the peas are tender. Serve immediately.

Snow Peas With Shiitake Mushrooms

Oyster sauce can be found at any Asian grocery and can often be found in supermarkets. Don't buy the cheapest one you can find. It might taste like a mud puddle. A good one has a very distinct richness and really adds character to this dish. You also can leave it out of this recipe if desired. I might object, but I likely won't be in your kitchen.

Serves: 4

Ingredients
12 ounces snow peas
1 cup shiitake mushrooms, remove stems
   and slice into 1/4-inch slices
2 tablespoons oyster sauce
2 tablespoon toasted almonds
2 tablespoons olive oil

Directions
Heat olive oil over medium-high heat in a large skillet. Add shiitake mushrooms and cook, stirring frequently, for 1 minute. Add the snow peas and cook a further minute. Add the oyster sauce and stir together. When sauce is hot and bubbly, remove from heat and serve. Garnish with toasted almonds.

Snow Peas With Herb Butter

The butter compounds listed in Chapter 5 are a very simple way to bring flavor and punch to any vegetables. This recipe calls for a fresh herb butter but could be prepared with any butter compound.

Serves: 6

Ingredients

1 pound snow peas, trim stems
   and remove strings
2 tablespoons fresh herb compound
   butter (see p. 282)
Salt and black pepper to taste

Directions

Bring 2 quarts of lightly salted water to a boil over medium-high heat. Add snow peas and bring water back to a boil. Reduce heat and simmer for 1-1/2 minutes until snow peas just cook, but are still a little crunchy. Drain in a colander and shake dry. Transfer to a mixing bowl and add the herb butter. Toss well and stir until butter is melted and snow peas are coated. Serve immediately.

Bay Scallop Broth With Snow Peas

A simple light soup with Asian flavors. For a vegetarian version, replace the scallops with half-inch cubes of tofu.

Serves: 8 as a starter

Ingredients

6 cups vegetable stock (see p. 289)
3 slices (1/4-inch thick) fresh ginger
3 garlic cloves, peel and lightly smash
   with the flat of a knife
3 tablespoons soy sauce
3 tablespoons sherry
1 teaspoon sesame oil
1-1/2 cups snow peas, remove stems and
   strings and cut in half diagonally
1 pound small bay scallops (about
   the size of a marble)
6 scallions, slice thin
Black pepper

Directions

Bring stock, ginger, and garlic to a boil over medium-high heat, reduce heat, cover and simmer for 15 minutes. Pick out the garlic and ginger and discard. Just before you are ready to serve the soup, add soy sauce, sherry, and sesame oil. Bring this to a boil over high heat. Add the snow peas, scallops, and scallions and bring back to a boil. Reduce heat and simmer for 1 minute. It is important not to overcook the scallops and snow peas with this soup. The snow peas should still have a little crunch and the scallops should still be plump and tender. Season to taste with black pepper and extra soy sauce.

CHEF'S NOTES

1. Peas do not store well and should be used or frozen within 2 to 3 days.

2. Peas freeze well, though they do soften. Blanch and shock before freezing in airtight containers or freezer bags.

2. When stir-frying snow peas, you can tell they are done when the pods puff up like balloons. This signals that they are warm inside. Further cooking will diminish their sweetness and crunch.

4. Eat sugar snap peas raw. They are like vegetable candy. In my house, they rarely make it to the refrigerator.

5. You need to remove the string from snow peas. It is tough and nasty. Pull the stem toward the thin side of the pod and the string should follow along with the stem.

6. You will see a theme with all the recipes offered here — short cooking and simple preparation. Save the complicated pea recipes for canned or dried peas. They need to be tortured into edibility.

PLUMS

In China, plums symbolize good fortune and it is distinct good fortune to eat a perfectly fresh plum. Tender and super sweet, the experience is completed when you've wiped the honey-like nectar from your lips with the back of your sleeve. Plums are a great hand fruit, found in many recipes, and are also a favorite fruit for country wines and liqueurs. Like many tree fruits, they are available from late summer to early fall.

Chilled Plum and Cranberry Soup

Serve bowls of this chilled soup as a dessert at your next barbecue.

Serves: 6

Ingredients

    4 large sweet apples
    8 large ripe plums
    2 cups fresh cranberries
    3/4 cup water
    3/4 cup sugar
    1/2 cup white wine
    1/4 teaspoon cardamom
    1/8 teaspoon cinnamon
    1/8 teaspoon grated nutmeg
    1/4 cup sour cream
    2 tablespoons fresh chopped mint
    Directions

Directions

Peel, core and roughly chop the apples. Slice the plums and discard the pits. Put cranberries, apples, plums, sugar and water in a saucepan and place over medium-high heat. Bring to a boil, reduce heat and simmer until apples are soft, 10 to 20 minutes. Add the wine, cardamom, cinnamon and nutmeg. Taste and add sugar if you like. Raise heat and bring back to a boil, stirring frequently. Remove from heat and transfer to a bowl. Chill completely in the refrigerator.

Place soup in a food processor and puree until very smooth. Ladle into shallow bowls and spoon a dollop of sour cream in the center. Sprinkle with the chopped mint.

Plum and Honey Spread

I don't really like plums, but if I have to eat them, I would prefer they are served up this way on an English muffin.

Yields: 1 pint

Ingredients

2 pounds plums
1 cup honey

Directions

Sanitize a pint jar in a boiling water bath. Remove the pits from the plums while cutting them into large chunks. Work over a mixing bowl to capture all of the plum juice. Transfer plums to a heavy-bottomed saucepan and add the honey. Place saucepan over medium heat and bring mixture to a boil while stirring frequently. Increase the heat and bring to a full boil. Skim off any icky stuff from the top that may form. Boil for 15 minutes, stirring gently but frequently, until mixture darkens. Remove the jar from water bath and fill to within 1/4 inch of the top. Process 10 minutes in a water bath as outlined in Chapter 7.

. . . .

Plum and Walnut Crisp

A great way to serve any stone fruit.

Serves: 8

Ingredients

1/2 cup packed light brown sugar
2 tablespoons corn starch
1/2 teaspoon ground cinnamon
2-1/2 pounds sliced pitted plums
2 tablespoons lemon juice
2 tablespoons butter, chop in small pieces
1 cup sugar
3/4 cup flour
1/2 teaspoon salt
3/4 cup chopped walnuts
1 large beaten egg

Directions

Preheat oven to 375 F. Combine brown sugar, cornstarch and cinnamon in a large mixing bowl. Add plums, lemon juice and butter. Toss this whole mess together until well combined and then spoon into a shallow baking pan. Place the sugar, flour, salt, and 1/2 cup of the walnuts in the bowl of a food processor. Process until the nuts are finely chopped. Add the beaten egg and process until just mixed, appoximately10 seconds. Spoon this mixture over the plums. Pull some of the plums up through the batter. Bake until well-browned and bubbling, 50 to 60 minutes. Serve warm with vanilla ice cream.

. . . .

CHEF'S NOTES

1. Underripe plums can be softened at room temperature. They will not get any sweeter. It is best to acquire them while very ripe and eat them within a few days.

2. Remove the pits before you freeze them. The pits will impart an off flavor. The best way to freeze plums is to remove the pits and skins; puree with a little honey and freeze in airtight containers.

From *The Everyday Cookbook*
· circa 1890 ·

Canned Plums

"To every pound of fruit allow three-quarters of a pound of sugar; for the thin syrup, a quarter of a pound of sugar to each pint of water. Select fine fruit, and prick with a needle to prevent bursting. Simmer gently in a syrup made with the above proportion of sugar and water. Let them boil not longer than five minutes. Put the plums in a jar, pour in the hot syrup, and seal. Greengages are also delicious done in this manner."

POTATOES

Many people, especially men, are fond of calling themselves "meat and potatoes" people. I suppose this is a warning to not try and trick them with anything new. Yet, everyone loves potatoes. And everyone, every American anyway, eats a truckload of potatoes. Much of this comes in the form of chips and fries, but even very unsophisticated eaters find reasons to like very sophisticated potato dishes. Potatoes always deliver that familiar comfort and, no matter how you dress them up, they still invariably find that home in your heart. They are always available and always true.

The colors and types of potatoes are many and varied, from tiny creamy reds to hefty russets that could sidecar any steak. There are golden Yukons, Peruvian purple and ultra white new potatoes. They all have subtle differences and preferred uses. I've offered a selection of recipes that will find a home for any type of potato. In most CSAs, you will get a large sack of potatoes late in the season to store and carry you well into the winter. Keep these in a dark place at 55 For below for the longest shelf life.

Potatoes a la Berrichonne

Berry is a region of France, located in the Loire valley, famous for its rustic slow-cooked dishes. This works best with small waxy red potatoes or any of the fingerling varieties.

Serves: 4

Ingredients

2 pounds small waxy potatoes
5 slices bacon
2 medium onions, diced
Salt and pepper to taste
2 to 4 cups meat or vegetable stock (see p. 289)
Sprig of thyme
Sprig of parsley
Sprig of rosemary
Sprig of oregano
1 bay leaf
2 tablespoons chopped fresh herbs

Directions

Tie herbs and bay leaf into a bundle with string or make an envelope with cheesecloth. Cut bacon into small strips and cook with onions over medium-high heat in a 5-quart pan. When onions are well browned, add the potatoes, salt and pepper. Add just enough stock to cover the potatoes. Add herb bundle. Bring to a boil. Reduce heat and simmer until potatoes are tender, approximately 25 to 35 minutes.

Remove herb bundle. Serve hot with a garnish of chopped herbs.

Potato Gnocchi

Gnocchi can be made with nearly any type of potato. When you get tired of mashed potatoes, give these little dumplings a try. They carry any pasta sauce well, can be sautéed or pan-fried and you can flavor them innumerable ways.

Serves: 4

Ingredients

    3 pounds fresh peeled potatoes, divided
    1 cup flour
    1/2 teaspoon grated nutmeg
    Salt and pepper to taste
    2 eggs

Directions

Dice 1 pound of potatoes in large pieces. Cook in boiling salted water for about 20 minutes until soft enough to mash. Drain well.

While potatoes are cooking, grate the remaining potatoes with a hand grater. Place the grated potatoes on a large piece of cheesecloth. Pull the edges of the cheesecloth together. Twist and squeeze the cheesecloth to wring out as much liquid from the potatoes as possible.

Mash the cooked potatoes in a large bowl. Add the grated potatoes and blend together. Mix in flour, nutmeg, salt and pepper. Blend 2 eggs together and mix into the potato mixture, a little at a time. Mixture should be a thick paste.

Bring a large pot of salted water to a boil over medium-high heat. Make small nickel-size nuggets with a pair of teaspoons and drop them one at a time into boiling water. Cook in the boiling water for 6 to 8 minutes. Scoop gnocchi from water with a skimmer or a slotted spoon and drain well. Use in a recipe immediately or cool in the refrigerator for later use. They will keep in the refrigerator for 3 days in a covered container.

Macaire Potatoes

Make these with leftover mashed potatoes with Lyonnaise sauce and serve alongside roasted meats.

Serves: 4

Ingredients

    2 cups leftover mashed potatoes
    1/4 cup butter or oil for frying
    Salt and pepper to taste

Directions

Heat the butter or oil over medium-high heat in a large skillet. Split the potatoes into 4 ball-shape portions and place in the pan. Flatten with the back of a spatula, season with salt and pepper and cook until well browned. Carefully flip the cake and brown the reverse side. You may have to cook these in batches depending on the size of your pan.

Lyonnaise Potatoes

Lyon is famous for its onions and the town lends its name to many classic preparations that are garnished with sautéed onions. This dish could also be called fried potatoes with onions. However, then you wouldn't buy a cookbook to find out how to make them. If you like a high falutin' name for your food, it might be more appropriate to name it after the patch of dirt your onions were pulled from, perhaps "Potatoes Ashtipula" or maybe "Potatoes a la farmer Dave's lower 40" and if you don't know, join a CSA.

Serves: 4 to 6

Ingredients

2 pounds fresh potatoes, any type will do
1/2 cup diced onion
3 tablespoons butter
Salt and pepper to taste
2 tablespoons chopped fresh parsley

Directions

Bring a large pot of salted water to a boil. If your potatoes are large, cut them into smaller pieces. Par cook the potatoes, peeled or unpeeled, until tender on the outside but still a little waxy in the center. Drain off water and cool enough so that they can be handled. Slice into 1/4-inch slices.

While the potatoes are cooking, melt 1 tablespoon of butter in a large skillet over medium heat. Add the diced onions and cook gently until soft and lightly browned. Remove the onions from the pan and set aside. Increase heat to medium-high and melt the remaining butter. Lay sliced potatoes in a single layer and brown on one side and season with salt and pepper. Add the cooked onions, stir gently and continue to cook for 1 to 2 minutes. Add chopped parsley and toss gently. Serve immediately.

Simple Potato Salad With Herbs

This recipe calls for oregano. I chose oregano because sometimes it can be difficult to find recipes for it and I have two big bushy oregano plants that always guilt me into finding a use for them.

Serves: 6

Ingredients

1-1/2 pounds waxy potatoes, reds, golds or fingerlings
1 red onion, cut into thin slices
2 tablespoons chopped fresh oregano
Salt and black pepper to taste
3 tablespoons olive oil
2 fresh tomatoes

Directions

Place potatoes in a pot full of salted water and place over high heat. Bring to a boil, reduce heat and simmer for 15 to 20 minutes until the potatoes are tender. Remove the pot from heat. Pour off water and cool slightly. When you can handle the potatoes, cut them into bite-size pieces.

Core the tomatoes and cut into thin wedges. Combine potatoes, onions, oregano, olive oil, salt and pepper in a large mixing bowl and gently toss with your hands. Pour into a serving bowl. Serve at room temperature.

Packet-Steamed New Potatoes With Herbs

This recipe is very good with any small or fingerling potato variety.
Feel free to substitute any available fresh herb.

Serves: 4

Ingredients

1-1/2 pounds new or fingerling potatoes
Salt and black pepper to taste
4 sprigs mint
4 sprigs parsley
1 tablespoon chopped mint
1 tablespoon chopped parsley

Directions

Preheat oven to 400 F. Lay a large sheet of foil on a cookie sheet. Grease the foil with pan coating or shortening. Place the potatoes in the center of the foil and liberally salt and pepper. Arrange the herb sprigs among the potatoes. Fold up the sides and then the ends of the foil to form a packet. Seal all the edges. Bake for 40 to 45 minutes until potatoes are tender. Open packet and remove herb sprigs. Place potatoes in a serving bowl and sprinkle with fresh chopped herbs.

. . . .

Fingerlings and Fennel

Potatoes and fennel are a natural. Serve this with broiled fish or pork.

Serves: 6

Ingredients

2 pounds fingerling potatoes, cut
    into 3/4-inch chunks
1 tablespoon butter
1 small fennel, dice fine
2 tablespoons chopped fresh mint
Salt and black pepper to taste

Directions

Bring a saucepan of lightly salted water to a boil over medium-high heat. Add potatoes and cook until potatoes are tender, 10 to 15 minutes. While the potatoes are cooking, heat butter in a large skillet over medium heat. Add fennel and cook, stirring occasionally for 5 to 8 minutes until fennel just browns. Drain the cooked potatoes and add to the pan with fennel. Salt and pepper liberally. Add chopped mint and gently toss all together. Serve immediately.

. . . .

Potatoes Rosti

The classic Swiss potato cake, rich with butter and onions.

Serves: 4

Ingredients

2 pounds baking potatoes
1 stick butter
1 onion, dice fine
Salt and black pepper to taste

Directions

Preheat the broiler. Place unpeeled potatoes in a large saucepan. Cover the potatoes with water and add salt. Place the pan over medium-high heat. Bring to a boil and cook for 8 minutes. Remove potatoes and set aside to cool completely. Peel potatoes and coarsely grate into a mixing bowl.

Melt 1 tablespoon of butter in a heavy-bottomed pan (cast iron works very well), over medium heat. Add the onions and cook for 5 minutes until soft. Stir onions into potatoes. Reserve 1 tablespoon of butter in a small microwaveable container. Place the remainder of the butter into the skillet and melt completely over medium heat. Place the potato mixture into the hot butter and form into a round cake. Cook for 15 minutes, shaking pan occasionally to loosen the cake, until bottom becomes crusty and brown. Melt the reserved butter in a microwave and drizzle over the top of the cake. Place under broiler and brown the top. Invert cake on a serving dish and cut in wedges.

. . . .

Potatoes Braised in Red Wine

A distinctive low-fat potato side dish.

Serves: 4

Ingredients

1-1/2 pounds potatoes, peel and
    slice into 1/4-inch slices
1-1/4 cups dry red wine
1 small onion, diced
3 tablespoons chopped fresh thyme
2 tablespoons chopped fresh parsley
Salt and black pepper to taste

Directions

Preheat oven to 375 F. Spread onions in the bottom of an ovenproof casserole dish. Arrange potatoes on top of onions and pour on red wine. Sprinkle with the chopped thyme and a liberal amount of salt and black pepper. Stir contents to coat potatoes with wine. Cover the dish with foil and bake, opening and stirring 2 to 3 times until potatoes are tender and most of the wine is absorbed, about an hour. Serve immediately with a sprinkling of chopped fresh parsley.

. . . .

Colcannon

This is a traditional Irish potato mash, but you don't have to be Irish to get comfortable with this dish.

Serves: 6

Ingredients

3 large potatoes, peel and cube
1/2 cup whipping cream
4 cups chopped cabbage
3 leeks, chopped
3 tablespoon chopped fresh chives
Salt to taste
White pepper to taste
2 tablespoons olive oil

Directions

Preheat oven to 350 F. Cook potatoes and cabbages and leeks at the same time using separate kettles. Bring both kettles of lightly salted water to a boil over medium-high heat. Place potatoes in one kettle and cabbages and leeks in the other.

Potatoes: Reduce the heat to medium and cook until tender, about 10 to 20 minutes, depending on the type of potato and size of chunks. Drain in a colander and set aside.

Cabbages and leeks: Bring water back to a boil, reduce heat and simmer for about 20 minutes until the cabbage is tender. Drain in a colander and set aside.

In a large bowl, combine the potatoes, whipping cream, salt, and white pepper. Mix for 5 to 10 minutes with an electric hand mixer until potatoes are very smooth. Fold in cabbage, leeks and chives. Spray a large casserole dish with pan spray and press potato mixture into the dish. Drizzle the top with olive oil. Bake for 30 minutes until top browns. Serve hot.

. . . .

Mashed Potatoes

You might have to search a long time to find someone who doesn't like mashed potatoes. Never mind the ridiculous phobia for carbohydrates that has half the world hypnotized; mashed potatoes are good for you. A plate of mashed potatoes lets us make friends with ourselves. The body and spirit craves the warm joy of familiar food. Mashed potatoes connect us with what food should be — a meaningful reward for a well-lived life.

This is a basic recipe that is easy to make followed by some tasty variations. You can mash any potato and many mash them with the skins on. It is best to mash potatoes with a hand masher if you like a lumpier texture. For smoother potatoes, use a food mill. You may also push the potatoes through a fine mesh sieve if you don't have a food mill. You will see recipes for potatoes mashed in a food processor. Try to avoid this. The likely result will be a stiff "gloppy" mess.

Serves: 6 to 8

Directions

Place potatoes in a pot and cover with plenty of cold water. Bring to a boil over medium-high heat. Reduce the heat to medium and cook until tender, about 10 to 20 minutes depending on the type of potato and size of chunks.

While potatoes are cooking, combine milk

and cream in a small saucepan and warm over medium-low heat until butter melts. Keep warm over very low heat until potatoes are ready. Drain potatoes in a colander. Mash potatoes with a hand masher or run through a food mill or sieve. Quickly stir in warm milk and butter, salt and pepper. Mix gently and serve immediately.

. . . .

Mashed Potato Variations

It is hard to improve on the basic recipe, but if you just can't leave well enough alone, try any of these innovations. They are scaled for use in the mashed potato recipe above. Adjust amounts if making larger or smaller batches.

1. Replace butter with 1/4 cup olive oil.

2. Replace the milk or cream with buttermilk. This will lend the potatoes a pleasant tart background.

3. Mix in 1/4 cup of persillade (see p. 146) after potatoes are mashed.

4. Mix in 1/4 cup of your favorite pesto recipe. There are wonderful pesto recipes throughout this book.

5. Replace 1/4 cup of the milk with 1/2 cup sour cream.

6. Mix in 1/2 cup of mascarpone or ricotta cheese after the potatoes are mashed. Mascarpone is a rich, sweet Italian soft cheese. Ricotta has a lighter fresh flavor.

7. Add 4 large garlic cloves to the pot with the potatoes while cooking. Mash garlic along with the potatoes.

8. Add 2 tablespoons Dijon mustard and 1 tablespoon toasted mustard seed (toast mustard seed by browning lightly in a dry skillet over medium heat to 3 to 5 minutes).

9. Mix in 1/4 cup of any fresh chopped herb or combination of fresh chopped herbs. Rosemary, oregano, basil, chives, dill, thyme, sage, chervil, even mint in small quantities are great additions.

10. Squeeze the cloves out of a head of roasted garlic (see p. 129). Either mash with the potatoes or stir in whole.

11. Mix 2 tablespoons of minced fresh jalapeno chili to mashed potatoes if you would like a spicy mash or minced poblano chili if you would like a milder mash.

12. Add 1/2 cup roasted sweet or chili peppers (diced into ¼-inch pieces) to mashed potatoes.

13. Cook 1/2 cup thinly sliced leeks in 1 tablespoon of butter over medium heat until tender and well browned, about 10 minutes. Mix into mashed potatoes.

14. Garnish mashed potatoes with thin slices of lightly browned garlic slices. Slice 4 garlic cloves as thin as possible and cook in 1 tablespoon of olive oil over medium-low heat, stirring frequently, until soft and golden. Sprinkle garlic over the top of the potatoes.

Mashed Potato Variations
Continued...

15. Stir in 1/2 cup of any cheese you desire. Some favorites are grated Parmesan, grated Swiss cheese, cheddar, nuggets of goat cheese, feta, bleu and queso fresco.

16. Stir in 1/2 cup finely chopped raw or grilled onions. To grill onions, simply cook in a skillet over medium heat with 1 tablespoon of butter until tender and brown.

17. Roughly chop 1 cup of wild or button mushrooms. Cook mushrooms gently in 1 tablespoon of olive oil over medium-low heat for about 10 minutes. Add 1 tablespoon chopped fresh thyme and stir into mashed potatoes.

18. Stir in 1/2 cup of crispy crumbled bacon and 2 tablespoons of chopped fresh chives.

19. Stir in 1/3 cup prepared jarred horseradish.

20. Flake 1/2 cup of any smoked fish and combine with 1 tablespoon of chopped fresh thyme. Gently stir into mashed potatoes.

CHEF'S NOTES

1. Waxy potatoes are best in potato salads or in any recipe that you want the potato to hold its shape. New potatoes, red potatoes, Yukon gold and most fingerlings are considered waxy.

2. Starchy potatoes are best for baking or mashing. They tend to be moister and sweeter. Russets and most large baking potatoes are considered "starchy" potatoes.

3. Cooked potatoes absorb a lot of salt. You may need to be liberal with salt to bring out the entire flavor.

4. If you don't have any teeth or you want a very smooth mashed potato, a food mill or ricer will remove all the lumps.

5. If using potatoes that have been stored for a while, boil them in water with a little sugar to enliven the flavor.

6. When storing potatoes, add a few apples to the bag or box. This will keep them from sprouting.

Down on the Farm

The humble potato is one of the most widely consumed vegetables in the world. Its adaptability makes it possible for it to be grown in many places. Originating in South America, it is a plant that is able to store lots of energy (carbohydrates) in its storage organs, or tubers, which we eat. The best commercial farms are now able to produce more than 70,000 pounds of potatoes per acre, or 29.5 million calories per acre. But the potato is not only a good source of energy; it contains a lot of fiber (especially if you eat the skin!), vitamin C and potassium. It is also low fat, unless you put on the butter, sour cream, or fry it in oil, as many of us like to do.

Potatoes come in many shapes and colors. We are familiar with the reds, russets, whites, and yellows we see in our supermarkets and we are now being introduced to other types — blue potatoes, potatoes with red flesh, fingerlings and other exotic color combinations. (Potatoes that have flashy colors tend to be higher in certain antioxidants.)

A culinary marvel, you can do many things with them: mash, fry, bake, roast, put on the grill or eat raw if so inclined. They also can be dehydrated and made into flour and alcohol — Some people like potato vodka.

Overall, potatoes can be used for many things. We should be thankful for them as they sustain us during those long winters we experience in the northern latitudes.

— Chris Malek, Malek Family Stewardship Farm, Stevens Point, Wisconsin

RADISHES

My grandfather, Jake, could sit down with a shaker of salt and eat an entire bowl of radishes. I would look on with horror as he happily crunched away on these nasty pills of bitterness. I'm sure there is some sort of metaphorical life lesson in the ability to enjoy a big bowl of raw radishes, and Jake, God rest his soul, was a gruff and stolid working man, but it was lost on me then and is elusive now. So rather than attempt to have the radish change me, I've sought to change the radish. The recipes in this chapter are an attempt to present radishes in a way that allows even the young Randy to eat an entire bowl.

Most of us are familiar with the ping-pong ball-size globe radishes that are almost exclusively found untouched on relish platters or fresh vegetable displays. The flavor is so sharp that one or two raw is about all anyone can stomach. However, there are many varieties that offer more subtlety and interest. Long white-tipped French radishes or all-white icicle radishes are milder and make great cocktail sandwiches. Large daikon-style radishes are also turning up in CSAs and farmers markets. These are very mild and add a refreshing crunch to salads or soups. You also can cook any radish, which will make them mild and sweet. Radishes are among the first items to appear each season. Perhaps this is the season to remove them from their relish platter exile.

Radish, Coconut and Carrot Slaw

Search the Internet for a video on how to safely open and peel a coconut. It's a bit physical, but fresh coconut makes all the difference in this South Asian-inspired slaw.

Serves: 4 (as an appetizer)

Ingredients
1/2 cup shredded radish (any type)
1/2 cup fresh shredded coconut
1/2 cup shredded carrots
1/4 teaspoon salt
1/3 teaspoon cayenne pepper
3 tablespoons chopped fresh cilantro
2 tablespoons butter
1/4 teaspoon celery seed
1/4 teaspoon fennel seeds
1/4 teaspoon cumin

Directions
Place shredded radish, coconut and carrot in a fine strainer and press out as much liquid as possible. Move salad to a mixing bowl and add salt, cayenne pepper and cilantro.

Heat butter in a small saucepan over medium heat. Add dry spices and cook until they darken slightly. Pour over slaw and toss until well mixed. If this slaw is served a second time, you should allow it to come to room temperature and toss to re-incorporate the butter.

Radish Finger Sandwiches

You can make these with any radish, but I think the long oval-shaped French breakfast radishes make the best sandwiches. Make plenty — they are addictive.

Ingredients

Crusty baguette or ciabatta, cut
   into 1/4-inch slices
Radishes, slice thin
Room temperature butter
Salt and freshly ground black pepper

Directions

It is best to slice the radishes as thin as you can. The slicing blade of a food processor might be helpful if you are not handy with a knife. Spread butter evenly on one side of each slice of bread. Season the bread with salt and black pepper. Place radish slices in a single layer on half of the bread slices. Form sandwiches with the other half of bread slices. Cut sandwiches into small 1- to 2-inch pieces.

. . . .

Creamed Radishes

A rich, slightly tart side dish for roasted meats.

Serves: 4

Ingredients

1-1/4 pounds of radishes, remove
   greens and quarter
1 tablespoon butter
1 tablespoon cider vinegar
1/2 cup whipping cream
Salt and pepper to taste
1 tablespoon chopped fresh chives

Directions

Melt butter in a large skillet over medium-high heat. Add the radishes and stir to coat with the butter. Add vinegar, salt, and pepper to taste to the skillet. Cook for 5 minutes, stirring constantly. Add the cream and boil for 5 to 10 minutes until cream thickens and coats the radishes. Transfer to a serving bowl and sprinkle with fresh chives.

. . . .

Radish Pickle

I love this alongside grilled sandwiches. You can use any radish, but daikon or French breakfast radishes make it special. Try it on your sub sandwich too!

Yields: 4 pints

Ingredients

1-1/2 pounds radishes
2 carrots
2-1/2 cups rice wine vinegar
1 cup water
2 tablespoons honey
2 teaspoons fresh grated ginger
2 cloves garlic, mince
4 dried or fresh cayenne or Thai chilies
2 tablespoons soy sauce

Directions

Sterilize the pint jars in a boiling water bath. Cut radishes and carrots into julienne strips. If you are not confident in your knife skills, simply slice thinly with the slicing blade of your food processor. Toss radishes and carrots together. The pieces need to be small enough to absorb the marinade. Combine vinegar, 1 cup water, honey, ginger, garlic, chilies, and soy in a saucepan. Bring to a boil over medium heat. Remove jars from water bath and immediately pack with the radishes and carrots. Pour the vinegar mixture into jars, filling to within 1/4-inch of the top. Cover jars, seal and process for 10 minutes as outlined in Chapter 7.

Radishes Braised in Vinegar

When radishes are cooked they loose their sharpness and eat much like turnips or parsnips. This dish can be served as a warm salad.

Serves: 4

Ingredients

1 pound radishes, trim off tops and bottoms
2-1/2 tablespoons sugar
1/2 cup water
1/3 cup red wine vinegar or
    other flavored vinegar
1 tablespoon butter
Salt and pepper to taste
1 tablespoon chopped fresh chives

Directions

Combine all ingredients in a large skillet. Bring to a boil, reduce heat, and simmer covered for 10 minutes. Remove cover and simmer 10 minutes more until radishes are tender. Scoop radishes out of the pan with a slotted spoon and keep warm. Continue to boil liquid in the pan for 2 to 3 minutes until it thickens slightly. Return radishes to the pan, salt and pepper to taste. Toss radishes to glaze with pan juice. Place in serving bowl and sprinkle with chives.

Radish Leaf Soup

Serve this with shaved Radish Finger Sandwiches early in the summer.

Serves: 4

Ingredients

4 ounces radish greens
2 tablespoons butter
6 cups vegetable stock (see p. 289)
3 medium potatoes, peeled and diced
1/4 cup sour cream
Salt and pepper to taste

Directions

Melt butter over medium heat in a small soup kettle. Add radish greens and cook until soft. Add stock and potatoes to the kettle and simmer gently for 30 minutes. Place soup in the bowl of a food processor and puree until smooth. Return processed ingredients to the kettle and reheat. Add sour cream and stir until well mixed. Serve immediately topped with chopped fresh herbs.

CHEF'S NOTES

1. Buy early season radishes with the greens attached. They are tender and flavorful. Use them raw in green salads or braise very quickly as you would spinach.

2. Good News! — Radishes are thought to relieve flatulence. Perhaps they are the perfect chaser for sunchokes?

3. Use thinly sliced radishes in place of onions on burgers or cold roast beef sandwiches.

4. Radishes are best early in the season and late in the season while the weather is still a little cool. They get very sharp over the summer months.

RAMPS

Sometimes called wild leeks, these are a wonderful treat. They appear early in the spring and can be the first taste of something fresh each season. They are a sharp jolt of onion and garlic that is most profound seconds after you pull them out of the ground, dust off the dirt and munch them leaves and all. This may be the most significant way to eat any early season offering; our bodies and souls slightly greedy, truly needy and impatient for a renewal. Of course, you don't need a cookbook to eat ramps this way; I recommend taking a few home to give a more formal treatment.

Ramps Cooked With Bacon

In Appalachia where the ramp is revered, you often will find them simmered with hunks of smoky bacon. The flavors are a natural pair. A great side dish with any roasted meat.

Serves: 4

Ingredients
1 pound whole ramps, just barely trim off root ends
3 slices bacon, finely chopped
Salt and pepper

Directions
Heat bacon in a large skillet over medium heat. Cook bacon, stirring occasionally, until bacon fat liquefies and meat turns crispy, about 10 minutes. Scoop bacon from pan with a slotted spoon and set aside. Place ramps in skillet with bacon fat and cook about 6 to 8 minutes, gently stirring and turning the ramps until tender. Return the bacon to the pan, season with salt and pepper and serve immediately.

Poached Ramps With Mustard Vinaigrette

This is my favorite ramp recipe. I serve them chilled as a simple side with sandwiches or a light soup.

Serves: 4

Ingredients

1 pound ramps, greens attached
2 cups vegetable stock
(see p. 289) or salted water
1/2 cup prepared mustard vinaigrette
(see p. 279)

Directions

Pour stock or water into a large skillet and bring to a boil over medium-high heat. Trim the root end of the ramps as closely as possible. If you trim too much, the ramp will came apart. Place ramps in boiling water and cook for 5 to 10 minutes until they soften and start to become a little translucent. Pour off liquid and rinse under cold running water to stop cooking. Place in a serving dish and ladle on vinaigrette.

. . . .

Poached Ramps With Brown Butter

A variation of the recipe above. The sharpness of the ramps plays well off the smokiness of the butter.

Serves: 4

Ingredients

1 pound ramps, greens attached
2 cups vegetable stock
(see p. 289) or salted water
1 recipe brown butter (see p. 282)

Directions

Pour stock or water into a large skillet and bring to a boil over medium-high heat. Trim off the root end of the ramps as closely as possible. If you trim too much, the ramp will come apart. Place ramps in boiling water and cook for 5 to10 minutes until they soften and start to become a little translucent. Drain in a colander and keep warm. Prepare brown butter. Toss ramps and brown butter together in a mixing bowl. Serve immediately.

. . . .

198

Ramps With Eggs

A simple breakfast or brunch dish.

Serves: 4

Ingredients

1/2 pound leeks, roughly chop
8 eggs
2 tablespoons olive oil
Salt and pepper
1 tablespoon grated Parmesan cheese

Directions

Preheat oven to 350 F. Place ramps in a pan of lightly salted water and bring to a boil over medium-high heat. Cook 3 to 5 minutes until ramps are slightly tender. Drain in a colander. Arrange ramps in the bottom of a deep pie pan and sprinkle with salt and pepper. Whisk eggs together with olive oil, salt and pepper. Pour over ramps and bake, uncovered, for 10 to 20 minutes until eggs are set. The center should still jiggle a little when shaken. Remove from oven and sprinkle on Parmesan cheese. Return to oven for 5 more minutes. Drizzle top with a little olive oil and serve with hunks of crusty bread.

. . . .

CHEF'S NOTES

1. You can substitute ramps for scallions or spring onions in any recipe.

2. Unlike leeks, ramp greens are tasty and palatable. Ramp greens, boiled for 3 to 5 minutes and chilled, make a great addition to any salad.

3. Ramps will flavor everything in your refrigerator.

4. Ramps are best eaten immediately. If you must store them, wrap in several layers of plastic and place well away from other food.

5. The best way to deal with a glut of ramps is to use them to make pesto and freeze the pesto. Blanch and shock (see p. 287) the greens and the bulbs, blend them into a pesto and freeze. This pesto packs a punch that is more suited to use as a seasoning than as a sauce.

6. For a great vegetable dip or potato topping, combine 1/2 cup mayonnaise, 1/2 cup sour cream.

RHUBARB

I have a perverse fondness for rhubarb. Our neighbor, Mr. Miller, had a tremendous stand of rhubarb in his backyard that my sister and I would raid regularly. We would skulk into his yard around dusk, both clutching cheap plastic steak knives, and cut down great stalks of rhubarb. We would drag them to our garage sanctuary to be dipped into carefully prepared bowls of sugar. That was some wickedly delicious rhubarb. Sadly, the rhubarb lost some of its savor when he caught us one day. And instead of dialing up Five-O, he grabbed a shears and commenced to cut down what seemed like a wheelbarrow full and offered us the whole pile to bring back to our mom. To my boyish sensibilities the rhubarb had suddenly become as interesting as mashed potatoes but a hint of that "schadenfreud" is still raised every spring when the rhubarb comes up.

Most of us either grow rhubarb or have a Mr. Miller in the neighborhood willing to share. It is one of the first things to sprout up each season. Cultivated rhubarb is found at markets for those of you without friendly neighbors. If buying rhubarb, look for the thin stalks available early each spring. Once they grow large they get tough and woody.

Rhubarb Compote

*This is beautifully simple. It's great by itself, but really shines
as an ingredient in turnovers or with ice cream.*

Yields: 2 quarts

Ingredients

5 cups rhubarb, dice into 3/4-inch pieces
1/4 cup lemon juice
3 cups water
1-3/4 cups sugar
1 cinnamon stick
2 cloves
1/2 teaspoon grated nutmeg
1/4 cup spiced rum
1/4 cup raisins

Directions

Bring water, sugar, and spices to a boil in a large pot over medium-high heat. Stir mixture to dissolve the sugar completely. Add rhubarb and reduce heat to simmer. Cook until rhubarb is soft and liquid forms a thick syrup. Stir in rum and raisins and cook 2 more minutes. Remove from heat. Remove cinnamon stick and cloves. Serve warm or cold.

Pan-Fried Catfish With Rhubarb

My grandfather and I used to catch the small catfish called bullheads. My grandmother would fry them and serve them with creamed rhubarb. I was too young to care about the recipe, but I do remember the dish being a perfect end to a perfect day. This is a good guess at the recipe.

Ingredients

2 pounds catfish filets
3 tablespoons butter
1 cup thinly sliced rhubarb, peel if necessary
3/4 cup heavy cream
1 teaspoon sugar
2 tablespoons chopped fresh basil
Salt and black pepper

Directions

Heat butter in a large skillet over medium heat. Salt and pepper catfish filets and place in skillet. Fry gently for a few minutes on each side until filets are cooked through. Remove from heat and keep warm. Place rhubarb in the same pan the fish were cooked in. Cook in the remaining butter until lightly browned. Add heavy cream, salt and pepper to taste. Increase heat and boil cream and rhubarb until it reduces by half and thickens. Stir in sugar and basil. Place filets on individual plates or in a large serving dish. Pour hot sauce over fish and serve immediately.

Rhubarb Chutney

A great alternative to applesauce to pair with pork.

Yields: 4 pints

Ingredients

2 oranges
2-1/2 pounds rhubarb, cut into 1-inch chunks
5-1/3 cups light brown sugar
4 cups rice wine vinegar
2 cups dried cranberries
2 onions, diced
1 tablespoon mustard seeds
12 allspice berries
12 whole black peppercorns

Directions

Sterilize 4 pint-size canning jars in a boiling water bath. Grate zest from both oranges with a zester or hand grater and set aside. Peel the oranges, removing the white pith completely. With a paring knife cut sections out between the white membranes of the orange. Roughly chop the orange sections and place in a large mixing bowl along with any juice collected on the cutting board. Squeeze juice from the remaining membranes. Add the rhubarb, sugar, vinegar, raisins, onions, allspice, and peppercorns. Toss together and transfer to a saucepan. Place saucepan on stove top over medium heat. Bring to a boil then reduce heat and simmer, stirring frequently for 1 to 1-1/2 hours, until mixture is thick. Remove jars from boiling water. Ladle rhubarb into jars. Fill to within 1/4 inch from the top. Cover jars, seal, and process for 10 minutes as outlined in Chapter 7.

From *The Everyday Cookbook*
· circa 1890 ·

Rhubarb Sauce

"Wash the rhubarb and cut into one-inch pieces; cover with two cups of sugar to one quart of rhubarb. Stand aside for one hour. Use just enough water to moisten the sugar. Cook until rhubarb is tender. Serve cold. This is a delicious dish served with whipped cream."

Minted Strawberry and Rhubarb Juice

This is a great juice for the tart early season strawberries you may find when the rhubarb is still young and tender.

Serves: 2

Ingredients

1 quart strawberries, remove greens
3 stalks rhubarb, cut into chunks
1 orange
1/4 cup tightly packed mint leaves
3 tablespoons honey
1/2 teaspoon ground cumin

Directions

Using a paring knife, peel orange by cutting thin vertical strips from top to bottom and rotating the orange until fully peeled. Cut peeled orange into quarters. Feed strawberries, rhubarb, orange pieces, and mint leaves though your juicer and extract juice completely. Add honey and cumin. Pour into 2 glasses.

CHEF'S NOTES

1. It's hard to find a better way to eat rhubarb than just dipping in sugar and crunching away. Only when you tire of that should you try some of these recipes.

2. Rhubarb freezes best in light syrup. Prepare syrup with 1 part honey to 4 parts hot water. Cut rhubarb into desired sizes. Blanch for 2 minutes, shock to stop cooking (see p. 287). Drain rhubarb well and cover with honey syrup. Freeze in airtight containers or freezer bags.

3. In 16th century Europe, a tea of rhubarb and parsley was used as a treatment for venereal disease.

SALSIFY

Salsify is one of those vegetables you can't identify, occasionally found on the menu of an elegant restaurant. It has a sexy name and you envision it must be so yummy that it will change your life. When you get it, you realize the only thing interesting about it is the name. It's not much more than a bland white carrot. However, it is occasionally present in your CSA box or available at farmers markets and you may want to impress your friends by serving the exotic vegetable. Any of these recipes do their best to turn something unremarkable into something mildly exciting. Bon Appétit!

Salsify Fritters

This is a tasty snack that can be served alone or in a tempura vegetable platter.

Serves: 4

Ingredients
3-1/2 cups salsify, peel, blanch
    and shock (see p. 287)
2 cups tempura batter (see p. 286)
Vegetable oil for frying
2 lemons or limes

Directions
Heat oil in a countertop fryer to 350 F (please don't fry in a pan on the stove top).

Cut salsify into consistent sizes. Dip pieces into batter and fry until golden. (Avoid putting too many pieces in the fryer basket at once.) Turn pieces, if necessary, to cook evenly. You will have to cook in batches. Remove the salsify from fryer with basket or skimmer and place on a plate lined with paper towels.

Place on a serving platter or in a bowl and serve with lemon or lime wedges. You may also serve with a favorite dipping sauce (see Chapter 5).

. . . .

Salsify Horseradish Mash

As an alternative to mashed potatoes, this would be perfect alongside a peppered tuna steak.

Serves: 6 to 8 as a side

Ingredients
2 pounds salsify, clean and cut into small chunks
1 clove garlic
2-1/2 tablespoons butter
3/4 cup milk
1 tablespoon horseradish
Salt and pepper to taste

Directions
Place salsify and garlic into a saucepan with water. Bring to a boil over high heat. Cook for 10 minutes until salsify is soft enough to mash. Add butter, milk and horseradish. Mash salsify and ingredients together with a potato masher or puree in a food processor. Salt and pepper to taste.

. . . .

Roasted Beet and Salsify

Serves: 6 to 8 as a side

Ingredients

- 1 pound fresh beets
- 1 pound salsify
- 1/4 teaspoon grated nutmeg
- 1/4 teaspoon ground cumin
- 1/4 teaspoon salt
- 2 tablespoons olive oil
- 2 tablespoons honey

Directions

Preheat oven to 350 F. Blend together honey and olive oil in a small bowl. Set aside.

Peel beets with a stout vegetable peeler. Cut into large chunks and arrange on a cookie sheet. Peel salsify with a sharp knife. Cut into large chunks and place on the same cookie sheet. Sprinkle with nutmeg, cumin and salt. Drizzle with honey/oil mixture and toss vegetables gently to coat. Roast in the oven for 45 to 60 minutes or until vegetables are soft.

Braised Curry Salsify

Starchy root vegetables absorb the sharp curry flavors well. This recipe is great with wilted greens and panir cheese (see page 285).

Serves: 4 as a side

Ingredients

- 1 pound salsify, clean
- juice
- 1 tablespoon butter
- 1 small diced onion
- 2 tablespoons white wine
- 1/2 cup béchamel sauce (see p. 277)
- 1 teaspoon curry powder

Directions

Cut salsify into thin slices and place in cold water with a little lemon juice. Bring a pot of lightly salted water to a boil over high heat. Place salsify in boiling water and cook until soft, about 8 minutes. Drain completely and place in a serving dish.

While salsify is cooking, melt butter in a skillet over medium-high heat. Add onions and cook about 2 to 3 minutes, stirring frequently until onions are soft. Add wine and boil down by half. Add curry powder and stir to blend. Stir in béchamel and heat through. Pour hot sauce over salsify and serve immediately.

CHEF'S NOTES

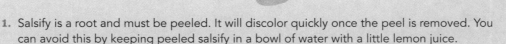

1. Salsify is a root and must be peeled. It will discolor quickly once the peel is removed. You can avoid this by keeping peeled salsify in a bowl of water with a little lemon juice.

2. Salsify is also known as oyster plant. Some say it tastes a little like oysters. I love oysters — I don't love salsify. There is no resemblance.

3. The roots stay fresh unpeeled for about a week in the refrigerator.

SHALLOTS

To the uninitiated, shallots are looked on as little onions. They do look like small globe onions, but have a personality all their own. While onions add a sharpness and pungency to food, shallots add a delicate sweetness that cannot be duplicated any other way. Shallots typically are minced fine and added to vinegar based sauces, but they also can be pickled whole and make a wonderful steak garnish. Shallots will be available locally from midsummer on.

Pan-Grilled Steaks With Shallots

Choose cuts of meat that are naturally tender. This is a quick-cooking method and will be nearly inedible with most cuts from the round or shoulder. I recommend sirloin, strip steak, or rib steak.

Ingredients

4 steaks, each 6 to 12 ounces
4 tablespoons butter, divided
4 tablespoons fresh shallots,
    slice in slivers or rings
4 tablespoons red wine vinegar
1 tablespoon red wine or stock (see p. 289)
Salt
Coarse ground black pepper

Directions

Liberally season both sides of steak with salt. Press coarse pepper into the meat on both sides. Heat 2 tablespoons butter over medium-high heat in a large skillet. When skillet is hot, lay steaks in pan and let sit for a few minutes to sear outside of meat. Cook until liquid starts to rise on uncooked side of meat. Turn the steaks over; add the shallots to the skillet and sauté. Cook steaks to preferred doneness and remove from pan. Add vinegar and wine or stock. Let liquid sizzle and sputter while scraping up bits of cooked meat from bottom of the pan with a wooden spoon. Boil liquid until it cooks down by half. Remove from heat and whisk in the remaining 2 tablespoons of butter. Spoon shallots and pan sauce over steak and serve immediately.

Buttermilk Mash With Golden Shallots

While this is a mashed potato recipe, the shallots are the stars. They bring an unexpected sweet richness to simple mashed potatoes.

Serves: 4

Ingredients

1 pound Yukon Gold or other waxy potato
1 tablespoon butter
3 shallots, cut in half and slice
    into very thin ribbons
1/2 cup buttermilk
Salt and pepper

Directions

Peel and quarter potatoes and immediately place in a saucepan of water. Add 1 teaspoon of salt. Bring pot to a boil over medium-high heat. Reduce heat and simmer for 20 to 30 minutes until potatoes are soft. While potatoes are cooking, melt butter in a skillet over medium-high heat. Add shallots and cook about 8 minutes, stirring frequently until shallots are golden brown and soft. Remove from heat and set aside. Drain potatoes in a colander and return to pan. Mash with a potato masher. Stir in shallots, buttermilk, salt, and pepper to taste. Serve hot.

. . . .

Shallot Sauce for Oysters

In the States we love our hot sauce, but try this for a change of pace.

Ingredients

2 large shallots, dice fine
2 tablespoons white wine vinegar
Coarse salt
Fresh ground black pepper

Directions

Combine all ingredients in a small mixing bowl and adjust seasoning. Serve atop shucked oysters.

. . . .

CHEF'S NOTES

1. Shallots are very good storage vegetables. If kept in a cool dry place, they will outlast onions.

2. Boil shallots whole until tender and cook with a little butter and garlic for an elegant side dish.

3. Minced shallots go well with any acidic food. Add minced shallots to any vinaigrette recipe.

SHELL BEANS

I have to confess to not working with shell beans much. They are the fresh versions of many of the dried beans you see on store shelves. They are available locally during very short windows.

I played around with a few recipes using canned versions of these beans and the results were tasty. I can only imagine the revelation once I get a chance to try these fresh. Perhaps the next book can be an investigation of the items I'm unfamiliar with. I'm sure that's a position many home cooks find themselves in.

Simple Shell-Bean Salad

This can be made with any available shell bean.

Serves: 4

Ingredients

1 cucumber, peel, remove seeds and dice fine
1 pound shell beans
1 tomato, dice
1/2 cup fresh chopped mint
1/2 cup chopped fresh parsley
1/2 diced red onion
1/4 cup tahini (sesame seed paste)
1/4 cup lemon juice
2 garlic cloves., minced
Pinch of cayenne
Salt and black pepper
Red or green butter lettuce leaves for a salad bed

Directions

Bring a saucepan of salted water to a boil over medium-high heat. Add beans and cook until soft. The time will vary based on the type of bean (10 to 20 minutes). Drain beans in a colander and rinse with cold water. Place tahini in a large mixing bowl and thin with 1 tablespoon of water. Add all other ingredients except for lettuce. Toss completely and serve on a decorative platter lined with lettuce leaves.

. . . .

Fava Beans With Savory

*This is the classic preparation for fava beans. It also will work
well with lima beans or cranberry beans.*

Serves: 4

Ingredients

3 cups fresh fava beans, shelled
2 whole sprigs summer or winter savory
2 tablespoons butter
2 tablespoons chopped fresh savory
Salt and fresh ground black pepper

Directions

Bring a pot of salted water to a boil. Add beans and
sprigs of savory. Cook until tender but not mushy,
about 3 to 5 minutes. Pour off water and return
pot full of beans to medium heat and add the
butter. Add chopped savory, salt and pepper. Stir
gently while butter melts. Serve at once.

Bissara

*The Southern and Eastern Mediterranean areas are famous for delicious blended dips. This is
an example from Algeria. Serve this with warm flatbread or break off hunks from a crusty loaf.*

Makes 4 cups

Ingredients

3-1/2 cups fresh fava beans, shelled
1 jalapeno or other hot chili,
   remove seeds and chop
1 teaspoon paprika
1 teaspoon cumin
2 garlic cloves
1/2 cup extra virgin olive oil
1 lemon
Salt and fresh ground pepper

Directions

Zest lemon with a zester or hand grater into a
small bowl and set aside. Cook beans in salted
boiling water until beans are tender, but not
mushy. Drain. Place beans in the bowl of a food
processor and add chili, paprika, cumin, garlic
cloves and the juice of the zested lemon. Puree
bean mixture and slowly drizzle in olive oil until
well incorporated. Season with salt and pepper.
Pour onto a shallow serving platter. Garnish with a
drizzle of olive oil and a sprinkling of paprika and
lemon zest.

SORREL

Sorrel, also called garden sorrel or lemon sorrel, is a green that many in North America are unfamiliar with. It has been a staple in Europe for centuries. Its Latin name is translated as "I suck," which refers to the sour taste and not to any particular Roman's failing self-image. A delightful tartness is sorrel's most distinctive and exciting attribute. It wakes up any dish you serve. My first taste of sorrel, only a few years ago, was a revelation. I had no idea lettuce could explode with so much flavor. Used in small quantities it enhances the flavor of any green salad. In larger quantities, used in a pesto sauce or a soup, sorrel provides a lemony tartness that is a perfect partner with fish and seafood. Sorrel is available from late spring to midsummer.

Germiny Soup

Finely chopped sorrel makes a fine soup. This soup and Chilled Sorrel Soup (p. 210) use similar thickened egg bases and illustrate how a very sharp and alive flavor can be carried nicely in a rich base. This soup easily could double as a sauce for light-fleshed fish.

Serves: 6 to 8

Ingredients

1 pound sorrel leaves
1 tablespoon butter
6 cups vegetable, chicken, or
   beef stock (see p. 289)
6 egg yolks
2 cups heavy cream
Salt and pepper
6 to 8 sliced croutons, 3/4-inch thick

Directions

Cut out stems and tough center ribs from sorrel leaves. Finely chop the sorrel leaves. Heat 1 tablespoon of butter in a large pot over medium-high heat. Add sorrel and cook until soft. Pour in stock and bring to a boil. Reduce heat to a simmer.

Blend together egg yolks and cream in a mixing bowl. Whisk 1/4 cup of soup into cream mixture then slowly pour cream into soup while whisking. Continue to stir the soup until it thickens slightly. Remove from heat just before boiling. Season to taste with salt and pepper.

Place a crouton in the bottom of shallow soup bowls. Pour soup over crouton and sprinkle with chopped sorrel.

Hard Cooked Eggs With Sorrel

The tartness of the sorrel makes this creamy egg dish bolder than you might expect. A great start to the day with buttered English muffins.

Serves: 4

Ingredients

1 cup sorrel leaves, remove ribs and finely mince
1/4 cup finely diced shallots
3 tablespoons butter
1 tablespoon flour
1-3/4 cups milk
Salt and pepper
4 hard-cooked eggs, quarter

Directions

Heat 3 tablespoons butter in a large skillet over medium-low heat. Add sorrel and shallots. Cook slowly until liquid from sorrel is evaporated. Sprinkle on 1 tablespoon of flour and cook for 5 minutes, stirring constantly. Increase heat to medium high and add milk. Continue stirring until mixture starts to boil. Reduce heat to low and simmer for 10 minutes, stirring frequently. The sauce should be the thickness of thin gravy; if it's too thick, add a little more milk. Salt and pepper to taste.

Arrange quartered eggs in a serving dish and ladle over sorrel sauce. Serve immediately.

. . . .

Chilled Sorrel Soup

A fine lunch on a hot day.

Serves: 6 to 8

Ingredients

4 cups fresh sorrel
4 cups water
1 tablespoon lemon juice
2 egg yolks
Salt and pepper to taste
Sour cream for garnish

Directions

Cut out stems and tough center ribs from sorrel leaves. Tie up stems and ribs in a bundle with string. Chop leaves into short strips. Bring water to a boil in a soup pot. Add lemon, sorrel leaves, stem bundle, salt and pepper. Reduce heat and simmer for 20 minutes. Remove and discard stem bundle.

Beat egg yolks in a small mixing bowl. Slowly add 2 tablespoons of hot soup to beaten egg while stirring. Slowly add egg mixture back into simmering soup stirring constantly. Soup will thicken slightly. Remove from heat just before soup boils. Chill completely in the refrigerator.

Serve in shallow bowls. Garnish with a spoonful of sour cream and a sprinkling of sorrel.

. . . .

CHEF'S NOTES

1. Like most greens, sorrel needs to be eaten quickly. It will not keep for long. If you find yourself with an unmanageable quantity, blend it into a pesto and freeze.

2. The simplest way to prepare sorrel: quickly cook in a skillet with a little butter, salt and water.

3. Add chopped sorrel leaves to any pureed cream soup. Cream of potato, cauliflower, asparagus — even pea soup, are enlivened by the dazzling tartness of sorrel.

4. When freezing sorrel, it is best to blend it into a pesto first.

Garden Sorrel Pesto

Garden sorrel is sometimes called lemon sorrel because of its very pronounced tartness. A dab of this mixed with butter is a natural on broiled fish.

Yields: 3-1/2 cups

Ingredients
2 cups garden sorrel
1/3 cup parsley
2 garlic cloves
1/3 cup grated Parmesan cheese
1/4 cup roasted pine nuts
Salt to taste
1/4 cup olive oil

Directions
Place all ingredients except oil in a food processor; process until smooth while drizzling in olive oil. Will keep several weeks in the refrigerator and can also be frozen.

· · · · · · · · · · · · · · · · ·

Down on the Farm

July 17

I surely hate to keep bringing you the same news, but another week has passed with little more than nothing for rain. I greeted part of the drought with a welcome, since it gave us a chance to get the garlic in the barn and the shallots in the hoop houses without interruption. My overall anxiety about the lack of water was not diminished by the clanking of a bulldozer and a crane a quarter of a mile from where we were pulling garlic. The neighbor was digging his irrigation hole deeper to make up for the lowering water table. My method of getting water from the ground with sand points and little Honda pumps is limited in its ability to reach down for water, and I expect soon that I will be sucking air and will no longer be able to irrigate. That will be the test of how well my soil can hold water. Water rights will soon be a major issue both for agriculture and municipalities as we deplete our underground reserves and pollute what little is left. There are those of us that think that water will enter its final crisis before fuel does. Ultimately water will be more important, because we can't drink gasoline.

— David Peterson, Maplewood Gardens

SPINACH

Of course, I can't introduce the chapter on spinach without a Popeye reference. I believe Popeye was just a propaganda vehicle to get kids to eat spinach. Kids, at least kids in my day, are vehemently opposed to spinach, I think mostly because it usually was some nasty green mess served up out of a can. It seemed slimy and foreign and altogether unfit for human consumption. Popeye didn't see it that way and gobbled that nasty stuff up like it was ice cream or cotton candy, but it didn't fool any of us. If Popeye were adapted for current tastes, he would be eating a bowlful of fresh baby spinach with strawberries and a light vinaigrette. I think that kids are much more refined and discerning nowadays.

Baby spinach starts appearing early in the season and will be available throughout the summer and fall. It does not keep well, so use it or freeze it as soon as possible.

Spinach and Rice Soup

This soup is very light. It will taste much better with a rich and flavorful stock.

Serves: 4

Ingredients
1-1/2 pounds fresh spinach
3 tablespoons olive oil
1 onion, dice
2 garlic cloves, mince
1 small red chili, remove seeds and chop
1/2 cup cooked rice
5 cups rich vegetable stock (see p. 289)
1/4 cup grated Parmesan cheese
Salt and black pepper

Directions
Heat a large skillet over medium-high heat. Add the spinach and 1 tablespoon of water. Cook the spinach, stirring and turning, just until it wilts. Remove from the heat and transfer to a clean cutting board. Chop the spinach with a knife until nearly minced. Set aside.

Heat a large saucepan over medium heat and add the olive oil. Add onions, garlic and chili and cook, stirring regularly, until onion is soft, about 5 minutes. Add the rice and mix well. Pour in the stock. Raise the heat and bring to a boil then lower the heat and simmer for 10 minutes. Add the chopped spinach, bring back to a simmer and cook 5 to 7 minutes more. Salt and pepper to taste. Serve in shallow bowls with a sprinkling of grated Parmesan cheese.

Calf's Liver Florentine

A Florentine garnish typically contains spinach and tomatoes. If you don't like liver you won't eat this. If you do, this is a lively and colorful presentation.

Serves: 4

Ingredients

4 slices calf's liver, each 4 ounces
Flour for dusting
6 tablespoons butter or oil, divided
Salt and pepper to taste
1 pound fresh spinach
2 large tomatoes, slice
2 medium onions, slice thin
l lemon

Directions

Season flour with salt and pepper. Coat liver slices with seasoned flour. Set aside. Heat 2 tablespoons butter or oil over medium-high heat in a large skillet. Add onions with a little salt and pepper and cook, stirring occasionally, until onions are soft and translucent. Remove from pan and keep warm.

Arrange tomato slices in the pan and cook on one side until lightly browned. Remove from pan and keep warm. Add a little more butter or oil and very quickly cook the spinach, seasoning with a little salt. The spinach will cook very quickly and should be removed as soon as it wilts and changes color. You may have to cook in batches. Set aside and keep warm.

Heat the remaining oil or butter and place the slices in a single layer in the pan. Cook 5 to 7 minutes on one side, turn the slices and cook a few more minutes until cooked through. Lay wilted spinach in the bottom of the serving platter. Arrange slices of liver on top of spinach. Shingle grilled tomatoes over liver and top all with the cooked onions. Garnish with lemon wedges.

. . . .

Spinach Stir-Fry With Peanuts

Great with seafood or with a hunk of crusty bread.

Serves: 4

Ingredients

1 pound of spinach leaves
1 tablespoon sesame oil
1 clove minced garlic
1 teaspoon fresh minced ginger
1/4 teaspoon crushed red pepper
1 teaspoon Thai fish sauce
1 tablespoon soy sauce
1 teaspoon sugar
1/2 cup chopped roasted peanuts

Directions

Heat the sesame oil in a very large skillet or wok over medium-high heat. Add the garlic, ginger, and crushed pepper. Stir immediately to keep the garlic from scorching. Cook 20 to 30 seconds and add spinach. Continue to stir and toss until the spinach just wilts. You will have to do this with tongs to hold fresh spinach down to the hot pan. Add the fish sauce, soy sauce, sugar, and peanuts. Stir and cook 1 minute longer. Serve immediately.

. . . .

Wilted Spinach Salad With Panir Cheese

Panir is a mild unripened cheese (has a very subtle flavor). It's unusual in that it can be cut in pieces and fried without melting. It's difficult to find but very easy to make. Follow the recipe on page 285.

Serves: 6

Salad Ingredients

8 cups fresh spinach, trim off stems
1 cup fresh panir cheese, dice
    into 1/2-inch pieces
1/4 cup oil for frying
1 roasted red pepper, cut in strips (see p. 288)
1/3 cup toasted chopped walnuts

Dressing Ingredients

1/4 cup extra virgin olive oil
2 tablespoons sesame oil
2 tablespoons walnuts, chop fine
2 tablespoons lime juice
2 tablespoons chopped fresh cilantro
2 teaspoons sugar
1/4 teaspoon paprika
1/4 teaspoon prepared yellow mustard
Salt and pepper to taste

Directions

Combine all dressing ingredients except oil in a mixing bowl. Vigorously stir with whisk while slowly adding sesame and olive oil. Set aside.

Heat 1/4 cup olive oil over medium-high heat in a skillet. Add diced panir cheese and fry, occasionally stirring to brown cheese on all sides. Remove from pan and drain on a paper towel.

Place the spinach in a large mixing bowl; add the browned cheese and roasted red pepper.

Heat the salad dressing in a saucepan. Whisk briefly and, while still hot, pour hot dressing all over spinach. Toss gently and transfer to serving bowl. Garnish with chopped walnuts and serve immediately.

. . . .

CHEF'S NOTES

1. You must clean the stems from spinach. They are stringy and tough even when cooked. Baby spinach can be eaten with the stems.

2. Spinach usually hides a fair amount of sand in its leaves. Rinse several times in cold water before using.

3. Nutmeg, pepper and sugar are very good seasonings with spinach.

4. Spinach can be substituted for other leafy greens such as chard or mustard greens in recipes.

5. Mix cooked spinach with a little cream, parmesan cheese and bread crumbs for an elegant stuffing for fish or chicken.

Spinach and Herb Pate

Use this recipe as an excuse to buy a mortar and pestle. The crushing more perfectly extracts the oils that allow this Pate to set. Serve slices of this as a snack with strong tea.

Serves: 4

Ingredients

1 pound spinach leaves
1 large clove of garlic
1/3 cup chopped pistachio nuts
Salt
1/2 teaspoon ground coriander
Pinch of cayenne pepper
1/4 cup chopped cilantro
2 tablespoons chopped fresh parsley
1 small onion
2 teaspoons rice wine vinegar
Black pepper
2 tablespoon olive oil
1 tablespoon sour cream

Directions

Finely grate onions with a hand grater. Set aside. Heat 1 tablespoon of oil in a large skillet over medium heat. Add spinach to pan and cook, stirring frequently, until spinach has just wilted, about 2 minutes. Add the garlic clove and cook 2 minutes longer. Remove the pan from the heat, remove the garlic, and set aside. Place spinach in a bowl to cool. When spinach is cool enough to handle, squeeze the spinach by hand to extract as much liquid as possible. Squeeze in batches until it is entirely wrung of liquid. Save 2 tablespoons of the liquid. Place pistachioes, salt, the cooked garlic, coriander seeds, and cayenne in the bowl of a mortar. Pound and grind with the pestle until the mixture is pasty. Mix in 2 tablespoons spinach water. Combine spinach, nut mixture, onions, cilantro, and parsley. Add the vinegar and knead the mixture together with your hand. Oil the inside of a bowl or cup that can fit 1-1/2 cups. Pack mixture in and press firmly. Cover with plastic film and refrigerate overnight. Serve at room temperature. Invert and unmold onto a plate. Cut thin wedges and garnish with a dab of sour cream.

STRAWBERRIES

You may go a long time before you find someone who doesn't like strawberries. They are members of the rose family and thus it is no surprise that they are a part of many romantic and erotic customs. Strawberries and champagne are a signal for a celebration of love and strawberries and chocolate perhaps suggest a more overtly physical manifestation of that love. But you don't have to be in love to enjoy strawberries. Even the most confirmed bachelor in the world could raise a smile eating a bowl of strawberries and cream. They may sometimes bring love but they always bring happiness. Strawberries start to arrive in the late spring and the high season lasts until the high heat of mid-summer.

Strawberry Mousse

Fruit mousses are easy, sexy and particularly good with the freshest just-picked berries.

Yields: 1 quart

Ingredients

    4 cups strawberries, tops removed
    3/4 cup plus 1 tablespoon sugar
    Splash of rum, kirsch or any handy fruit liqueur
    4 egg whites
    1/2 teaspoon lemon juice

Directions

Place strawberries and 3/4 cup sugar in the bowl of a food processor and process until berries form a smooth puree. Add a little water if necessary to smooth out puree. Remove 1 cup of puree, add the lemon juice and set aside.

Place the balance of the puree into a large mixing bowl. Place egg yolks in the bowl of a countertop mixer or in a large mixing bowl. Whip egg whites with a balloon whip or a hand mixer. Add 1 tablespoon sugar and whip until the eggs form stiff peaks as you pull out the beaters.

Using a rubber spatula, gently fold the egg whites into the strawberries. The trick is to scrape around the sides and bottom of bowl in a circular motion to gently mix the two ingredients. Add egg white a little at a time until the ingredients are well blended and an even color. It takes a little time and patience to do this right. Spoon the mousse into decorative dishes or stemware. Top with a spoonful of the reserved strawberries, whipped cream or a quartered fresh berry.

Strawberry Cilantro Smoothie

I love smoothies and the flavoring possibilities are endless. Herbs are not usually included in most smoothie recipes, but the sweetness of really fresh strawberries is perfect with the piquancy of cilantro.

Serves: 4

Ingredients

16 ounces nonfat or low-fat vanilla yogurt
1 cup ice cubes
2 cups fresh strawberries
1 cup skim milk
3 tablespoons honey
1/4 cup chopped cilantro

Directions

Throw this whole mess into a blender and blend until smooth. Be sure to blend long enough to incorporate some air and make light and frothy. Pour into tumblers and garnish with a sprig of cilantro.

Maltese Strawberries

This light dessert can be made at the last minute. The strawberries are improved with a lengthy soak in the orange liqueur, but still will be very good if that's not possible.

Serves: 6

Ingredients

3 medium oranges
1 pint of strawberries
3 tablespoons sugar, divided
1/4 cup Curacao or Triple Sec
1/2 cup heavy cream
6 sprigs of mint

Directions

Place very cold cream in a mixing bowl. Add 1 tablespoon of sugar and beat with a hand mixer, starting at medium speed and slowly increasing speed as cream thickens. Blend until very stiff. Keep cold in refrigerator.

Cut oranges in half. Trim off a little of the end of each orange half so that they can stand upright.

Scoop out the flesh from the orange halves and place in a sieve resting over a medium-size bowl. With your hands, squeeze the oranges to let the juice run through the sieve and into the bowl. Discard the orange flesh.

Rinse the strawberries and cut off the green tops. Cut them in halves or quarters if they are too large. Place them in the bowl with orange juice. Add Curacao or Triple Sec and 2 tablespoons of sugar. Gently stir and toss strawberries with other ingredients. Spoon the strawberry mixture into the orange halves and place the orange half in small glass dishes or on a platter of crushed ice. Top with a generous dollop of whipped cream and a sprig of mint.

Down on the Farm

June 17

It is a beautiful harvest day today in the gardens. The temperatures for the past two weeks have been consistently ten or more degrees below normal and the cloud cover has been above normal. This has created conditions that have left the development of most garden plants far behind schedule. Some things are now more than three weeks behind where they were last year, and that makes it very difficult to put together a normal box of food. The gardens are looking fine and the work is progressing well, but very little is reaching harvest size as soon as we had hoped. Last year there were strawberries in the boxes on the fifth of June, and this year, while there are a huge number of berries on the plants, I have not yet seen even one turning red. We can thank our lucky stars that the weather has treated us better than some of our organic friends down in the southwestern part of the state where flooding and cold weather have left many CSA farmers with nothing to put in their members' boxes.

— David Peterson, Maplewood Gardens

Minted Strawberry and Cucumber Crudités

A crudités display is simply a decorative arrangement of raw fruits and vegetables. This one is very simple. It is dressed with a light citrus vinaigrette; experiment with other dressings if you like.

Serves: 4

Ingredients

1 pound fresh cucumbers
2 pints fresh strawberries
2 tablespoons lemon juice
2 tablespoons orange juice
1/4 cup chopped fresh mint
1/4 cup paprika
1 tablespoon sesame oil
1 tablespoon olive oil

Directions

Peel cucumbers and discard peel. Cut in half lengthwise and scoop out seeds and soft flesh with a spoon. Cut cucumber into 2- or 3-inch sections and further cut each section into 4 wedges. Arrange wedges in an attractive pattern on a large serving platter.

Rinse strawberries and cut off green tops. Slice each in half lengthwise. Arrange in a pile in center of platter or spread out between cucumber wedges. Whisk together lemon juice, orange juice, mint, paprika, sesame oil and olive oil until well blended and frothy.

Strawberries Romanoff

This is my go-to dessert when I don't have a lot of time. It works with sweet super-ripe strawberries and the tart wild strawberries that are often the first to appear each spring.

Serves: 4

Ingredients

1 pint orange sherbet
2 cups fresh strawberries
2 tablespoons champagne or white wine
2 tablespoons powdered sugar
1 cup whipping cream
1 orange
1/4 teaspoon vanilla extract
2 tablespoons sugar

Directions

Cut off the tops of the strawberries and slice strawberries into 1/8-inch slices. Place in a small bowl with the powdered sugar, champagne or white wine. Mix well and set aside for at least one hour. Zest orange with a zester or hand grater and set zest aside.

Cut orange in half and squeeze the juice into a chilled mixing bowl. Add whipping cream. Whip with a hand blender, starting slow and increasing speed as cream thickens. When cream is partially whipped, add sugar and vanilla. Continue to whip on high until cream is very stiff. Keep chilled until ready to use.

Scoop a billiard ball-size scoop of sherbet into a 4 martini glasses or glass dishes. Spoon 1/2 cup of strawberries over each scoop of sherbet. Top with a generous scoop of the whipped cream. Garnish with the orange zest.

. . . .

Strawberry Rhubarb Jam

The play of sweet and tart in this classic combination is perfect slathered on an English muffin but also a terrific tart or pie filling.

Yields: 10 cups

Ingredients

2 pounds strawberries
1 pound rhubarb
1 lemon
2 cups sugar

Directions

Sanitize desired size canning jars in a hot water bath. Trim the tops from the strawberries and cut strawberries into uniform sizes. Place in a large saucepan. Cut rhubarb into 1/2-inch chunks and add to the saucepan. With a vegetable peeler, peel thin ¼-inch strips of lemon from end to end from end to end. Add to the pan with strawberries. Add 1 cup water and then place pan over medium-high heat and bring to a boil. Reduce heat and simmer 15 minutes. Cut lemon in half and squeeze the juice into the pan. Add the sugar, one half cup at a time, making sure the sugar dissolves completely before adding more. Reduce heat to medium and cook for 10 minutes, stirring frequently. Remove from heat. Skim off the foam.

Remove the jars from the water bath and fill with the jam to within 1/4-inch of the top. Cover jars, seal and process for 10 minutes in a boiling water bath as outlined in Chapter 7.

. . . .

Strawberries With Zabaglione

Zabaglione is rich wine-flavored custard that dresses berries for fine evening events.

Serves: 4

Ingredients

1 pint strawberries, tops removed
1 recipe (2 cups) prepared zabaglione
   (see p. 283)
4 sprigs fresh mint

Directions

Cut strawberries into pieces that fit on a fork. Place berries in four small dishes or wine glasses. Top each with 1/2 cup of prepared zabaglione and garnish with a mint leaf.

. . . .

Mixed Berry and Apple Juice

I usually don't talk about nutrition; I find it hard to keep myself awake for those conversations. But this juice will deliver a righteous nutrient jolt — and it tastes pretty good.

Serves: 2

Ingredients

1 quart strawberries
1 pint blueberries
1 pint blackberries
2 apples
1 lime

Directions

Cut apples into quarters. Peel the lime by squaring off the ends and holding firmly on a cutting board. With a paring knife sliding just between the flesh and the peel, cut thin strips of peel from the lime. Rotate and repeat until lime is fully peeled. Feed all fruit through your juicer and extract juice completely. Pour into 2 glasses. Drink and feel an incredible lightness of being.

. . . .

Strawberries in Balsamic Syrup

Serve with ice cream or thin slices of biscotti.

Serves: 6

Ingredients

4 cups strawberries, tops removed and cut in half
1/4 cup good balsamic vinegar
3 tablespoons fine sugar
1 tablespoons lemon juice
1/4 cup packed whole mint leaves

Directions

Combine vinegar, sugar and lemon juice in a small saucepan over medium heat. Cook, stirring frequently, until sugar dissolves, about 5 minutes. Remove from heat and let cool. Place strawberries in a mixing bowl and pour vinegar mixture over strawberries. Toss together with the mint leaves. Cover and refrigerate for at least 1 hour.

. . . .

Strawberry Coulis

If you can find superfine caster sugar, it dissolves more completely, but it's not vital.

Yields: 3 cups

Ingredients

1 pound fresh strawberries,
   cleaned and quartered
1/2 cup sugar
1 lemon

Directions

Puree strawberries in a food processor. Add sugar a little at a time, tasting as you go until you have the desired sweetness. You must do this by taste because the sweetness and tartness of the berries will vary based on variety and ripeness. Add the lemon juice and taste in the same way until you have a tasty balance of sweet and tart. If the berries are immature and very tart you may want to skip the lemon juice. Once you have the flavor just right, process the remainder until very smooth. Strain berries through a sieve if you would like to remove the seeds.

This is a great topping for ice cream or cheese-cake, but I think most of you have guessed that this belongs in a margarita or daiquiri.

. . . .

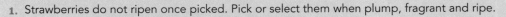

CHEF'S NOTES

1. Strawberries do not ripen once picked. Pick or select them when plump, fragrant and ripe.

2. Use strawberries as quickly as possible. They do not store for long. If they start to mold remove the culprit immediately before it spreads to neighboring berries.

3. Strawberries taste best at room temperature. Remove from the refrigerator for an hour before serving.

4. The best way to freeze strawberries is to toss with a 50/50 mixture of honey and water. Freeze in airtight containers or sturdy freezer bags. They may also be spread in a single layer on a baking sheet, frozen individually and then packed in freezer bags.

5. The tartness of rhubarb and the sweetness of strawberries are a natural flavor combination.

STRING BEANS

There is evidence from Latin America that a wild form of string beans were served on family tables over 10,000 years ago. It's safe to assume that the phrase "sit still and eat your vegetables" has echoed throughout our homes for a very long time.

String beans are so named because of the long, fibrous and barely edible string that runs along the side of the pod. Thankfully, most varieties that are currently grown are stringless, thereby saving us the fussy tedium of removing it. Strings or no strings, snapping fresh beans into a bowl always strikes me as a comforting communal experience — something done with loved ones while chattering about the joys and difficulties our circle of acquaintances present us. Don't get me wrong; it's still a piece of drudgery. I go to great lengths to avoid snapping beans, but it is a heart-warming comfort to know that in some kitchen somewhere, someone is snapping beans.

String beans come in a wide variety of shapes and colors — from the large Romano bean to the thin, tasty French "haricot verts," with varieties available in green, yellow, purple and a sort of marbled purple. They are interchangeable in recipes, but note that the purple varieties will turn an unattractive shade of green when cooked.

If you are a CSA member, you likely will be buried with string beans from midsummer through fall. Don't fret, because of their relatively tough outer pods, they handle the stresses of freezing and canning well.

Following is a sampling of recipes for sautéed green beans. This is a cookbook not a textbook so feel free to come up with a few of your own.

Simple Sautéed String Beans

To sauté is to cook quickly in oil or butter. The sturdy rind of green beans makes them the perfect vehicle for the delicate brown that sautéing can bring to many foods. The technique is fast and easy.

Ingredients

Green beans, as many as desired
Butter or oil

Directions

Preheat a skillet over medium-high heat. Heat enough butter or oil to cover the bottom of the pan with a thin film. Add precooked beans in a single layer into the hot pan and let sizzle for a minute or two to brown one side. Don't walk away; it won't take long. Stir gently until warm and serve immediately.

. . . .

String Beans With Caramelized Onions

Serves: 4

Ingredients

Ingredients
1 pound string beans
1 small red onion
2 tablespoons butter
1 teaspoon sugar

Directions

Sauté green beans per the instructions at the beginning section of the string bean section. Shave red onions very thin and sauté in butter until dark brown. Remove from heat and add a little sugar. Lay atop sautéed beans in a serving dish. Serve warm.

. . . .

String Beans With Cranberries and Walnuts

The dried cranberries are a gorgeous accent to the dark green of the beans.

Serves: 4

Ingredients

2 tablespoons olive or canola oil
1 pound string beans
1/4 cup sweetened dried cranberries
1/4 cup chopped walnuts
Optional: Crushed red pepper

Directions

Sauté green beans per the instructions at the beginning section of the string bean section. Add a handful of sweetened dried cranberries and chopped walnuts to the green beans. If you like a little heat, add some crushed red pepper to taste.

. . . .

String Beans With Fresh Herbs

As an alternative, mix cooked beans with any of the pesto recipes in Herb section.

Serves: 4

Ingredients
1 pound green beans
2 tablespoons fresh herbs
2 tablespoons butter

Directions
Sprinkle on any combination of fresh herbs: parsley, basil, chervil, tarragon, fresh dill, chives, thyme or mint.

. . . .

Classic String Bean Almandine

It's a classic for a reason; it's delicious and simply elegant.

Serves: 4

Ingredients
1/2 cup sliced or slivered almonds
1 pound string beans
2 tablespoons olive oil

Directions
Preheat oven to 350 F. Sauté green beans. Roast sliced or slivered almonds on a shallow pan in the oven for 10 minutes until lightly browned. Toss with sautéed beans or sprinkle on top nuts on top.

. . . .

String Beans Braised in Olive Oil

A truly noble way to prepare many vegetables is to braise them in olive oil. The long cooking does tend to minimize the nutrient content, but the flavor and texture are astounding. Accent with whole cloves of garlic, fresh tomatoes, or bits of citrus and the result is sweet, rich and satisfying.

Serves: 4

Ingredients
1 pound string beans, trim ends
1/4 cup olive oil
1 cup minced onion
Salt and pepper
2 tablespoons sugar
3 garlic cloves
1 lemon (juice and zest)
1 large tomato, diced
1/2 cup tomato juice
1/2 cup water
1 sheet of parchment paper

Directions
Preheat oven to 300 F. Give the garlic cloves a little smash with the flat of a knife. Arrange beans in the bottom of a Dutch oven or baking dish. Add water, tomato juice and olive oil. Spread garlic, diced tomatoes, and minced onion over beans. Sprinkle with sugar, salt, pepper, lemon juice, and lemon zest. Soak parchment in water and spread over the top of the beans. Cover pan tightly with lid or foil.

Cook in slow oven for 2-1/2 to 3 hours until most of the liquid has been absorbed and pan juice is a little syrupy. This can be served immediately, but is best served room temperature after resting a bit. It will keep for several days in the fridge so make a big batch.

. . . .

String Beans With Ginger Red Lentils

This is a simplification of a somewhat complex Indian recipe. Red lentils are available at most supermarkets. They add a hearty substance (not to mention protein) and color to the dish. Coconut adds a touch of sweetness, and the ginger and seasoning lend a little mystery and zest to the humble green bean.

Serves 6 to 8

Ingredients

2 pounds green beans
1/2 cup red lentils
1 tablespoon fresh grated ginger root *
1 teaspoon ground or grated nutmeg
2 tablespoons olive oil
1/4 cup diced onion
1/2 teaspoon black mustard seed
1/2 teaspoon cumin
1/2 teaspoon ground coriander
1/2 cup coconut
1tablespoon lemon juice
Salt and pepper to taste

*Keep your ginger root handy in a resealable bag in the freezer. You can grate the root straight out of the freezer with a small handheld cheese grater. No need to peel the root; very little of the peel will go though the grater.

Directions

In a small saucepan cover the lentils with unsalted water. Cook lentils until they are tender but not mushy. Pour lentils into a fine sieve and run cold water over them to stop the cooking. Toss lentils with ginger and nutmeg. Set aside.

Heat oil over medium-high heat and add black mustard seed. Cook until seed pops like popcorn. Add onion, cumin, and coriander to pan and cook, stirring occasionally, until onions are translucent. Add beans and cooked red lentils. Warm through and season with salt and pepper. Remove from heat and toss with coconut and lemon juice.

Roasted Beans With Bleu Cheese

Roasted string beans can be a savory side dish or the centerpiece on a plate of salad greens.

Serves: 4

Ingredients

1 pound string beans, trim ends
    (preferably thin "haricot verts")
3 tablespoons olive oil, divided
2 cloves garlic, minced
2 teaspoons cider vinegar
Salt and pepper to taste
1/2 cup bleu cheese crumbles

Directions

Preheat oven to 425 F. Toss beans in a large bowl with 1 tablespoon olive oil, salt and pepper. Arrange in a single layer on a cookie sheet and roast in oven roughly 15 minutes, stirring once during cooking.

Combine vinegar, garlic and a pinch of salt and pepper in mixing bowl. Drizzle remaining 2 tablespoons of olive oil into vinegar while whisking. Place roasted beans into bowl, add bleu cheese and toss gently. Serve warm as a side or room temperature as a salad.

Green Bean and Radish Salad

A light and vibrant vegan salad. Tahini can be found in the ethnic aisle of many supermarkets.

Serves: 4

Salad Ingredients

8 ounces whole green beans,
   preferably "haricot verts"
1 carrot, cut into matchsticks the size of the beans
3 ounces radishes, cut into matchsticks
   the width of the beans
1 tablespoon chopped fresh cilantro

Dressing Ingredients

9 ounces tofu
2 tablespoons tahini
2 tablespoons soy sauce or tamari
1 teaspoon sugar
1 lime
1 tablespoon sesame seeds

Directions

Combine beans, carrots and radishes in a pan of boiling water. Blanch for 2 minutes and shock (see p. 287). Drain completely and pat dry. Place tofu in a food processor and process until smooth. While processing add tahini, soy sauce, and sugar. Squeeze in the juice from the lime. If dressing is too thick, add a little water. Arrange vegetables on 4 small or 1 large plate. Spoon dressing over salad and garnish with sesame seeds and chopped cilantro.

Asian-Style String Beans

This sweet and spicy adaptation is the perfect accompaniment to simple grilled chicken or salmon.

Serves: 4

Ingredients

1 pound string beans
2 tablespoons soy sauce
1 teaspoon cornstarch
1 teaspoon brown sugar
1 teaspoon sesame oil
1/2 teaspoon crushed red pepper
1 teaspoon minced garlic
1 teaspoon minced ginger root

Directions

In a medium mixing bowl, combine soy sauce, cornstarch, brown sugar, sesame oil, crushed red pepper minced garlic and minced ginger root and mix until the cornstarch dissolves. Set aside.

Sauté beans as instructed in beginning String Bean section and turn heat down a bit. Add spice mixture and stir constantly and enthusiastically until cornstarch sets and sauce becomes shiny syrup. Remove from heat and garnish with a sprinkling of sesame seeds.

String Beans With Cream

Very simple — great for a rainy day supper.

Serves: 4

Ingredients
- 1 pound string beans
- 1/4 cup whipping cream
- 2 tablespoons chopped fresh herb
- Salt and pepper to taste

Directions
In this technique, it is not necessary brown the beans. Cover pre-cooked beans with heavy cream; salt and pepper to taste. Simmer beans and cream until liquid cooks down by half, becoming a rich sauce the consistency of chocolate syrup. Serve immediately with a sprinkle of your favorite fresh herb.

. . . .

String Beans With Wild Mushrooms

The mushrooms give this a delicious richness.

Serves: 4

Ingredients
- 1 pound string beans
- 3 tablespoons olive oil
- 1 cup chopped shiitake, oyster, portabello, or any other mushroom you find at the farmers market

Directions
Sauté mushrooms until thoroughly cooked to fully develop the flavors. Add to pan while you sauté green beans. Serve warm.

. . . .

String Beans With Cherry Tomatoes

This is a great midsummer side.

Serves: 4

Ingredients
- 1 pound string beans
- 1 cup cherry or grape tomatoes
- 2 cloves garlic, minced
- 2 tablespoons olive oil
- 1 teaspoon balsamic or cider vinegar

Directions
Cook green beans as directed in beginning String Bean section. In a separate pan, lightly brown minced garlic in olive oil. Cut tomatoes in half; add to the pan with the garlic. Cook the tomatoes, stirring often, until they soften and start to fall apart. Add the tomatoes to the beans at the end of their cooking and add a splash of balsamic or cider vinegar. Serve warm as a side dish or room temperature as a salad or relish.

. . . .

String Bean and Garbanzo Salad

A great summer salad with Eastern Mediterranean flair.

Serves: 4

Ingredients

2 cups cooked whole green beans
4 cups coarse chopped tomatoes
1 cup shaved or thinly sliced red onion
1/2 cup feta cheese crumbles
2 tablespoons chopped fresh mint
2 tablespoons red wine vinegar
2 tablespoons extra virgin olive oil
16-ounce can garbanzo beans
Salt and pepper to taste

Directions

Place all ingredients in a big mixing bowl and toss with a couple of big spoons or your hands. Arrange on a platter and serve.

String Beans With Onions and Mint

The mint really wakes up this dish!

Serves: 4

Ingredients

1 pound string beans
2 tablespoons olive oil
1/4 cup diced onions or shallots
2 tablespoons chopped fresh mint

Directions

Sauté diced onions or shallots in the same pan you will use to sauté the beans. Brown green beans with onions. Take off heat and sprinkle with chopped fresh mint.

String Beans With Garlic

Try either garlic variation of this simple recipe.

Serves: 4

Ingredients

1 pound green beans
1 minced garlic clove or 3 or 4 whole cloves
2 tablespoons olive oil

Directions

Add minced garlic to beans while cooking. If using whole cloves, lightly smash with the flat of a knife and brown lightly in pan before adding the beans. The flavor is similar, but the appearance of the dish is bolder and more descriptive. The garlic cloves will sweeten slightly with the cooking.

CHEF'S NOTES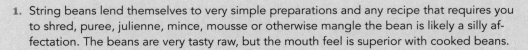

1. String beans lend themselves to very simple preparations and any recipe that requires you to shred, puree, julienne, mince, mousse or otherwise mangle the bean is likely a silly affectation. The beans are very tasty raw, but the mouth feel is superior with cooked beans.

2. Spread blanched beans on a cookie sheet and freeze overnight. They will freeze separately and be much easier to handle, measure and cook when you need them.

3. String beans will form pale brown spots called rust with time. The rust is harmless, but it is a signal that the beans are past their prime. Use or preserve the beans within a week to avoid this.

4. In my opinion, the look of a plate of beans is almost always improved by leaving the beans whole with the pointy ends intact. You may disagree, but if I ever dine at your house I'll voice an objection.

5. For a pretty presentation, tie cooked string beans in a bundle with a blanched and shocked strip of leek or scallion. Wrap the ribbon around a small handful of beans arranged so the ends all point in the same direction. Tie into a bow and slip in a small sliver of red pepper as an accent. Reheat the beans with a quick dip in boiling water or in the microwave. Please don't waste this effort on someone you don't like very much.

6. Pickled green beans are a fantastic cocktail garnish (Bloody Mary's anyone!). Make sure you set aside a few for canning (see Chapter 7).

SUNCHOKES

Until I started researching this book, I had never cooked or eaten a sunchoke (also called a Jerusalem artichoke for reasons that have nothing to do with Jerusalem or artichokes). I had walked by them at farmers markets and super-market displays without a thought. I tried and was introduced to yet another surprise that nature has to offer us.

I suspect this is the case with many of us and one of the things I hope a book like this can do is open some doors to experiences that you may have been reluctant to face. Today a sunchoke, tomorrow a change in careers! It could happen.

Sunchokes are moist and crunchy like a water chestnut. They have a mild nutty flavor that is pleasant and fresh. Sunchokes are tubers that develop on sunflowers late in the season after they flower. They are harvested well into the winter.

Sunchoke Salad

This salad is similar to a basic potato salad with a richer, nuttier flavor. You may boil the chokes, but you will have to be very careful not to overcook them. And be prepared with ice water to shock them immediately. They will get mushy in an instant.

Serves: 6 to 8

Salad Ingredients
    2 pounds sunchokes, peel and
        dice into 1/2-inch pieces
    1/2 cup diced red pepper (sweet or chili)
    2 tablespoons chopped fresh chives or other herb

Dressing Ingredients
    1/4 cup sunflower or canola oil
    1/4 cup rice wine vinegar
    1 tablespoon sugar
    Salt and black pepper to taste

Directions
Fill a large bowl with ice water. Bring about 1 inch of water to a boil in a large soup pot. Place sunchokes in a bamboo or stainless steel steamer basket and set in the boiling pot; cover. Steam until just starting to soften, the time will vary based on the size and density of the sunchokes. Immediately put steamed sunchokes into bowl of ice water to stop the cooking. Cool completely. Drain and shake dry. Transfer sunchokes to a mixing bowl with peppers and chives. Whisk together dressing ingredients in a small bowl. Pour dressing over sunchokes and toss well.

Roast Pork With Sunchokes

Like potatoes, sunchokes absorb pan juices very well and offer a rich side to roast meats.

Serves: 4

Ingredients

2 pounds pork loin or pork butt
1-1/2 pounds sunchokes, peel and
    cut into large pieces
2 tablespoons olive oil
1 tablespoon dried thyme
Salt and pepper
1/2 cup white wine
1 tablespoon butter

Directions

Preheat oven to 400 F. Rub pork liberally with salt, pepper and thyme. Heat olive oil in a Dutch oven over medium heat and brown pork on all sides. Cover pan and roast for 25 minutes. Remove pan from oven and arrange sunchokes around pork. Stir the sunchokes in the pan juices to coat and return to oven. Roast uncovered for 25 minutes until internal temperature of pork reaches 165 F. Remove pork from pan and let rest 10 minutes before slicing. Slice pork and arrange on serving platter. Place sunchokes around sliced pork. Heat Dutch oven over medium-high heat and pour in white wine. Let wine sizzle and boil while scraping off tasty bits on the bottom of pan. Cook for 2 minutes and stir in the butter. Pour pan sauce over pork and sunchokes.

Sunchoke Soup

A simple onion and garlic-flavored soup.

Serves: 4

Ingredients

2 1/2 cups sunchokes, scrub well, remove
    hard knobs and roughly chop
2 tablespoons olive oil
2 large onions, slice in strips
2 garlic cloves, minced
2 cups vegetable stock (see p. 289)
1 orange peel strip (approx. 2 inches long
    with as little white as possible)
Salt and pepper
1/4 cup whipping cream

Directions

Heat oil over medium-high heat in a large saucepan. Add onions and cook, stirring occasionally, until onions are soft and translucent. Add the garlic and cook 5 minutes until garlic is soft. Add the sunchokes and mix until chokes are well coated with oil. Add stock and bring to a boil. Add the orange peel. Cover, reduce heat and simmer for 10 minutes. Remove from heat. Pick out and discard the orange peel. Transfer to a food processor and process until smooth. Return to the pan and reheat. Salt and pepper to taste. Mix in the whipping cream. Serve immediately with crusty bread.

Warm Sunchoke and Quinoa Salad

The chickpeas and sunchokes make this a hearty vegetarian main dish. Quinoa is a rice-like grain native to South America. It is available at many supermarkets or co-ops.

Serves: 6

Ingredients
- 1/2 cup quinoa
- 2 tablespoons sesame oil or olive oil
- 1/2 cup diced onion
- 1-1/4 cups vegetable stock (see p. 289)
- 3/4 cup canned chickpeas (garbanzo beans)
- 1 cup peeled and diced sunchokes
- 1/2 cup diced tomatoes
- 1 tablespoon lemon juice
- 1/2 teaspoon crushed red pepper
- Salt and black pepper

Directions
Place quinoa in a large bowl and cover with cold water. Strain in a colander and repeat this rinse 4 times. Let quinoa drain well. Heat the oil over medium-high heat in a large saucepan and then add the quinoa. Cook, stirring occasionally for 5 minutes (until quinoa starts to pop). Add the onions and continue to cook until the onions are soft and translucent. Add the vegetable stock and bring to a boil. Add the chickpeas, sunchokes and crushed red pepper. Bring back to a boil, reduce heat, cover and simmer for 20 minutes. Remove from heat and let rest for 5 minutes. Add tomatoes, lemon juice and season with salt and pepper. Gently stir all ingredients to combine and fluff. Serve with slices of fresh fruit.

. . . .

Spicy Sunchoke Pickle

Serve this on a relish tray or as a salad garnish.

Makes 4 pints

Ingredients
- 1-1/2 pounds sunchokes
- 3 cups white vinegar
- 1/4 cup honey
- 2 teaspoons turmeric
- 4 dried or fresh cayenne or Thai chilies
- 4 cloves garlic, peel
- 1 tablespoon whole black peppercorns
- 4 bay leaves
- 1 tablespoon mustard seed

Directions
Sterilize canning jars in boiling water. Combine vinegar, honey and turmeric in a saucepan and bring to a boil over medium heat. While mixture is heating, scrub the sunchokes and cut into ¼-inch slices. Remove jars from boiling water and pack them while they are still hot. Each jar should contain 1 pepper, 1 garlic clove, 1/4 tablespoon peppercorns, 1/4 tablespoon mustard seeds, 1 bay leaf and equal amounts of the sliced sunchokes. Fill each jar with the boiling vinegar mixture making sure to cover the sunchokes. Cover jars, seal and process for 10 minutes in a boiling water bath as outlined in Chapter 7.

. . . .

Sunchokes With Roasted Chili Butter

The chilies make this an exciting side for a simple supper of soup and crusty bread.

Serves: 4

Ingredients

- 1 pound sunchokes, peel and dice into 1/2-inch pieces
- 1/2 cup (half recipe) roasted chili butter (see p. 281)
- 1 tablespoon fresh chopped cilantro

Directions

Place sunchokes in a saucepan and cover with water. Place over medium-high heat and bring to a boil. Reduce heat and simmer until sunchokes are tender, about 10 minutes. Drain sunchokes in a colander. Shake dry and return to the saucepan. Add the butter and stir until the butter is melted and the sunchokes are well coated. Transfer to a serving dish and sprinkle with cilantro.

CHEF'S NOTES

1. Sliced sunchokes make a great alternative to fried potatoes for breakfast. Simply slice chokes, with or without peel, and brown in hot oil or butter. Season to taste and sprinkle with chopped parsley.

2. Sunchokes can make you gassy so you may want to avoid them while on a date.

3. Do not overcook sunchokes. They are best raw or lightly cooked to maintain that intriguing crunch and sweetness.

SWEET POTATOES

Quite often I'm asked, "What is the difference between a yam and a sweet potato?" My answer is invariably "I don't know. I don't believe I've ever eaten a yam." A quick Google search tells me that yams are native to Africa and not widely available in North America. So, if you felt compelled to pick up a book on cooking local foods, you should probably look closely at the yams in your market basket because they are either not yams or not local. However, sweet potatoes, in their many varieties, are available all over the world and wherever you get them they will deliver an intoxicating mix of sweetness, color and richness.

The many types have subtle differences in flavor and texture but they are interchangeable with each other in most recipes. The smaller varieties start appearing in late summer and the larger varieties are available until the very end of the season. Just like standard potatoes, sweet potatoes will keep for a very long time if stored in a cool, dry place. You should be able to enjoy them well into the winter.

Baked Sweet Potato

You also could dress these with olive oil and chopped fresh herbs.

Serves: 4

Ingredients

4 medium-size sweet potatoes
1/2 cup butter or flavored butter
    compound (see p. 282)
Salt and pepper to taste

Directions

Preheat oven to 400 F. Poke potatoes with a fork around circumference and place on a shallow baking sheet. Bake the potatoes for 25 minutes. Turn the potatoes over and bake another 25 minutes. Test the potatoes for doneness by squeezing the middle. If they give and feel soft, the potatoes are done. Remove from the oven and cut a slit along the long axis. Squeeze the potato open like a coin purse and top with a nugget of butter. Salt and pepper to taste.

Baked Sweet Potato Salad With Maple and Lime

Make this with leftover baked sweet potatoes. It's a substantial and manly dish, perfect for a barbecue side or a winter salad.

Serves: 6 to 8

Ingredients

2 pounds (approx.) fresh sweet potatoes
4 tablespoons maple syrup
3 tablespoons orange juice
3 tablespoons lime juice
Salt and pepper to taste
1/2 cup olive oil
1/2 cup chopped parsley or cilantro
2 tablespoons grated fresh ginger
1-1/2 cups crushed or chopped tomatoes

Directions

Preheat oven to 350 F. Prick sweet potatoes with a fork in several places. Bake in oven for 30 to 45 minutes until potatoes are soft when you squeeze them. Let them cool completely. Peel and cut potatoes into 1/2-inch cubes. Set aside.

In a large mixing bowl, combine maple syrup, orange and lime juice, salt and pepper to taste, olive oil, fresh herbs and fresh ginger. Whisk vigorously until well blended and frothy. Add the potatoes to the bowl and toss gently with the dressing.

Let marinate in refrigerator for at least an hour. Toss tomatoes with potatoes and serve on a bed of leaf lettuce or spinach.

. . . .

Sweet Potato and Dried Chili Relish

A satisfying dish on its own, it also makes a wonderful buffet salad or an accompaniment to grilled fish or chicken.

Serves: 4 as a side

Ingredients

1-1/2 pound sweet potatoes, peel
2 tablespoons orange juice
1 tablespoon crushed dried chilies
4 green onions
1 teaspoon lime juice
Salt to taste

Directions

Bring a pot of water to a boil over medium-high heat. Dice the sweet potatoes into 1/4-inch pieces. Add potatoes to the boiling water and cook for 8 to10 minutes, until just soft. Drain in a colander and rinse with cold water. Shake off as much water as possible. Set aside.

Slice the green onion very thin and add to a mixing bowl. Add the orange juice, chilies and lime juice. Add the sweet potatoes and gently toss mixture; salt to taste. Serve chilled.

. . . .

Sweet Potato Pancakes

Great for breakfast or as a side to fried foods.

Serves: 4

Ingredients

2 eggs
1 tablespoon chopped fresh parsley
1 pound sweet potatoes, peel
1/2 pound red potatoes, peel
1/4 cup minced onions
4 tablespoons flour
Vegetable oil for frying
Salt and pepper

Directions

Grate sweet potatoes and red potatoes with a hand grater or the grating attachment of a food processor. Transfer grated potatoes to a large double-layer of cheesecloth or a clean kitchen towel. Twist and wring the potatoes to remove as much liquid as possible. You may have to do it in batches.

Whisk together eggs and parsley in a large mixing bowl. Add the potatoes and onions to the bowl and salt and pepper to taste. Add flour and mix well. Batter should be the consistency of loose cookie dough. Add a little more flour if necessary. Place 1/8-inch layer of oil in skillet or griddle and heat over medium heat. Place billiard ball-size scoops of batter in hot pan and flatten. Fry pancakes for 3 to 5 minutes until golden brown on one side. Flip pancakes and brown the other side. Place pancakes on a cookie sheet in an oven set on low to keep warm. Fry the pancakes in batches, adding oil as needed until all the batter is used. Serve for breakfast with maple syrup or honey or for dinner with sour cream or cranberry relish.

· · · · · · · · · · · · · · · · ·

Spiced Sweet Potato and Pear Juice

A very rich and flavorful juice. Tahini can be found in the ethnic section of most well-appointed markets.

Serves: 2

Ingredients

2 medium sweet potatoes
1 beet, remove greens
1 carrot
2 pears
2 scallions
3 tablespoons roughly chopped ginger
2 tablespoons Tahini (sesame paste)
Pinch of ground cloves
Pinch of grated nutmeg

Directions

Cut sweet potatoes, beet, carrot, pears and scallions into pieces that can fit into your juicer. Feed through the juicer and extract juice completely. Transfer juice to a blender and add Tahini, cloves and nutmeg. Blend ingredients well. Serve in 2 glasses.

· · · · · · · · · · · · · · · · ·

Sweet Potato Pie With Cognac Cream

If you call someone "my little sweet potato pie" you'll likely raise a smile. There's a reason for that...

Yields: 9-inch pie and ½ cup cream

Pie Ingredients

- 1 recipe basic pie dough (see p. 285)
- 2 cups uncooked rice or dried beans
- 4 large sweet potatoes (1-1/2 pounds)
- 2 eggs
- 1/3 cup packed light brown sugar
- 1/4 teaspoon salt
- 1/4 teaspoon grated nutmeg
- 1/2 cup whipping cream
- 3 tablespoons cognac
- 1/2 teaspoon vanilla extract

Cognac Cream Ingredients

- 1/2 cup chilled whipping cream
- 1 tablespoon packed light brown sugar
- Pinch of ground cinnamon
- 1 teaspoon cognac
- 1/4 teaspoon vanilla extract

Pie Directions

Preheat oven to 375 F. Roll out the dough and fit into a 9-inch pie tin. Trim edge, leaving a ½-inch overhang. Fold overhang over toward the inside of pie tin and crimp with your fingers or a fork. Chill dough for 30 minutes. Cover crust completely with foil and fill bottom of pie with uncooked rice or dried beans. Bake 15 minutes. Remove from oven and carefully lift out foil and rice or beans. Return to oven and bake a further 10 minutes. Crust should be golden all over. Cool crust on a rack. Increase oven to 400 F.

Prick the potatoes with a fork all over. Bake on a cookie sheet until tender, about 1 hour. Potatoes should be quite soft when you squeeze the sides. Reduce oven to 350 F. Remove from the oven and allow to cool enough to handle. Cut potatoes in half and scoop out the flesh into the bowl of a food processor. Add eggs, sugar, salt and nutmeg and process until smooth. Add whipping cream, cognac and bourbon and pulse the processor a few times to just combine the ingredients.

Pour filling into pie crust. Bake on the middle rack of the oven until most of the pie is set but the center still wiggles a little when shaken, about 45 minutes. If crust edge starts to brown too much, wrap the edge in a piece of foil. Remove from oven and cool on a rack for 1 hour. Serve topped with cognac cream (below).

Cream Directions

Place a metal mixing bowl in the freezer for 30 minutes to facilitate whipping of the cream. Place all ingredients in chilled bowl and whip with an electric mixer until cream forms peaks. Top slices of pie with a gob of cream and serve immediately.

Sweet Potato Chips With Citrus

If you're gonna eat potato chips, make them yourself. After a batch of these, you will never in your life open another bag.

Yields: A big bowl of chips

Ingredients

Zest from 2 limes and 1 lemon
2 teaspoons coarse salt, kosher or sea
1-1/2 pounds sweet potatoes (2 large or 3 small)
Oil for frying

Directions

Preheat deep fryer to 375 F. Zest limes and lemon into a small bowl and mix with the salt. Peel the sweet potatoes and compost the peels. Shave as many chips as possible from each potato with a vegetable peeler. Drop chips into fryer in small batches and fry until chips are lightly browned and most of the bubbling stops. Remove from oil and drain on several sheets of paper towel. Continue to fry chips in small batches allowing oil temperature to recover between batches. Sprinkle a little of the salt mixed with lemon and lime zest on each batch. Toss all together when chips are all fried. Turn on the big game and enjoy.

Spicy Sweet Potato Wedges

Sweet potato wedges will be done in less than an hour and can cook while you prepare the rest of dinner, or pay your bills, or wash the car, or take the dog for a walk, etc.

Serves: 4 to 6

Ingredients

1 teaspoon coriander seeds
1/2 teaspoon fennel seeds
Seeds from 1 cardamom pod or 1/2
    teaspoon ground cardamom
1/2 teaspoon red pepper flakes
4 medium sweet potatoes
3 tablespoons vegetable oil
Salt to taste

Directions

Preheat oven to 425 F. Place coriander, fennel, cardamom and red pepper flakes in a mortar and pestle and crush until mix becomes a coarse powder. Mix in salt to taste. Cut potatoes into thick wedges and place in a large mixing bowl. Add spice blend and vegetable oil to potatoes and toss until potatoes are well coated. Arrange in a single layer on a cookie sheet and bake for 20 minutes. Turn wedges and bake an additional 15 to 25 minutes until potatoes are tender and browned.

CHEF'S NOTES

1. Sweet potatoes are best frozen well cooked and mashed. To retain the bright color, mix in 1 teaspoon lemon juice per cup of mashed sweet potato. Freeze in sturdy containers or freezer bags.

2. Do not store potatoes in the refrigerator. The cool temperatures will cause the potato to rot prematurely. A cool dark place is all that's required. They will keep for several months.

3. In ages past, sweet potatoes were thought to be an aphrodisiac — eat them with someone you like!

Down on the Farm

September 25

I am happy to announce that the sweet potatoes were enough of a success so that we will have some for our CSA boxes this week. However, they are almost impossible to dig without damage. Unlike regular potatoes, they seem to position themselves at random underground. Regular potatoes are in hills directly below the plants, but sweet potatoes might be anywhere within a couple of feet of the plant and very deep in the soil. We have tried really hard not to spear them with the fork while digging, but without complete success. We need to dig the rest before next week because we will be planting garlic in the garden where they were grown. We hope to see twice as many next week.

— David Peterson, Maplewood Gardens

TOMATOES

tomatoes

Tomatoes are the poster children for what's wrong with the way we produce and consume food in the West. I'm hardly the first to note how horrible supermarket tomatoes are most of the year. The problem isn't the grower; the problem is the expectation. Tomatoes were once a treat of the late and fulsome summer. A tomato salad was a joyous experience pinned to a place and time. We canned tomatoes to keep that memory alive until the next high summer explosion. When we started to demand a wedge of fresh tomato on every salad we ate every day of the year (or even to demand the salad), we were demanding what nature wasn't offering. The result of this tomato hubris is the nasty pink atrocities that adorn our supermarket shelves. If you are going to make one statement in support of a local food culture, make this one — refuse to eat tomatoes out of season. It should be an easy choice to make because they taste so crappy anyway.

The beauty of making this choice is that when the tomatoes do become available in your backyard or locally from your CSA or farmers market, they usually are the sweetest, most flavorful treats of the season. If you freeze and can them, an echo of that sweetness remains to offer a happy reunion later in the year.

Tomatoes from the farmers market or your CSA usually are adorned with the adjective "heirloom." The term has a specific meaning, having to do with older varieties that have largely vanished from consciousness. However, what it really communicates is that this tomato was grown by hand and picked by hand. You can be pretty sure that a tomato described as heirloom will be ripe and flavorful.

Grilled Shrimp With Tomato Coulis

Enjoy this for a midsummer barbecue. Scallops or any mild fish will also work well.

Serves: 6-8

Ingredients

1-1/2 pounds large shrimp, peel and devein
1-1/4 cups olive oil, divided
1 tablespoon sesame oil
2 cloves garlic, minced
1 tablespoon soy sauce
2 tablespoons white wine
2 tablespoons lime juice
2 tablespoons fresh chives
1 cup prepared tomato coulis,
    warm (recipe at right)
1/4 cup finely chopped basil

Directions

Preheat grill to medium heat. Mix 1/4 cup olive oil and chopped basil and keep at room temperature. Prepare marinade with 1 cup olive oil, sesame oil, garlic, soy, wine, lime juice and fresh chives in a large mixing bowl. Add the shrimp and marinate for 2 hours.

Lay the shrimp on the grill grate and sprinkle with salt and pepper. Baste with a little of the marinade being careful not to drip too much in the fire causing flare-ups. Cook for 2 to 3 minutes and turn. Baste again and cook a further 1 to 2 minutes. Be careful not to overcook. Shrimp should still be a little translucent on the inside. Remove from heat and keep warm.

Set out 4 dinner plates. Cover bottom of plates with warm tomato coulis. Carefully pile equal amounts of shrimp in the center of each plate. Sprinkle basil oil over dish causing attractive little pools of oil in the coulis. Serve with grilled vegetables and crusty bread

Caprese Salad

South of Rome is the region of Caprese, famous for its basil and tomatoes. When you bring home a bunch of beautiful sun-soaked tomatoes, follow the lead of the Capresans and eat them simply. When nature has delivered you a perfect tomato, just get out of its way.

Serves: 4

Ingredients

4 large or 6 medium tomatoes
1 cup fresh mozzarella slices
1 loose cup whole fresh basil leaves
1/4 cup extra virgin olive oil
Salt
Fresh ground black pepper
Optional: 1/4 cup thinly sliced red onion

Directions

Slice tomatoes about 1/4-inch thick. Pick leaves of basil and leave them whole. Slice pieces of fresh (buffalo) mozzarella. Arrange tomatoes, basil leaves, and mozzarella in an alternating shingle-style on a salad plate or buffet platter. Top the display with shaved red onion. Sprinkle with a very good olive oil and season with kosher salt and fresh ground pepper. This makes a great starter for a more substantial meal or a light, colorful, buffet item.

Caprese Dip

Serve this on hunks of crusty French or Italian bread.

Serves: 4

Ingredients
1 pound diced fresh tomatoes
1/2 cup fresh sliced (1/8-inch ribbons) basil
1 clove garlic
Extra virgin olive oil
Kosher salt
Fresh ground pepper
1/2 cup diced fresh mozzarella

Directions
This is a classic bruschetta and, as such, is really enhanced with the very freshest of ingredients. The best olive oil, just-picked vine-ripened tomatoes, and basil picked off of the branch, make this preparation a religious experience. The tomatoes you use should be of a smaller variety with less pulp and seeds. Slice tomatoes in half and scoop out soft insides (reserve for some other use). Dice remainder with a sharp knife. Smash clove of garlic with flat of knife and mince roughly. Dice fresh mozzarella the same size as tomato. Roll basil into a bundle and slice into thin ribbons. Mix in a bowl and simply dress with olive oil, salt and pepper to taste.

· · · · · · · · · · · · · · · · · ·

Tomato Coulis

This coulis, mixed with good vinegar and some chopped fresh basil, is a superior salad dressing. It is a very light and healthy sauce, yet the flavor is bold enough to carry a standalone dish. Sprinkle over a little olive oil and some finely chopped herbs for a very sexy garnish.

Yields: 1 quart

Ingredients
2 pounds fresh ultra-ripe tomatoes, peel, remove seeds and cut in half
Salt
Lemon
1 teaspoon sugar

Directions
Sprinkle salt on cut sides of tomatoes and turn over in a sieve. The salt will pull some of the moisture out of the tomatoes to allow for a thicker sauce. Set aside for 30 minutes.

Place tomatoes in the bowl of a food processor and add sugar and the juice of one lemon. Process until very smooth. If coulis is too thin, simmer in saucepan until it cooks down to desired thickness and then season with salt and pepper. Strain sauce and serve or store.

· · · · · · · · · · · · · · · · · ·

Gazpacho

Gazpacho has come to mean a bowl of chilled tomato juice with raw vegetables floating in it. The word itself means "soaked bread" in Arabic. This recipe recalls that earlier authentic meaning.

Serves: 4

Ingredients

4 garlic cloves, mince
2 fresh tomatoes
1 teaspoon salt
1/2 teaspoon cayenne pepper
4 tablespoons extra virgin olive oil
1 onion, shaved as thin as possible
1 green pepper, diced
1 cucumber, peel, remove seeds and dice
1/2 cup diced croutons (see p. 283)
3 cups cold water

Directions

Core and dice (peel if you like) the tomato. Place in a mixing bowl with minced garlic, salt and cayenne. Crush mixture thoroughly with the back of a spoon. Stir tomato mixture with wooden spoon while slowly drizzling in olive oil. Add onions, pepper, cucumber and croutons. Add cold water and mix thoroughly. Serve well-chilled.

· · · · · · · · · · · · · · · ·

Tomato Cheddar Tart

This dish does best with smaller tomatoes that have fewer seeds and moisture, but it can be successful with any tomato provided you cut them very thin. It's a great cocktail party item but also makes a terrific everyday snack.

Yields: 12 pieces

Ingredients

1 sheet puff pastry*
1 tablespoon prepared stone ground mustard
1 cup shredded cheddar cheese
1 shallot, mince
1 pound fresh tomatoes
1 teaspoon fresh thyme or chives
Salt and pepper

* Puff pastry is found in the frozen section of most supermarkets. It is available in sheets or squares.

Directions

Preheat oven to 375 F. Remove the puff pastry from freezer and thaw for 30-plus minutes. Unfold and flatten slightly with a rolling pin. The sheet should measure roughly 10 by 11 inches. Spray a baking sheet with nonstick spray and carefully transfer pastry to sheet. Spread sheet evenly with mustard and sprinkle on shallots.

Cut core out of tomatoes and slice as thin as possible. Arrange in a single layer covering the pastry. You may have to overlap them slightly. Leave a 1/2-inch space around the outside of the pastry. Sprinkle the thyme, salt and pepper over all. Pinch the outer edges all around to form a tart shell. Bake in oven for 30 minutes until pastry turns golden brown. Serve warm cut in squares.

· · · · · · · · · · · · · · · ·

Wilted Tomato Sauce

You may never have pasta any other way once you try this smoky, savory sauce.

Yields: 4 cups

Ingredients
1 tablespoon olive oil
1 recipe oven-wilted tomatoes (see recipe below)
1 onion, dice
1 tablespoon balsamic vinegar
3 cloves garlic, mince
Salt and pepper

Directions
Heat olive oil in a saucepan over medium heat. Add onions and garlic. Cook, stirring regularly, until onions and garlic are well browned, about 12 to 15 minutes. Add balsamic vinegar, salt, and pepper. Cook 5 minutes more. Mixture should be thick and syrupy. Add tomatoes and toss together until well combined. Remove from heat and place in a food processor. Process very gently to just chop the sauce. Serve or store.

Fresh Tomato and Feta Salad

A Greek-inspired version of the beautifully simple combination of tomato and fresh cheese.

Serves: 4

Ingredients
1 pound fresh tomatoes
1/4 cup sliced 1/8-inch strips onions
1/4 cup sliced 1/8-inch strips green peppers
1/2 cup feta cheese crumbles
1/4 cup prepared vinaigrette (see p. 278)
2 tablespoons chopped fresh basil

Directions
Cut tomatoes into fork-size pieces and arrange on a plate. Top with julienne peppers and onions. Spread feta cheese over vegetables. Dress with vinaigrette. Sprinkle on chopped fresh basil and serve.

Oven-Wilted Tomatoes

The long slow roasting of the tomatoes simultaneously browns and dries them. This concentrates the sugars and gives you a beautifully sweet and chewy tomato. Immersed in olive oil, they will keep for several weeks in the refrigerator.

Yields: 16 pieces

Ingredients
8 fresh ripe tomatoes, core and cut in half
1/4 cup olive oil
Salt and pepper

Directions
Preheat oven to 350 F. Lay tomatoes, cut-side up, on a shallow baking sheet. Drizzle each tomato with olive oil and season with salt and pepper. Roast in oven for 2 to 2-1/2 hours until tomatoes are shriveled but still a little moist in the center. Serve warm or let cool, place in a resealable container and cover with a good olive oil.

Wilted Tomato Brushetta

Serve this nice treat at a cocktail party.

Yields: 16 appetizers

Ingredients

16 pieces of oven-wilted tomatoes
(see recipe p. 245)
16 sliced croutons (see p. 283)
1/4 cup chopped fresh basil

Directions

Arrange croutons on a serving platter. Place one piece of tomato on each crouton. Sprinkle with chopped basil.

· · · · · · · · · · · · · · · ·

Simple Wilted Tomato Pasta

A very simple but elegant dish.

Serves: 4

Ingredients

1 pound string pasta, fettuccini,
linguini or angel hair
1/4 cup olive oil
3 cloves garlic, mince
16 pieces oven-wilted tomatoes (see Oven-
Wilted Tomatoes recipe p. 245)
1/4 cup shredded Parmesan
2 tablespoons fresh chopped parsley

Directions

Bring 1 gallon of salted water to a boil in a large saucepan. Add pasta and cook, stirring occasionally, until pasta is tender but not mushy. Drain pasta in a colander and rinse with cold water. Set aside.

Heat olive oil in a large skillet over medium heat. Add garlic and cook for 1 minute until garlic just browns. Add pasta and stir to completely coat the pasta. Add 2 tablespoons of water to the pan. Add the tomatoes. Cover and let cook for 5 minutes. Place pasta in a serving bowl and top with cheese and parsley. Serve immediately.

· · · · · · · · · · · · · · · ·

Criolla

A South American tomato salsa with a little spice that can be used with grilled fish or vegetables.

Yields: 2 cups

Ingredients

4 tomatoes, peel, remove seeds
and dice (see p. 288)
1 onion, diced
1 Serrano or Anaheim chili, mince with seeds
1 clove garlic, mince
1 tablespoon chopped fresh parsley
3 tablespoons olive oil
2 tablespoons red wine vinegar
Salt

Directions

Stir all ingredients together in a mixing bowl and allow the flavors to marry for 30 minutes.

· · · · · · · · · · · · · · · ·

Down on the Farm

July 10

One of the highlights of our week in the gardens was the ceremonial eating yesterday of the first tomato of the season. The tomato itself was some kind of a freakish giant of an orange, cherry tomato, measuring over an inch and a half in diameter. It was spotted Sunday all alone at the very bottom of one of our sweet orange cherry plants. I picked it and toted it home as the sun disappeared behind the trees at the end of the too hot weekend. I set it on the cutting board and admired it throughout the evening. Shortly after our gardening week began, I cut it into four quarters and carried it out to the garden where I presented it to the gathered workers. It was a solemn moment as we first presented it to the heavens and then popped it into our mouths. One of the assembled tomato eaters was heard to say that it was like being in church, some thought it even better. It was the earliest date of the eating of the first tomato in the history of Maplewood Gardens.

— David Peterson, Maplewood Gardens

Spiced Tomato Gravy

An Indian-influenced tomato sauce that is outstanding with fried food.

Yields: 2-½ cups

Ingredients

2 pounds ripe red tomatoes
3 tablespoons chopped cashews or pecans
1/4 teaspoon fennel seeds
1 teaspoon cumin seeds
2 red or green hot chilies, remove
    seeds and mince
1 tablespoon fresh grated ginger root
1/2 tablespoon brown sugar
1/2 teaspoon turmeric
1 tablespoon tomato paste
1/4 cup olive oil
3 tablespoons fresh chopped parsley
1/2 cup vegetable stock (see p. 289)
Salt

Directions

Peel, seed and dice the tomatoes (see p. 288). While seeding and dicing tomatoes, save as much of the juice from the tomatoes as possible and set aside. Place the nuts, fennel seeds and cumin seeds in a food processor and process until coarsely chopped. Add the reserved tomato juice, chilies, ginger, brown sugar, turmeric and vegetable stock and process until smooth. Heat olive oil in a saucepan over medium heat. When oil is hot, carefully slide contents of food processor into oil and cook for 5 to 10 minutes until oil and seasoning separate. Stir in the diced tomatoes and half of the parsley. Reduce heat and simmer, covered, for 30 minutes. Salt to taste and add the remaining parsley. Stir to blend.

Fiery Tomato Juice

This juice is not for "wusses!" — A bold start to the day.

Serves: 2

Ingredients

- 6 medium-size tomatoes, core and quarter
- 1 red bell pepper, core, remove seeds and cut into large chunks
- 1/4 red onion
- 2 scallions
- 2 cloves garlic
- 2 small or 1 large jalapeno chili, remove stem and seeds
- 1/4 cup cilantro
- Dash of Tabasco
- Salt

Directions

Process all vegetables through a juicer as directed in manual. Add a shake or two of Tabasco and salt to taste.

. . . .

Tomato and Basil Juice

High summer in a glass!

Serves: 2

Ingredients

- 6 medium-size tomatoes, cored and quartered
- 1 cup packed basil leaves
- 1 lime, peeled
- 2 cloves garlic
- 1/4 cup fresh chives
- Salt and pepper to taste

Directions

Feed all ingredients through your juicer to extract juice completely. Season to taste with salt and pepper.

. . . .

Heirloom Tomatoes With Vinaigrette

Sometimes you find tomatoes at the farmers market or in your CSA share that are so perfect, complex preparation will diminish them. When such a gift crosses your path, simply cut, dress and eat them.

Serves: 6

Ingredients

- 1-1/2 pounds heirloom tomatoes, room temperature and cut into fork-size wedges
- 1/2 cup of lemon vinaigrette (see p. 279)
- Salt

Directions

Place cut tomatoes in a serving bowl and drizzle with the vinaigrette. Sprinkle with a little salt and eat.

. . . .

tomatoes

Basic Tomato Sauce

This is the starting point for a hundred other sauces. Any recipe that calls for spaghetti or marinara sauce will be well-served with this sauce. Use immediately, refrigerate, freeze or can. Make huge pots of this and enjoy it all winter.

Yields: 6 cups

Ingredients

1 tablespoon olive oil
2 onions, finely diced
4 cloves garlic, minced
3 pounds tomatoes, roughly chop
1/4 cup red wine
1/4 cup tomato paste
1 teaspoon dried oregano
1 teaspoon sugar
1/4 teaspoon crushed red pepper
Salt and pepper

Directions

Heat olive oil in a large soup kettle over medium heat. Add the onions and garlic. Cook, stirring regularly, until onions are lightly browned and soft, about 8 minutes. Add all other ingredients, increase heat to medium-high and bring to a boil. Reduce heat to low and simmer uncovered, stirring occasionally for 30 minutes. Sauce is ready at this point but you can simmer longer; it will increase the sweetness of the sauce. Stir in a little water to thin if it gets too thick. Serve or store.

· · · · · · · · · · · · · · · ·

Roast Tomato Vinaigrette

This versatile sauce can be a salad dressing, pasta sauce or a light sauce for fish or seafood.

Yields: 1 quart

Ingredients

4 tomatoes, any variety larger than cherry tomatoes and smaller than slicers
1 cup extra virgin olive oil
1/4 cup white vinegar, cider or sherry vinegar
2 tablespoons balsamic vinegar
2 teaspoons kosher salt
2 teaspoons fresh ground pepper
1 tablespoon minced garlic
1 tablespoon sugar

Directions

Preheat oven to 450 F. Cut tomatoes in half and place in a roasting pan. Season with salt and pepper and coat with olive oil. Heat in the oven until lightly charred. Puree roasted tomatoes in a food processor making sure to include all the juices in the roasting pan. While processor is mixing, add white vinegar, balsamic vinegar, and slowly add 2 tablespoons olive oil. Season to taste with salt, black pepper, minced garlic, and sugar.

· · · · · · · · · · · · · · · ·

CHEF'S NOTES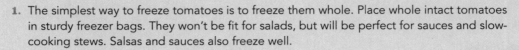

1. The simplest way to freeze tomatoes is to freeze them whole. Place whole intact tomatoes in sturdy freezer bags. They won't be fit for salads, but will be perfect for sauces and slow-cooking stews. Salsas and sauces also freeze well.

2. Buy local tomatoes when they are ripe. They should feel a little soft to the touch. If you must ripen them, place them in a paper bag and set aside at room temperature for a few days. Never refrigerate tomatoes unless you have already cut into them. They will stop ripening and any bruising will make them deteriorate very quickly.

3. Dried tomatoes are like tomato candy. They can be expensive to purchase but are easy to make with any commercial food dehydrator. Because they have high moisture content, they will take quite awhile to dry but will keep for months once dried. The concentrated sweetness is perfect in wintertime pasta dishes.

4. The surest sign of a perfectly ripe tomato is the smell. Sniff the stem end and if you smell tomato, eat it.

5. Tomatoes pair beautifully with nearly any herb. Experiment with combinations.

6. The longer you cook tomatoes in a sauce, the sweeter they become. A long slow-simmered sauce will have a full-bodied naturally developed sweetness. If you do not have time, you can add sugar to a sauce and get acceptable results.

TURNIPS AND RUTABAGAS

Due to my youthful obsession with Russian novels my esteem for the noble turnip has been damaged. When I think of turnips it always conjures images of a starving peasant family in a small thatched cottage. They are careworn and the dialogue goes something like this.

PEASANT HUSBAND: *"Goodwife, pray, what's for dinner?"*

PEASANT WIFE: *"Husband, I fear we have only turnips."*

PEASANT HUSBAND: *"Turnips again! Oh woe is us — we have only turnips to eat. We are sorrowful and grim."*

At least they had turnips. When all of your other glamorous garden goodies are but a memory, you still will have turnips. If stored properly, turnips will be wholesome well into the winter and, if prepared with some flair and imagination, may not fill you with sorrow.

Early in the season you will find wonderful mild baby turnips, usually with the greens attached. The greens are delicious and a bonus. Baby turnips are cute and lend themselves to very elegant presentations. They are an early season treat and generally get gobbled up pretty quickly. Just scrub under running water and simply prepare.

Later in the season, you will see the slightly larger, slightly sharper turnips (the ones that caused peasant husband and his good wife so much dread). These require some dressing up before they are fit for the table. They need to be peeled with a sharp knife and tortured into edibility.

In January, before you give in to the urge to grab a tomato trucked all the way from Arizona, remember that you have fresh local turnips in storage and don't be sad!

The rutabaga is larger and milder than the turnip. It also has a pleasing golden hue that the turnip lacks. Outside of that, the rutabaga cooks and eats exactly like a turnip. Any recipe that uses one can use the other.

Mushroom Stuffed Turnips

This recipe makes a noble treat out of the humble turnip.

Serves: 8

Ingredients

8 tennis ball-size turnips
1 cup prepared mushroom
    duxelle/stuffing (p. 162)
1/4 cup vegetable stock
2 tablespoons bread crumbs
2 tablespoons grated Parmesan cheese
2 tablespoons melted butter
Salt and pepper to taste

Directions

Preheat oven to 400 F. Peel turnips with a paring knife or a sturdy vegetable peeler. Cut a flat spot on one side and cut a 12-inch slice directly opposite. The turnip should be able to set on a flat surface without rolling with the larger flat surface facing up. Hollow out the turnip with a melon-baller or a grapefruit spoon. Heat a large pot of salted water to a boil over high heat. Place turnips in boiling water, allow water to return to a boil and cook for 8 to10 minutes. Turnips should be tender but not falling apart. Drain and quickly plunge turnips in ice water to stop cooking.

Fill each turnip with a generous spoonful of mushroom duxelle. Arrange in an ovenproof dish and pour in vegetable stock. Top each turnip with bread crumbs and grated Parmesan cheese. Drizzle butter over top and place in oven. Bake for 20 to 30 minutes until tops are browned.

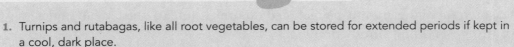

CHEF'S NOTES

1. Turnips and rutabagas, like all root vegetables, can be stored for extended periods if kept in a cool, dark place.

2. To freeze turnips and rutabagas, remove the skin and cut into usable pieces. Blanch and shock (see p. 287). Freeze in containers or freezer bags.

3. Turnips can be well cooked and pureed for use as a low-fat thickener in sauces and soups. Rutabagas are less suited for this due to the color.

4. Use turnips and rutabagas in place of or, in addition to, potatoes in pot roasts and stews. They carry the flavor of roast meats very well.

5. Toss grated raw turnip or rutabaga with any vinaigrette (see p. 278) for a quick and tasty slaw.

6. The greens of young spring turnips are delicious. Braise as you would chard or spinach.

Neeps

Neeps is one of the traditional accompaniments to haggis along with tatties (mashed potatoes). The notion of a sheep's stomach stuffed with guts makes most Americans a little queasy, but generations of Scotsmen grew bold and ruddy on the stuff and it can't be any more alarming than what is inside your average chicken nugget. Nonetheless, the overdelicate can enjoy neeps with roast chicken or beef and few would object to the Scottish custom of washing it down with a couple fingers of Scotch.

Serves: 4

Ingredients

1-1/2 pounds rutabaga, peel and
    cut into 3/4-inch chunks
Pinch of grated nutmeg
2 tablespoons butter
Salt and pepper

Directions

Place rutabagas in a large pot, cover completely with water and add salt to taste. Bring to a boil over high heat. Reduce heat and simmer for 20 to 30 minutes until rutabagas are fairly soft. Drain off the water in a colander. Return to the pot and add butter, nutmeg, salt and a generous amount of black pepper. Mash thoroughly with a hand masher and serve immediately. If you like your mash ultra smooth and creamy, you may process in a food processor or run through a food mill, though, I doubt old MacDougall needed such contrivances.

· · · · · · · · · · · · · · · ·

Rustic Turnip and Thyme Stew

Hearty and substantial, this stew will warm you up on a drizzly fall day.

Serves: 4

Ingredients

6 smallish leeks or 4 large leeks, white part only
3 Yukon gold potatoes
6 baby turnips
2 tablespoons butter
5 1/2 cups vegetable stock, divided (see p. 289)
3 or 4 sprigs of thyme
Salt and pepper to taste
2 tablespoons heavy cream
2 tablespoons chopped thyme

Directions

Slice leeks into rings crosswise, rinse and place in soup kettle. Cut turnips and potatoes into manageable pieces and roughly chop. Add to the kettle along with the butter, 1/2 cup vegetable stock and the thyme. Place kettle over medium-high heat and bring to a boil; stir well to combine butter and herbs. Add remaining stock, salt and pepper. Return stew to a boil. Reduce heat and simmer for 30 minutes. Taste and add salt and pepper if necessary. Stir in cream and remove thyme sprigs. Serve in shallow bowls with a sprinkling of fresh thyme.

· · · · · · · · · · · · · · · ·

Rutabaga and Pear Bake

This easily could be made with apples.

Serves: 4

Ingredients
3 cups sliced rutabaga
3 pears, core and slice
1/2 cup brown sugar
3 tablespoons butter
Salt and pepper

Directions
Preheat oven to 350 F. Bring a pot of lightly salted water to a boil over medium-high heat. Add the rutabagas and cook until barely tender, 10 to 15 minutes. Drain rutabagas in a colander. Combine with pears. Place half of mixture into a shallow baking dish. Sprinkle with 1/4 cup of brown sugar and dot with 1-1/2 tablespoons of butter. Repeat with the other half of ingredients. Cover and bake for 30 minutes. Serve warm or room temperature.

Turnip and Parsnip Juice

Sounds like something Bugs Bunny might order!

Serves: 2

Ingredients
1 medium-size turnip
1/2 pound cabbage (approx. 1/4 head)
1 parsnip
1 carrot
3 scallions
1/4 cup fresh parsley
3 garlic cloves

Directions
Cut core from cabbage and roughly chop. Trim green from parsnip and carrot and cut into pieces that fit into juicer. Cut turnip into quarters and roughly chop scallions. Feed all vegetables through a juicer along with parsley and garlic. Pour into 2 glasses and serve.

Glazed Turnips With Port Wine

Make sure to use a sweet Port in this recipe. Marsala, Madiera, or Sherry will work as well.

Serves: 4

Ingredients
24 baby turnips or 2 pounds large peeled turnips
1 tablespoon butter
2 tablespoons port wine
Salt and pepper

Directions
Cut baby turnips in half or cut large turnips into ½-inch chunks. Lay turnips in a single layer in a large skillet. Place over medium-high heat and fill the pan with water until turnips are half covered. Add butter, salt and pepper. Bring to a boil and then turn heat down to medium. Cover loosely with a sheet of foil and simmer for 15 minutes. Uncover the pan and continue to cook until all of the water is evaporated. When water has evaporated, turnips will start to brown in the remaining butter. Stir turnips and brown on all sides. Add the port and continue to cook, stirring occasionally, until port has evaporated. Serve immediately.

Cumin Roasted Rutabaga

Serve this as part of a winter relish tray with olives and pickled vegetables.

Serves: 6 to 8

Ingredients

3 pounds rutabagas, peel and
  cut into 1-inch chunks
2 tablespoons olive oil
2 tablespoons ground cumin
Salt and pepper
1/4 cup chopped cilantro or 1/8 cup
  cilantro pesto (see p. 148)
3 minced garlic cloves
1/2 cup crumbled feta or diced
  fresh mozzarella cheese

Directions

Pre heat oven to 425 F. Place all ingredients except the cheese in a large mixing bowl, toss well and let sit at room temperature for at least 30 minutes. Arrange on a baking sheet and roast for 1 hour until rutabagas are soft inside and crisp and brown outside. Remove from the oven and cool to room temperature. Toss gently with the cheese. Serve at room temperature.

Scalloped Turnips Gratin

This cheesy comfort food may be a vehicle to get your kids to eat turnips. Just tell them it's something like macaroni.

Serves: 4 as a side

Ingredients

1 pound turnips, peel and cut into 3/8 inch slices
1-1/2 cups prepared béchamel (see p. 277)
1 cup shredded cheddar cheese, divided
1/4 cup bread crumbs
Salt and pepper to taste

Directions

Preheat oven to 400°F. Choose an ovenproof dish that will roughly allow turnips to form a single layer. Heat or prepare béchamel. Stir 3/4 cup of cheese into warm béchamel. Remove from heat and stir until cheese is fully melted and smooth. Pour mixture over turnips. Sprinkle with a little salt and pepper. Cover tightly and bake for 30 minutes until turnips are tender and sauce is bubbly. Remove from oven, uncover and top with remaining cheese and bread crumbs. Return to oven for 10 minutes until top is golden brown. Serve immediately.

Baked Turnips

A great alternative to baked potatoes, and you can top it just like one.

Serves: 4

Ingredients

4 large turnips, peeled and quartered
1/4 cup melted butter
Salt and pepper to taste

Directions

Preheat oven to 375 F. Place turnips, butter, salt and pepper in a large mixing bowl. Toss well and arrange in a baking dish large enough to just hold them. Bake for 50 minutes until tender and brown.

WINTER SQUASH (PUMPKINS)

Every year millions of cans of pureed pumpkin and pumpkin pie fillings are shipped from somebody else's backyard to your backyard. In most parts of the world, pumpkin and squash are various, plentiful and at hand for long stretches of the growing season. In America, we have so many that we have to make scary sculptures out of them and roving gangs of ill bred youths giggle themselves silly smashing them in the street. That is the perfect place to start being more conscious of your cooking and eating choices. One large pumpkin or a modest purchase of squash with a little time commitment will give you all you need for an entire year. It is an easy choice to make — never buy canned or frozen pumpkin again.

Pumpkins are the most recognized of the winter squash but the varieties of winter squash are endless. There are beautiful golden butternuts and forest green acorns and spaghetti squash and perfectly round green and white marbled things that I can never remember the name of and little squash that looks like a banana and small white squashes you could use for a softball and tiny pumpkins used for centerpieces at Halloween parties. While there are differences between them, they all behave about the same when you cook them. They are among the last items available each season and if kept cool and dry will last all winter. I offer a few recipes to make sure that you can eat them all.

Spiced Butternut and Apple Juice

Wonderful color and flavor!

Ingredients
8 red apples, core and cut into wedges
1 butternut squash, peel, remove seeds
    and cut into 1-inch chunks
2 carrots, cut into 2-inch pieces
1/2 teaspoon cinnamon
1/4 teaspoon nutmeg

Directions
Place apples, squash and carrots through a juicer and process until juice is fully extracted. Add cinnamon and nutmeg. Serve in 4 glasses.

Baked Pumpkin or Squash Puree

This puree allows you to never buy another can of pumpkin ever. You may boil the pumpkin instead of baking it, this allows a cleaner flavor and a lighter color, but it requires you to trim off the peel while the pumpkin is still raw and the peel is hard to cut. Either preparation can be used in any recipe requiring canned pumpkin.

Ingredients
1 pumpkin

Directions
Preheat oven to 350 F. Cut off top of pumpkin and scrape out stringy bits and seeds. Save seeds for toasting. Cut pumpkin into large pieces and place on a baking sheet. Bake until very soft, about 45 minutes.

Scrape pulp from skin and discard the skin. Puree pulp until very smooth in a food processor. Process in batches if need be. Store for use in savory preparations or season and use for pumpkin pie filling. Puree will keep 1 week in refrigerator or indefinitely in the freezer.

To make pumpkin pie filling, simply add cinnamon, nutmeg, and ground cloves or any commercial pumpkin pie spice.

· · · · · · · · · · · · · · · · ·

Butternut Squash and Swiss Chard Strata

If it's late in the fall and you have run out of chard, you can sub sauerkraut or braised cabbage.

Serves: 6 to 8

Ingredients
2 pounds butternut squash, peel, remove
    seeds and cut into 1-inch chunks
3 tablespoons olive oil
Salt and black pepper
7 eggs
2-1/4 cups half and half or heavy cream
1/2 cup white wine
1 tablespoon Dijon mustard
10 cups stale bread or croutons,
    roughly cut into 1-inch pieces
1 cup minced shallots
4 cups tightly packed Swiss chard
1/2 pound shredded cheddar or Swiss cheese

Directions
Preheat oven to 400 F. Arrange squash on a shallow baking sheet and sprinkle with 1 tablespoon of olive oil and salt. Gently toss until well coated with oil. Place in oven and bake 25 minutes until squash is tender. Remove from oven and set aside.

Whisk together eggs, cream, wine, mustard, salt and pepper. Add bread to egg mixture and stir together. Let soak for 30 minutes. While bread is soaking, heat 2 tablespoons of oil in a large skillet over medium-high heat. Add shallots and cook until slightly softened. Add chard and cook just until it wilts. Remove from heat.

Spray an ovenproof lasagna pan with nonstick pan spray. Spoon half of the bread and egg mixture into the bottom of the pan. Top with one half of the chard mixture, one half of the squash and one half of the cheese. Place a second layer of bread, chard, squash and cheese in the pan. Cover with foil and bake for 20 minutes. Remove cover and bake 10 more minutes until cheese browns.

· · · · · · · · · · · · · · · · ·

Butternut Squash Salad With Feta

A hearty early autumn salad rich enough to be a main course.

Serves: 4

Ingredients

5 tablespoons olive oil
1 tablespoon balsamic vinegar
1 tablespoon tamari or soy sauce
10 to 12 shallots, peeled but left whole
3 red chilies, Thai or cayenne
1 butternut squash, peel, remove seeds
    and cut into 3/4-inch chunks
1 tablespoon chopped fresh thyme
1/4 cup chopped fresh parsley
1 clove garlic, minced
3/4 cup chopped walnuts
3/4 cup crumbled feta cheese

Directions

Preheat oven to 400 F. Combine olive oil, vinegar and soy sauce in a large mixing bowl. Bruise 2 of the chilies with a couple of whacks using the back of a knife to release the oils and add to soy mixture. Add the shallots and toss well. Place shallot mixture into a large, ovenproof roasting dish and roast, uncovered, for 30 minutes. Remove the pan from the oven and add the butternut squash. Stir to coat with oil and return to the oven for 30 to 40 minutes. Stir ingredients once more during cooking. Remove from oven when squash is tender and browned. Stir in chopped thyme and set aside to cool. Combine parsley, garlic and nuts in a small bowl. Seed and finely chop the remaining chili and add to the parsley mixture. Add parsley mixture to the roasting pan and gently toss until well mixed. Transfer to a serving dish and cool to room temperature. Mix in crumbled feta cheese.

Pumpkin Crème Brulee

This is as sexy as pumpkin can get!

Serves: 8

Ingredients

4 cups heavy cream
1 cup sugar
8 egg yolks
1 cup pumpkin pie filling (see p. 257)

Directions

This recipe is cooked in a double boiler. You may use a manufactured double boiler or simply set one up by resting a stainless steel mixing bowl atop a kettle of boiling water.

Combine all ingredients in double boiler. Cook, stirring constantly and scraping the bottom of the bowl until mixture thickens to the consistency of pancake syrup and coats the back of a spoon. Pour into 8-ounce ovenproof ramekins or soup cups.

Arrange ramekins or cups in shallow pan(s) filled with water. The water should reach halfway up the side of the cups. Bake for approximately 1 hour until set. They are done when just the very center jiggles if shaken. Remove from oven and water bath and cool.

Sprinkle liberally with coarse sugar and brown the top with a blowtorch, pencil torch or a very hot broiler. Set dishes aside until ready to serve.

Twice-Cooked Winter Squash Casserole

An excellent hearty vegan dish that can be enjoyed all winter.

Serves: 4

Ingredients

2 pounds winter squash, acorn,
   buttercup or pumpkin
2 teaspoons sugar
1/2 teaspoon ground cardamom
6 whole cloves
1/4 teaspoon saffron threads, steeped
   in 1 tablespoon warm water
14-ounce can unsweetened coconut milk
1/2 cup unblanched almonds, coarsely chop
Salt

Directions

Preheat oven to 375 F. Cut squash into pieces that can fit onto a cookie sheet. Scoop out seeds and poke cloves into flesh in an even, random manner. Lay squash, flesh-side down, in a single layer on the cookie sheet. Bake for 1 hour until the squash is soft. Remove from oven and cool enough to handle. Gently remove the flesh from the skin and cut into approx. 1-inch cubes. Transfer to a mixing bowl; add sugar, saffron in water, coconut milk, and salt to taste. Gently toss together and place in a shallow casserole dish. Squash should lie in a tight single layer. Sprinkle with almonds and return to the oven for 30 minutes and casserole is bubbly and thick and the top is golden. Serve immediately.

Roasted Butternut Squash Soup

I've never met anyone who didn't like this soup.

Serves: 6

Ingredients

2 large butternut squash
1/3 cup olive oil
2 leeks, chopped
4 stalks celery, chop
2 tablespoons butter
2 bay leaves
6 cups vegetable stock (see p. 289)
2 cups whipping cream
1 teaspoon nutmeg
1 teaspoon cinnamon
1 teaspoon ground cumin
Salt and pepper

Directions

Preheat oven to 400 F. Cut the squash lengthwise into quarters. Scoop out the seeds and discard. Arrange on a baking sheet and brush flesh with olive oil, salt and pepper. Roast until browned and tender, 30 minutes.

While squash is roasting, melt butter in a large skillet over medium heat. Add leeks and celery and cook, stirring occasionally until vegetables are very tender (about 15 minutes). Pour vegetables into a large soup kettle.

Remove squash from oven and cool enough to handle. Scrape flesh out of squash and place in the soup kettle. Add stock and bay leaves and bring to a boil over high heat. Reduce heat and simmer, uncovered, for 30 minutes. Remove the bay leaves and add whipping cream, nutmeg, cinnamon and cumin. Bring to a boil and remove from heat. Place in a food processor and process until smooth. You may need to do this in batches. Return to kettle and season with salt and pepper. Serve in shallow bowls and garnish with a drizzle of heavy cream.

Braised Garlic and Winter Squash

This seems like a crazy amount of garlic but the result is sweet and pungent.

Serves: 6

Ingredients

1 cup vegetable stock (see p. 289)
2 tablespoons butter
2 large heads garlic, cloves separate
   and remove skins
1/4 teaspoon grated nutmeg
3 pounds any firm winter squash, peel,
   remove seeds and cut into 1-inch cubes
2 tablespoons fresh chopped thyme
2 tablespoons fresh chopped sage
Salt and pepper

Directions

Preheat oven to 300 F. Place the stock, butter, garlic, salt, pepper and nutmeg in a large roasting pan or Dutch oven. Heat pan over medium-high heat and bring mixture to a boil, reduce heat and simmer for 10 minutes. Add the squash, thyme, and sage and stir to combine. Cover the pan and place in the preheated oven. Braise for 25 minutes, remove cover and gently stir. Braise for another 25 minutes until very tender. Remove from oven and transfer squash and garlic to a serving bowl with a slotted spoon. Place pan back over medium high-heat and boil pan juice down until it thickens. Add salt and pepper if necessary. Pour sauce over squash and serve immediately.

. . . .

Squash and Shrimp Broth

The Asian ingredients for this soup can be found at any Asian market or food store.

Serves: 4

Ingredients

1 butternut squash
4 cups vegetable stock (see p. 289)
1 cup green beans, cut into 1-inch pieces
1 tablespoon Thai fish sauce
8 ounces raw teaspoon-size shrimp
1/2 cup chili paste
1/2 teaspoon shrimp paste
1 small bunch basil leaves picked from the stem

Directions

Peel the squash and cut in half. Scoop out the seeds and cut into consistent 1/2-inch cubes. Set aside. Heat stock in a large pot over medium heat. Stir in the chili paste and shrimp paste. Add the squash and beans and bring to a boil. Once boiling, reduce heat and simmer for 15 minutes. Add the fish sauce, shrimp and whole basil leaves. Bring back to a simmer and cook for 3 to 5 minutes, depending on the size of the shrimp.

. . . .

Butternut, Parsnip and Potato Pancakes

Try these with your Friday fish fry.

Yields: 24 small pancakes

Ingredients

4 cups butternut squash, peel,
    remove seeds and grate
4 cups red potatoes, peel or
    leave skin on and grate
2 cups parsnips, peel and grate
1 cup minced shallot
1/3 cup unbleached flour
2 tablespoons chopped fresh chives
2 tablespoons chopped fresh parsley
2 tablespoons water
1 tablespoons tahini*
1 tablespoon minced garlic
1 teaspoon baking powder
1/2 teaspoon fresh grated nutmeg
1/4 teaspoon black pepper
Salt
Oil for frying

* Tahini is a prepared sesame-seed butter that can be found in the ethnic section of most markets.

Directions

In a colander, toss together the grated squash, red potatoes, parsnips, shallots and salt. Place the colander over a large bowl and drain mixture for 15 minutes. Squeeze the mixture tightly with your hands to extract as much liquid as possible. Don't be gentle; the idea is to wring as much liquid and starch as possible out of the vegetables. Pour off the watery liquid from the vegetables but reserve the starch that has settled to the bottom of the bowl. Add the grated vegetables to the vegetable starch, along with the flour, chives, parsley, water, tahini, garlic, baking powder, nutmeg and pepper. Toss well to combine and set aside for 5 minutes.

Cover the bottom of a large skillet with oil and place it over medium heat. When the oil is hot, drop 4 golf ball-size portions into the skillet and flatten slightly with the back of a spatula. Cook the pancakes over medium heat for 3 to 4 minutes per side or until golden brown. Carefully flip over the vegetable pancakes and cook an additional 3 minutes or until golden brown on the other side. Keep the pancakes warm in a 200 F oven while you continue frying the rest of the batch. You may have to add oil and/or clean out the pan along the way. Serve with sour cream or maple syrup.

Maple Squash Puree

A great Thanksgiving treat.

Serves: 6

Ingredients

3-1/2 pounds winter squash, peel,
    remove seeds and cut into chunks
2 tablespoons butter
1/4 cup maple syrup
Salt and pepper

Directions

Place squash in a large pot and cover with lightly salted water. Bring to a boil over medium-high heat, reduce heat and simmer for 10 to 20 minutes until squash is very soft. Time will vary based on the type of squash. Drain in a colander and place in the bowl of a food processor. Add remaining ingredients and process until smooth adding a little water or milk to thin to the right consistency. Serve warm.

Spicy Pumpkin Seed Sauce

You can plant the seeds, bake them and eat them like popcorn, or make this yummy sauce. Serve warm over boiled potatoes or grilled shrimp.

Yields: 4 cups

Ingredients

1 cup raw pumpkin seeds
1-1/4 pounds fresh tomatoes
2 garlic cloves, mince
1-1/4 cups vegetable stock (see p. 289)
1 tablespoon vegetable oil
3 tablespoons hot pepper sauce
Salt

Directions

Preheat oven to 400 F. Cut out cores from the tomatoes and quarter the tomatoes. Arrange on a baking sheet and roast in the oven for 1 hour until the edges are well charred. Heat a dry skillet over medium-high heat. Add pumpkin seeds and cook.

You must constantly stir the seeds and not allow them to scorch. They will pop eventually. When they have all popped, remove from the heat and transfer to the bowl of a food processor. Process seeds until minced and smooth.

Add the charred tomatoes and process until smooth. Add the garlic and the stock and process for a few more minutes. Combine the pepper sauce and the oil in a large skillet over medium-high heat and cook for 3 minutes. Add the pumpkin seed mixture and bring to a boil. Reduce heat and simmer uncovered, stirring regularly for about 20 minutes. Sauce should cook down by half. Serve immediately or chill and store. Sauce will keep refrigerated for a week.

CHEF'S NOTES

1. Cut squash does not keep very well. If uncut it will keep for several months.

2. There is no reason not to use local winter squash. It is available everywhere and stores well.

3. All winter squash absorb sweet flavors well. Cooking or roasting with honey, maple, sugar or molasses is always a winner.

4. To peel uncooked squash, cut into hand-size chunks and peel with a sharp knife.

ZUCCHINI

Many people think of zucchini as an Italian vegetable. This is not entirely true. Zucchini originated in South America, was developed in Italy and made popular in America by Italian immigrants. I often come across people who have heard of zucchini but have never tasted one. These same people rarely eat anything that does not come out of a can or a white plastic freezer bag. Zucchini does not do well served out of either of those conveyances. For most applications, except the ubiquitous zucchini bread, zucchini must be fresh.

No vegetable illustrates the fecundity of the earth more than zucchini. Any backyard gardener will tell you that under the right conditions, in mid to late summer, you can almost watch zucchini grow. As such, zucchini is a beautiful metaphor for the natural alchemy of soil and sun that growing and eating fresh embraces. Nothing more fully says plenty like an overflowing basket of shiny forest green squash. Yet, after you appreciate zucchini in poesy, you still might have to deal with the realities of a box full of the stuff. Some zucchini are as big as rugby balls, and one can only eat so much zucchini bread. This selection of recipes may help you through this gustatory challenge. Be forewarned, there is not a single zucchini bread recipe included. For that, please call your mother, or aunt, or cousin or sister-in-law. … Or better yet, just send them the zucchini.

Stuffed Zucchini

Let's face it; zucchini by itself is pretty bland and uninteresting. You have to introduce bold flavors to get a taste bud's attention and, because zucchini are shaped like boats and easy to hollow out, you can add that boldness by stuffing them with all kinds of savory goodies. Zucchini can be stuffed with anything handy by simply cutting on the long axis and scooping out the tender seeds and flesh. You can incorporate the flesh and seeds in the stuffing or discard them for compost. You also can cut small cups along the short axis and scoop with a melon-baller. They can be very shallow for an appetizer or taller for an attractive accompaniment to a main course. All recipes are for three zucchinis that are six to eight inches long.

Bacon and Tomato Stuffed

C'mon it's bacon — How could it be bad?

Serves: 4

Ingredients

    3 zucchinis, 6 to 8 inches long
    6 slices bacon, dice very small
    1 large onion, dice
    2 cloves garlic, mince
    1 cup diced tomato
    1 tablespoon chopped parsley
    1 egg scrambled
    1/2 cup bread crumbs
    1/4 cup grated Parmesan cheese
    Drizzle of olive oil or butter

Directions

Preheat oven to 350 F. Cut zucchinis on the long axis and scoop out the tender seeds and flesh. You can incorporate the flesh and seeds in the stuffing or discard them for compost. You also can cut small cups along the short axis and scoop with a melon-baller.

Fry bacon and render in a shallow pan over medium-high heat. Remove from heat and set aside cooked bacon, reserving about 1/2 of the fat in the pan. Sauté diced onion in the reserved fat. Add minced garlic and brown slightly. Add the tomato to the onion and garlic. Cook until the tomato breaks down a bit and forms a paste. Remove from heat. Stir together tomato mixture, cooked bacon, chopped parsley, scrambled egg, and enough bread crumbs to form a loose paste.

Spoon into hollow zucchinis. Top with grated Parmesan, drizzle with olive oil or butter and bake until top is browned (5 to 7 minutes). Serve as is or with your favorite sauce.

. . . .

Blue Cheese and Walnut Stuffing

This recipe is very simple, but incredibly rich and satisfying. The zucchini should be removed from the oven just as the blue cheese melts. If you bake it too long, the stuffing will become oily.

Serves: 4

Ingredients

    3 zucchinis, 6 to 8 inches long
    1 cup blue cheese crumbles
    1 cup coarsely chopped walnuts
    1/4 teaspoon black pepper
    Dash of paprika

Directions

Preheat oven to 350 F. Cut zucchinis on the long axis and scoop out the seeds. Par cook lightly seasoned lightly salted unfilled zucchini in oven until they start to soften. Remove from the oven and set aside to cool slightly.

In a small mixing bowl, toss together blue cheese crumbles, chopped walnuts and black pepper.

Fill cavities of par cooked zucchini generously with cheese mixture; the cheese will settle as it melts. Put zucchini back into the oven and cook until cheese just melts, approximately 5 minutes. Serve immediately.

. . . .

Eggplant and Smoke Oyster Stuffed

Here's your chance to use up that can of smoked oysters left over from last Christmas.

Serves: 4

Ingredients

3 zucchinis, 6 to 8 inches long
2 tablespoons olive oil
1/4 cup diced onion
1/4 cup diced bell pepper (red or green)
2 green onions, dice
1 tablespoon minced garlic
1 small eggplant, dice
3.75-ounce can smoked oysters, do not drain
2 whipped eggs
1/2 cup cream or milk
1 cup bread crumbs or bread cubes
1/4 cup grated Parmesan cheese
Salt, pepper and cayenne pepper to taste

Directions

Preheat oven to 350 F. Cut zucchinis on the long axis and scoop out the tender seeds and flesh. You can incorporate the flesh and seeds in the stuffing or discard them for compost. In a large skillet, heat olive oil and add diced onion, diced bell pepper, diced green onions and minced garlic; sauté until peppers and onions are soft. Add diced eggplant and cook until very soft. Remove from heat and transfer to a mixing bowl.

Roughly chop smoked oysters and add to vegetable mixture along with any oil in the can. Fold in whipped eggs, cream, bread crumbs and grated Parmesan cheese. Season to taste with salt, pepper and cayenne pepper. Mix well and stuff zucchini with mixture. Bake until stuffing browns and zucchini are soft, about 20 minutes.

. . . .

Double-Baked Purple Potato Stuffed

You may use any waxy potato for this recipe. The bold color of the purple potatoes and satisfying heft of this dish make it an attractive and delicious main course if served with a fresh salad, grilled tomatoes, or wilted greens.

Serves: 4

Ingredients

3 zucchinis, 6 to 8 inches long
6 medium (approx. 1 pound) purple potatoes
1/4 cup milk
Salt (kosher) and pepper to taste
1 teaspoon grated nutmeg
1/4 cup grated cheese
2 tablespoons plain yogurt
2 tablespoons chopped fresh parsley
Drizzle of olive oil

Directions

Preheat oven to 350 F. Cut zucchinis on the long axis and scoop out the seeds. Bake potatoes for about an hour until they are very soft. Remove from oven and cool just enough to handle. Cut the potatoes in half and scoop the baked flesh into a mixing bowl. Add milk, kosher salt and coarse pepper to taste, grated nutmeg and your favorite grated cheese.

Spoon the mixture into zucchini. Drizzle with olive oil and bake until potatoes brown and zucchini softens. Top with a dressing of plain yogurt mixed with chopped herbs.

. . . .

Salami and Olive Stuffed

Use very small baby zucchini in this preparation for a stunning antipasti display. Arrange on an attractive platter with a colorful selection of pickled vegetables, drizzle with olive oil and sprinkle with fresh basil.

Serves: 4

Ingredients

3 small baby zucchini
1 pound salami
1/4 cup black or kalamata olives
1/4 cup stuffed green olives
1/4 cup finely diced red onion
1/4 cup finely diced bell pepper
1 clove garlic, minced
Black pepper to taste
1/4 cup extra virgin olive oil
2 tablespoons chopped fresh basil

Directions

Preheat oven to 350 F. Cut zucchinis on the long axis and scoop out the seeds. Par cook unfilled, lightly seasoned zucchini in oven until they begin to soften. Remove from oven and set aside.

Roughly chop your favorite sliced salami into large pieces and place in bowl of food processor. Roughly chop black or kalamata olives and stuffed green olives; add to salami. Pulse salami and olives a few times until they have the consistency of a salsa; remove to a mixing bowl.

Fold red onion, bell pepper, minced garlic, black pepper and extra virgin olive oil into salami and olive mixture. Fill par-cooked zucchini with mixture. Top with a drizzle of olive oil and a sprinkle of chopped fresh basil. Serve at room temperature.

Summer Squash With Cherry Tomatoes

A quick midsummer side dish.

Serves: 4

Ingredients

2 tablespoons olive oil
3 to 4 summer squash
1/4 cup chopped roasted pepper, chili or sweet (see p.288)
12 cherry tomatoes
1 ear of sweet corn
2 tablespoons chopped fresh basil

Directions

Trim the ends from the summer squash, slice them in half and cut across to form 1/4-inch thick half moons. Remove the kernels from the ear of corn with a stiff knife. Heat the olive oil in a large skillet over medium-high heat. Add squash and cook, stirring frequently for 3 to 4 minutes. Add peppers, tomatoes and corn. Lower the heat to medium-low and cook for 5 minutes while stirring. Vegetables are done when squash just starts to soften. Remove from heat, stir in basil and serve immediately.

Cheddar Zucchini Gratin

In my native Wisconsin, it might be a state law to add cheddar cheese to every recipe. Here is a salute to the motherland.

Serves: 4

Ingredients

2 cups sliced zucchini
1-1/2 cups sliced mushrooms, any type
1 medium onion, slice into rings
1 cup shredded sharp cheddar
2 tablespoons bread crumbs
Salt and pepper to taste
2 tablespoons chopped fresh basil

Directions

Preheat oven to 350 F. Arrange zucchini, onions, mushrooms and 3/4 cup of cheese, lasagna-style, in a shallow baking pan; season with salt and pepper. Top with the last of the cheddar cheese. Cover pan with foil and bake for 20 minutes.

Uncover pan and top with bread crumbs. Return to oven, uncovered, for 10 minutes and top is brown and bubbly. Serve warm.

. . . .

Vodka Stewed Zucchini

Kind of like a "zucchini martini?"

Serves: 4

Ingredients

1 pound zucchini, slice into 1-inch thick rounds
1/2 cup canned tomato or spaghetti sauce
1/2 cup vodka
1 clove garlic, minced
1 tablespoon chopped fresh oregano
1 cup diced tomatoes
1/4 cup crumbled blue cheese
Salt and pepper to taste

Directions

Bring tomato sauce and vodka to a boil over medium-high heat in a large skillet. Add zucchini, diced tomatoes and garlic. Return to a boil; reduce heat and simmer, uncovered, for 6 to 8 minutes until zucchini is softened. Add salt and pepper to taste. Transfer to a serving dish and sprinkle with blue cheese and oregano. Serve immediately.

. . . .

Midsummer Harvest Juice

The ingredients in this juice can't help but remind you of verdant fragrant fields — A time when scarcity seems far off.

Serves: 2

Ingredients

4 zucchini, approx. 6 inches long
3 ripe tomatoes
2 celery stalks
2 scallions
2 garlic cloves
1/4 cup oregano leaves, firmly packed
Salt and pepper

Directions

Trim stem ends from zucchini. Core tomatoes. Trim root ends from scallions. Cut all vegetables into pieces that will fit into your juicer. Feed all vegetables and oregano through juicer. Season the juice to taste with salt and plenty of black pepper.

. . . .

Zucchini Refrigerator Pickles

Here's one more way to find a home for those ubiquitous late summer squash.

Yields: 4 pints

Ingredients

4 pounds small zucchini
1 pound pearl-size bulb onions, peel (or
    1 pound slivered yellow onion)
1 quart cider vinegar
1 cup honey
2 teaspoons celery seeds
2 teaspoons turmeric
2 teaspoons dry mustard
2 teaspoons mustard seeds

Directions

Trim ends from zucchini and cut into 1/4-inch wheel-shaped slices. Combine vinegar, honey, celery seeds, turmeric, dry mustard and mustard seeds in a saucepan. Bring to a boil over medium heat. Remove from heat and add zucchini and onions to mixture. Let stand 1 hour. After 1 hour, place pan back on medium heat and return to a boil. Boil for 3 minutes. Pour equal amounts of mixture into 4 pint-size canning jars. Cover and refrigerate. Will keep at least 2 months in the refrigerator.

CHEF'S NOTES

1. While the entire zucchini gives you edible biomass, the crunchy and slightly bitter skin is the part I prefer. Scrape the flesh out of the zucchini and cut in half until the walls are about 1/8-inch thick. Cut into thin French fry-shaped strips and serve raw in salads or cook like you would green beans. Reserve the flesh for another use.

2. Zucchini grills well. Cut in half lengthwise, scoop out seeds, season with a little olive oil, salt, pepper and garlic and char-grill over charcoal or wood for a simple side dish.

3. Zucchini does not freeze well but, in season, you get so much of it you may be tempted to freeze it just to save it from spoiling. Blanch, shock (see p. 287) and grate it before you freeze it. This frozen version will be acceptable in a mid-winter zucchini bread. You also can freeze strips of the skin (see note 1). They survive freezing much better than the flesh.

4. The sexiest zucchinis are the very small ones you get early in the season. Fry these whole in a little butter with chopped fresh herbs.

5. The flesh from those ridiculously huge zucchini can be juiced and used as a soup stock or as a base for more complex juices. It can be frozen as well. Simply remove the seeds, scoop the flesh from the zucchini and juice according to your juicer's directions.

6. Peel slices of fresh zucchini with a vegetable peeler for thin crunchy ribbons that are a great addition to salads and make an attractive plate garnish.

THE SEASON AS IT COMES

This chapter is required reading for CSA shareholders. The beautiful varieties of items that come in your CSA shares each week are just begging to find a home. You are confronted with a rainbow of vegetables all at the same time. Dishes that allow you to use a number of items at once to show off the seasonal variety as it presents itself. The good earth delivers when she feels it is right — and it is only right that you are ready for that.

I've tried to offer a collection of recipes that will cover the entire growing season. This is a cookbook and it is full of recipes, but when it comes to enjoying what's offered, when it's offered, you must have a little imagination. Substitutions are encouraged. Mix vegetables freely, play around with fresh herbs and spices and have a little fun.

Black Bean and Bulgur Salad With Asparagus, Arugula and Strawberries

A very good lunch salad on its own or with some good bread.

Yields: 5 cups

Salad Ingredients
1 cup cooked black beans (see p. 287)
1 cup soaked bulgur wheat
1 cup blanched asparagus (see p. 287)
1 cup wilted arugula
1 cup sliced strawberries

Dressing Ingredients
3 tablespoons cider vinegar
3 tablespoons lime or lemon juice
3 tablespoons chopped fresh cilantro
1/2 cup olive oil
Salt and pepper

Directions
Combine all salad ingredients in a large mixing bowl. In a smaller mixing bowl, whisk together vinegar, lime juice and cilantro. Continue to whisk and slowly drizzle in oil. Dressing should be cloudy and frothy. Pour over salad ingredients and toss well.

Spring Vegetable Stew

Make this mess on a rainy day with the goodies from your first CSA share of the season.

For the dried mushrooms, any variety will do, but morel or porcini are preferred. If you hit the jackpot and have some fresh spring morels, sauté them in butter and serve on the side.

Serves: 6 to 8

Ingredients

1/2 ounce dried mushrooms
6 radishes, with the greens
1 cup sugar snap peas
6 baby turnips, with the greens
1 head garlic, separate and peel all cloves
6 baby leeks or ramps, greens included,
    dice into 1/2-inch pieces
1 cup fresh peas, shelled
14 ounces chickpeas (garbanzo beans), drain juice
2 tablespoons olive oil
1 cup white wine
4 cups vegetable stock
1/2 teaspoon red pepper flakes
2 tablespoons butter
2 tablespoons lemon juice
1 teaspoon dried chives
1/4 cup chopped fresh dill
1/4 cup chopped fresh parsley

Directions

Cover mushrooms with warm water and let steep for at least 30 minutes. Strain the liquid through a fine strainer or a piece of cheesecloth and into a bowl. You will use this liquid in the stew. Rinse the mushrooms under cold running water, shake dry and set aside.

Trim the greens from the radishes and the turnips, discard tough stems and roughly chop greens. Set aside. Cut radishes and turnips in half.

Heat oil in a large Dutch oven or roasting pan over medium heat. Add leeks, turnips, radishes, garlic and red pepper flakes. Cook 5 to 8 minutes, stirring occasionally, until vegetables brown. Add wine and cook 5 minutes to reduce alcohol. Add vegetable stock, chickpeas, thyme, salt, pepper and reserved mushroom liquid. Bring back to a boil and then reduce heat, cover and simmer for 20 to 30 minutes until turnips are tender. Add sugar snap peas, fresh shell peas, turnip greens and radish greens. Increase heat to medium and bring to a boil. Cover and cook until peas are soft, but not mushy, about 10 minutes. Remove from heat and stir in butter, chives and parsley. Serve immediately in shallow bowls with lots of crusty bread.

CHEF'S NOTES

1. Often the most complicated thing about combining vegetables in a recipe is getting everything cooked at the same time. Just cook all your vegetables separately and combine them at the end. You can make a simple sauté by combining precooked vegetables in a pan with a little butter, salt and pepper. Cook until warm and serve.

2. Chopped fresh herbs are interchangeable in most recipes.

3. Try to combine colors when you can. The beauty and appreciation of any food is heightened with visual appeal.

Fingerling Salad With Early Summer Vegetables

You should see the first new crop of fingerlings in mid-June.
Show them off in this easy colorful picnic salad.

Serves: 6

Ingredients

2 pounds fingerling potatoes, cut into 1/2-
    inch slices, blanch and shock (see p. 287)
1/2 red pepper, dice
3 chopped green onions, white and green parts
1/4 cup packed arugula leaves,
    cut into 1/4-inch ribbons
1 cup diced string beans, blanched
    and shocked (see p. 287)
1/2 cup baby carrots, slice ¼-inch thick,
    blanch and shock (see p. 287)
1 finely chopped jalapeno pepper
1-1/2 cups mayonnaise

1/4 cup chopped fresh parsley
1 tablespoon lemon juice
Salt and white pepper to taste

Directions

In a small bowl, whisk together mayonnaise, parsley, salt and pepper. Combine all vegetables in a large bowl. Add mayonnaise to vegetables and gently toss until salad is well mixed. Keep refrigerated.

. . . .

Curried Tomato and Zucchini Compote

This is a wonderful vegetarian lunch served with any warm flatbread and a green salad.

Serves: 4

Ingredients

2 jalapeno chilies, remove tops and seeds
1 teaspoon grated fresh ginger
3 tablespoons cashews
1-1/2 tablespoons coriander seeds
1 teaspoon cumin seeds
1/4 teaspoon fennel seeds
3 tablespoons butter
2 tomatoes (1 pound total), peel, remove
    seeds and chop (see p. 288)
1-1/2 pounds zucchini, cut into ½-inch cubes
1/2 teaspoon turmeric
3 tablespoons chopped fresh cilantro
Salt

Directions

Place jalapenos, ginger, cashews, coriander seeds, cumin seeds, fennel seeds and 1/4 cup water in a food processor; process until very smooth. Heat butter in a large saucepan over medium heat. Pour in the spice blend and cook until bubbly and thick. Stir in the tomatoes and bring back to a boil. Add the zucchini, turmeric, salt and half of the cilantro. Reduce heat to low. Stir to blend well, cover and cook for 10 minutes. At this point you need to look in the pan every few minutes and stir and scrape the vegetables off the bottom of the pan. Add a little water if it is getting too sticky. Cook this way for 20 minutes, until zucchini is very soft. Remove from heat and transfer to a serving bowl. Serve warm or room temperature.

. . . .

Sinhalese Sauce

"Sinhalese" means in the style of Ceylon (Sri Lanka). This is a bit deceptive because the only thing South Asian about this dish is a simple curry blend of spices. Nonetheless, this tasty relish is perfect with poached or smoked salmon.

Ingredients

1/2 cup finely diced and seeded zucchini
1/2 cup finely diced red pepper
1/2 cup finely diced green pepper
1/2 cup finely diced tomato, seeded
1/2 cup finely diced cucumber,
    peel and remove seeds
4 hard-cooked eggs, separate whites and yolks
1 tablespoons curry powder
2 tablespoons extra virgin olive oil
1 tablespoon lime juice
Salt and pepper to taste
1 tablespoon chopped fresh parsley
1 tablespoon chopped fresh chives

Ingredients

In a large mixing bowl, toss together the diced vegetables. Force the egg yolks through the mesh of a fine sieve into the vegetable mixture. Finely dice the egg whites to use as a garnish for the salmon. Add curry, oil, lime juice, parsley, chives, salt and pepper. Toss all ingredients until thoroughly mixed. Let sit 30 minutes before serving.

Roasted Root Vegetables

There are many ways to season roasted vegetables; this is one of the most straightforward and perfect. Four ingredients, butter, honey, salt and lots of black pepper give you just the right amount of sweet and savory. In the fall, when all the green tomatoes and cucumbers are gone, roast up a tray of these for a taste of the good earth. You can roast any combination of potatoes, turnips, beets, rutabagas, parsnips, carrots, sweet potatoes, celeriac or kohlrabi. Do all of one kind or mix and match. Make enough butter and honey mixture to just coat whatever amount of vegetables you prepare.

Ingredients

1 part melted butter
1 part honey
Salt
Fresh ground black pepper

Directions

Preheat oven to 400 degrees. Stir together butter and honey in a mixing bowl. Set aside. The trick is to cut the root vegetables in sizes that are about the same size. This will ensure that everything finishes at the same time. Place the cut vegetables in a large mixing bowl along with the butter and honey. Toss all ingredients and place in a single layer on a shallow baking pan. Sprinkle liberally with salt (root veggies absorb a lot of salt) and lots of fresh ground black pepper. Roast in the oven until vegetables are soft and brown on the edges. Serve immediately or you might serve at room temperature as an appetizer platter.

Grilled Summer Vegetable Panzanella

Serve as a vegetarian main course or top with grilled chicken or fish — A traditional savory, Italian bread salad.

Serves: 4

Dressing Ingredients

12 chopped kalamata olives
1/4 cup red wine vinegar
2 tablespoons capers
Black pepper
1/4 cup olive oil

Salad Ingredients

3 cups day-old whole-grain bread, cut into
    1-inch chunks. (If using fresh bread
    toast before cutting into chunks.)
2 tomatoes, core and cut into wedges
2 small zucchini, remove tops and
    cut in half lengthwise
1 red onion, slice into ½-inch rounds
1 bell pepper, core, cut in half and smash flat
1 chili (any type) pepper, core, slice
    in half and smash flat
1/2 cup olive oil
Salt and pepper
2 tablespoons fresh chopped basil

Directions

Place all dressing ingredients in a blender or food processor and blend until smooth and creamy.

Prepare a gas or charcoal grill. Heat should be medium-high or the coals should have stopped flaming and formed a white ash around the outside.

Arrange all vegetables on a sheet pan and brush or drizzle each piece with olive oil on all sides. Use more oil if necessary. Liberally salt and pepper the vegetables. Place tomatoes on grill and grill the cut side until a little black char forms on the tomatoes. Remove the tomatoes before they turn to mush. Place in a large mixing bowl. Place the remainder of the vegetables on the grates. Grill (only grill one side) until vegetables are soft. This will take different times for each vegetable. When the piece is well browned and a little soft, remove from the grill to a cutting board. When all vegetables are grilled, allow them to cool to the touch and cut into 1-inch pieces. Place in the bowl with the tomatoes, add the bread and pour over the dressing. Gently toss until pieces are well dressed. Serve in a decorative salad bowl and sprinkle with chopped basil.

Spicy Dill Brine for Refrigerator Pickles

Try this simple all-purpose savory brine.

Yields: 6 pints

Ingredients

3 cups white vinegar
6 cups water
1 cup canning salt
12 sprigs fresh dill
6 fresh or dried hot peppers, bruise
    with the back of a knife

Directions

Bring vinegar, sugar and pickling spice to a boil over medium-high heat. Boil for 5 to 10 minutes until sugar is fully dissolved. Fill 6 pint-size jars with vegetables and fill with brine to within 1/4 inch of rim. Cover, seal and refrigerate for up to six months.

Midsummer Frittata

The frittata is an Italian version of an omelet. The difference between the two, outside of traditional Italian seasoning and ingredients, is that a frittata is not folded and it is cooked much slower and at a lower temperature. The size of your frittata is only limited by the size of your pan. Once cut and attractively presented, it makes a fantastic family brunch treat.

We call this a mid-summer frittata because these are vegetables you might find in your farmer's field in the middle of July, but you can put in any vegetables you have available. In fact, you pretty much can put anything edible into it. Just keep in mind that the vegetables will cook very little over such low heat, so any items that you don't want raw will have to be pre-cooked in some way.

Serves: 3 to 5

Ingredients
6 large eggs
Splash of milk
2 tablespoons olive oil or salad oil
1 medium zucchini or yellow squash, dice
1/4 cup chili or sweet chopped peppers
1/4 cup onions
1/4 cup chopped tomatoes
1 carrot, dice and blanch (see p. 287)
1/4 cup diced and blanched radishes
1/4 cup chopped fresh spinach
Salt and pepper
1/4 cup shredded Italian cheese
A few chopped fresh herbs

Directions
Whip the eggs vigorously with a little milk. You want to mix a little air into the mixture to make it all fluffy and light. Preheat a medium-size nonstick skillet, preferably with rounded sides (it's easier to remove the eggs), over medium-low heat. Coat the pan with oil. Pour in egg mixture and let eggs "set" in the bottom of the pan. Sprinkle vegetables into pan and cover. Do not stir. Let frittata slowly cook until eggs are set, but not tough. This may take a little time depending on how deep the eggs are. Sprinkle with cheese and re-cover until cheese melts. Slide out of pan and cut with a pizza cutter. Arrange slices on platter and sprinkle with fresh herbs. A truly gorgeous breakfast!

. . . .

Sweet Pickle Brine for Refrigerator Pickles

Simple all-purpose sweet brine.

Yield: 6 pints

Ingredients
4 cups white vinegar
4 cups sugar
2 tablespoons pickling spice

Directions
Bring vinegar, sugar and pickling spice to a boil over medium-high heat. Boil for 5 to 10 minutes until sugar is fully dissolved. Fill 6 pint-size jars with vegetables and fill with brine to within 1/4 inch of rim. Cover, seal and refrigerate for up to six months.

. . . .

seasonal

Early Season Refrigerator Pickles

The types of vegetables can be changed depending on what is available.
This is a pickle that might be made out of an early season CSA share.

Yields: 6 pints

Ingredients

- 2 cups radishes, cut into 3/4-inch chunks
- 3 cups sliced shiitake mushroom
- 3 cups asparagus, cut into 1-inch pieces
- 3 cups sugar snap peas
- 1 cup garlic scapes or 6 cloves garlic
- 1 cup chopped scallions

Directions

Sterilize 6 pint-size jars in a boiling water bath. Bring a gallon of water to a boil in large pot over medium-high heat. Add radishes and mushrooms and bring back to a boil. Cook for 5 minutes. Add peas, asparagus, garlic scapes or garlic cloves and scallions and bring back to a boil. Reduce heat and simmer for 3 minutes. Pour off water and fill pot with cold water and ice to stop the cooking. Drain cold water from vegetables and shake dry. Remove jars from water bath. Pack vegetables in pint jars. Fill jars with sweet or spicy pickle brine (see p. 273) to within 1/4 inch of rim. Cover and seal jars. Will keep six months in the refrigerator.

· · · · · · · · · · · · · · · ·

Midsummer Refrigerator Pickles

You will have a great assortment of vegetables to choose from this
time of year. This is just a suggestion. Use what you have.

Yields: 6 pints

Ingredients

- 3 cups cauliflower florets
- 3 cups green beans, cut in 2-inch pieces
- 3 cups zucchini, remove seeds and
  cut into 1/2-inch slices
- 1 cup diced red pepper
- 1 cup diced onion
- 3 cups sliced 1/2-inch wide cucumber slices
- 6 cloves garlic

Directions

Sterilize jars of desired size in a boiling water bath. Bring a gallon of water to boil in a large pot over medium-high heat. Add cauliflower, beans, zucchini, red pepper, onions and garlic. Allow water to come back to a boil and cook for 5 minutes. Drain off water and fill pot with cold water and some ice to stop the vegetables from cooking. Drain vegetables and shake dry. Add cucumbers to vegetables. Remove jars from water bath and pack with vegetables. Pour over sweet or spicy pickle brine to within ¼-inch of rim. Cover and seal jars. This will keep 6 months in the refrigerator.

· · · · · · · · · · · · · · · ·

Autumn Refrigerator Pickles

This is an unusual pickle but very good.

Yield: 6 pints

Ingredients
- 3 cups butternut squash, cut into 3/4-inch chunks
- 3 cups rutabaga, cut into 3/4-inch chunks
- 3 cups pumpkin, cut into 3/4-inch chunks
- 2 cups celeriac, cut into 1/2-inch chunks
- 2 cups sunchokes, cut into 3/4-inch chunks
- 6 cloves garlic

Directions
Sterilize desired size of jars in a boiling water bath. Bring 1 gallon of water to a boil in a large pot over medium-high heat. Add squash, rutabaga, pumpkin, celeriac and garlic. Allow water to come back to a boil and cook for 10 minutes. Remove from heat and drain off water leaving vegetables in pot. Fill pot with cold water and a little ice to stop the cooking. Drain cold water from vegetables and shake dry. Add the sunchokes. Remove jars from water bath and pack with vegetables. Pour over sweet or spicy pickle brine (see p. 273) to within 1/4-inch of the rim. This will keep 6 months in the refrigerator.

. . . .

Winter Vegetable Brochettes

Have one more barbecue before the snow flies.

Serves 4

Ingredients
- 2 precooked 4-ounce Italian sausage links, cut into 8 chunks
- 1 pumpkin, cut into 8 one-inch chunks
- 1 potato, cut into 8 one-inch chunks
- 1 large onion, quarter
- 1/2 cup red wine
- 1/2 cup olive oil
- 2 tablespoons lemon juice
- 2 tablespoons cider vinegar
- 1 tablespoon soy sauce
- 1 tablespoon dried thyme
- Salt and pepper

Directions
Bring 2 saucepans of salted water to a boil over medium-high heat. Place winter squash in one and potatoes in the other. Allow water to come back to a boil. Reduce heat, and simmer until vegetables are just cooked but still firm. Drain in a colander and cool with cold running water. Set aside.

In a mixing bowl whisk together red wine, olive oil, lemon juice, cider vinegar, soy sauce, thyme, salt and pepper. Build brochettes by alternating chunks of sausage, squash, potatoes and onions on metal skewers. Lay the skewers in a shallow baking dish and pour the marinade over the top. Cover pan and refrigerate at least 3 hours.

Prepare a gas or charcoal grill. Heat should be medium on a gas grill and the charcoals should still have a little flame. Place skewers on the grate and baste with a little of the marinade. Cook for 5 minutes on one side; turn over and baste skewers again. Continue to cook and baste until vegetables are charred and sausage is cooked through. Serve immediately with cooked rice.

. . . .

MULTI-PURPOSE RECIPES

Bechamel

Rich, creamy sauces are out of style at the moment but this classic sauce is a valuable tool in a good cook's toolbox. It is an ingredient and/or starting point for many recipes. You can get adequate results with skim milk; however, the taste and texture improve with heavier dairy products.

Yields: 5 cups

Ingredients

- 1/2 cup butter or other fat (chicken fat, lard, shortening)
- 1/2 cup all-purpose flour
- 1 quart milk or cream
- Pinch of grated nutmeg
- Salt and white pepper to taste

Directions

Using a large saucepan, bring 1 quart of milk to just boiling over medium heat. Stir occasionally while scraping the bottom of the pan with a wooden spoon. Reduce heat to very low and continue to stir.

While milk is heating, melt butter over medium-high heat in a pan large enough to hold the milk. When butter is melted, add flour and mix into a paste. Continue to stir and brown for 2 minutes.

Pour in the hot milk while stirring vigorously with a wire whisk. Continue to stir until all of the lumps have dissolved and the sauce is thickened. Reduce heat to low. Season with salt and white pepper and simmer for 15 minutes, stirring occasionally to cook the pasty taste out of the flour. Stir in milk or water to adjust the consistency of the sauce.

Sauce will keep one week in the refrigerator and can be frozen for 3 months.

VINAIGRETTES

Standard vinaigrette is simply an emulsion of an acidic liquid and oil. An emulsion is a mixture of two items that don't normally get along well. You force them to coexist by frantically whipping them together drop by drop or by adding an emulsifier, typically egg yolk or food starch.

Vinaigrettes are perfect as dressings for raw and cooked vegetables and fruit. The oil improves mouth feel and the acid and salt open the pores of the tongue and allow you to more fully taste many subtle flavors that might otherwise be hidden. The only ingredients that are mandatory in vinaigrette are oil and an acidic liquid such as vinegar, fruit or vegetable juice; salt and pepper are helpful but not absolutely necessary. Try any combination of the following oils and acids. This list is by no means exhaustive but should give you permission to experiment a little.

Oils
Red or white wine vinegar
Cider vinegar
Herb-infused vinegars
Rice wine vinegar
Lemon juice
Orange juice
Lime juice
Tomato juice
Cranberry juice

Acids
Olive oil
Salad oil (soybean)
Sunflower oil
Grape seed oil
Walnut oil
Herb-infused oil
Citrus-infused oil
Sesame oil
Hot chili oil
Peanut oil

. . . .

Basic Vinaigrette

I've offered two basic vinaigrette recipes and a handful of variations to try. I encourage you to experiment with different types of oils, flavored vinegars, juices, herbs and seasonings.

Yields: 1 cup

Ingredients
3/4 cup extra virgin olive oil
1/4 cup vinegar or citrus juice
Salt and pepper to taste

Directions
Stir vinegar and salt in a small mixing bowl until salt dissolves (salt will not dissolve in oil). Contrive a way to keep the mixing bowl steady while you whisk in oil. The bowl placed in a nest made out of a damp dish towel is one way or draft a patient family member to hold the bowl for you. Slowly drizzle in the oil while energetically whisking. The result should be smooth and satiny. Adjust the seasoning to taste.

This recipe will separate eventually, when it does, simply whisk it back to obedience.

. . . .

Vinaigrette With Emulsifier

If you are squeamish about raw egg, use frozen pasteurized egg yolk, or you can force the yolk from a hard-cooked egg through a fine sieve.

Yields: 1 cup

Ingredients

3/4 cup extra virgin olive oil
1/4 cup vinegar or citrus juice
1 egg yolk
Salt and pepper to taste

Directions

Whisk together vinegar and salt to dissolve. Whisk in egg yolk. Slowly drizzle in olive oil while whisking mixture furiously as directed in Basic Vinaigrette recipe. Taste and adjust salt and pepper to taste.

This recipe will be thicker and richer and it will not separate.

. . . .

Lemon Vinaigrette

Replace all or part of vinegar with lemon juice.

Roasted Garlic Vinaigrette

Prepare 1/2 cup Basic Vinaigrette as directed, but mash 1 large clove of roasted garlic (see Garlic section) and add to the vinegar before drizzling in the oil.

Mixed Herb Vinaigrette

Add one or several finely chopped fresh herbs just before serving — basil, chervil, flat leaf parsley, tarragon and chives are great options.

Maple Walnut Vinaigrette

Replace 1/4 cup of oil with a fine maple syrup and mix with vinegar. Add 1/4 cup chopped walnuts just before serving. This is very good with spinach and tree fruit.

Dijon Vinaigrette

Add 1 tablespoon Dijon mustard to vinegar before adding oil. Dijon vinaigrette is particularly good on a salad with dark greens.

Garlic Anchovy Vinaigrette

Mash together 4 small anchovy filets and 1 small, garlic clove with a mortar and pestle or the flat of a large knife. Add this mash to the dressing before adding the oil. Try this on a platter of grilled asparagus and tomatoes.

Lime Cilantro Vinaigrette

Replace 1/2 of the vinegar with fresh squeezed lime juice. Replace 2 tablespoons of oil with honey. Mix together vinegar, lime juice, honey and a pinch of cumin before drizzling in oil. Add 1/4 cup loosely packed finely chopped cilantro just before serving. You may want to use lighter oil, such as canola or sunflower oil to allow the lime and cilantro to show off a little. Use this as a light sauce on grilled chicken or toss with fresh pears or apples.

Asian-Style Sesame Vinaigrette

Replace 1/4 cup of oil with sesame oil. Replace salt with 1 tablespoon of good soy sauce and 1 tablespoon brown sugar. Use rice wine vinegar as your acid. Mix vinegar, soy and brown sugar and drizzle in both oils. Add 2 tablespoons sesame seeds to the vinaigrette just before serving. This makes a terrific slaw.

Tomato Basil Vinaigrette

Replace 1/4 cup of oil with tomato puree. Mix puree with vinegar and drizzle in oil. Stir in 1 peeled, seeded and diced fresh tomato and 1/4 cup loosely packed finely chopped fresh basil.

. . . .

FLAVORED COMPOUND BUTTERS

Butter is a fantastic carrier of flavor. There are limitless possibilities for adding the flavors of the farm into butter. These compounds can be used as an elegant spread for bread, as an ingredient, or as a garnish to top hot food and drinks. Use them to add interest in any place you would use regular butter. They are simple to make and can be wrapped and frozen for up to one year, ready for instant use.

Supplies Needed for Technique
    Good butter at room temperature
    Electric mixer
    Sheets of wax or parchment paper

Directions
Whip the butter using the mixer and add the flavoring compound. Continue to blend until well incorporated. Spoon the mixture onto wax paper and form a long 1-inch roll. Carefully roll the butter in the wax paper to form a wrapped tubular roll of butter. Wrap this in freezer-proof plastic wrap and store in the freezer. Simply cut slices of butter off of roll with a sharp knife as you need them, and remove the bits of wrap.

Here are samplings of recipes. They are all scaled for 1 cup of grade AA salted butter.

Tip: Roasted garlic is much sweeter than raw garlic.

. . . .

Roasted Garlic Butter

Supplies Needed for Technique

8 large garlic cloves
1/4 cup olive oil
Salt and pepper to taste

Directions

Preheat oven to 350 F. Toss garlic cloves with olive oil, salt and pepper. Arrange on a sheet pan and roast in the oven until soft and browned on the edges, about 20 -25 min utes. Remove from the oven and let cool. Place garlic into a small bowl and mash thoroughly with the back of a spoon. Whip mashed garlic with butter and prepare as instructed in the Directions for Flavored Compound Butters.

Tip: Roasted garlic is much sweeter than raw garlic.

Roasted Chili Butter

Supplies Needed for Technique

1 large or 2 small hot chilies
Pinch of cayenne pepper
Pinch of salt

Directions

Roast the chilies as outlined on page 288. Put the chilies into a food processor and chop the chilies until finely minced. Whip the chilies into the butter; add cayenne pepper and salt. Prepare and store as instructed in the Directions for Flavored Compound Butters.

Tip: Float a nugget of this on hot soup.

Shallot Butter

Supplies Needed for Technique

3 large shallots, finely diced
Salt and black pepper to taste

Directions

Cook the shallots for 2 to 3 minutes in salted boiling water. Drain water and pat dry.

Place shallots into a blender or food processor and puree with a little salt and black pepper to taste. Whip shallots into butter. Prepare and store as instructed in the Directions for Flavored Compound Butters.

Tip: Let a knob of this butter melt atop grilled steaks or salmon just before serving.

Minted Honey Butter

Supplies Needed for Technique

1/4 cup finely chopped fresh mint
1/4 cup fine local honey
Salt and pepper to taste

Directions

Mix mint with honey and whip with butter. Add salt and pepper to taste.

Prepare and store as instructed in the Directions for Flavored Compound Butters.

Tip: This butter is outstanding on baked apples or pears.

Fresh Herb Butter

Supplies Needed for Technique
- 1/2 cup finely chopped fresh herb, any desired herb
- 1 lemon zest
- Salt and pepper to taste

Directions
Combine herbs with the lemon zest. Whip with butter and a little salt and pepper to taste. Prepare and store as instructed in the Directions for Flavored Compound Butters.

Maple Butter

Supplies Needed for Technique
- 1/2 cup farm-cooked maple syrup
- Salt and pepper to taste

Directions
Whip maple syrup with butter. Add salt and pepper to taste. Prepare and store as instructed in the Directions for Flavored Compound Butters.

Tip: Of course, you can smear this on your French toast, but it also serves very well as table butter for warm rolls and bread.

Raw Garlic Butter

Supplies Needed for Technique
- 4 cloves of garlic
- 1 teaspoon chopped parsley
- Salt and pepper to taste

Directions
Mince or puree garlic in a food processor or with the flat of a knife (see Garlic section). Whip garlic into butter, season with salt and pepper and add chopped parsley. Prepare and store as instructed in the Directions for Flavored Compound Butters.

Tip: This is an obvious choice to flavor pasta.

Brown Butter

Brown butter is simply butter cooked until the solids brown. It is simple to make, yet requires you to pay close attention to the butter as it cooks. It has a rich nutty taste that is perfect with cooked green vegetables; asparagus, broccoli, chard or cabbages are suggestions. It is also a fine sauce for cooked apples or pears.

Makes 1/2 cup

Supplies Needed for Technique
- 1 stick (1/4 pound) butter, cut into 1-inch chunks
- Juice from 1 wedge of lemon
- Pinch of salt
- 1 teaspoon chopped fresh parsley

Directions
Place the butter into a medium skillet over medium-high heat. Melt butter completely. Let butter cook and bubble without stirring for 3 to 5 minutes. Butter is done when solids settle to the bottom and become a rusty brown. The best way to check for doneness: Raise the pan off of the heat and look at the color on the bottom. When the solids are browned, remove the pan from the heat and immediately squeeze in lemon. It will sputter a bit. Add the chopped parsley and a pinch of salt. Set aside until ready to serve.

Zabaglione

Zabaglione is a rich, sweet sauce for desserts that has its roots in 16th century Italian cooking. If cooked to a thick custard state, it can stand alone; however, it really shines as a topping for fresh berries.

Yields: 2 cups

Supplies Needed for Technique
- 5 egg yolks
- 1 teaspoon lemon juice
- 1/8 teaspoon vanilla extract
- 3/4 cup sugar
- 3/4 cup Marsala wine or sweet vermouth

Directions

Fill a medium-size pot about half full of water. Bring water to a boil over high heat. While you are waiting for the water to boil, combine the egg yolks, lemon juice, vanilla and sugar in a stainless steel mixing bowl large enough to rest on top of the pot — like a golf ball on a tee. Whisk these ingredients together vigorously until the mixture pales slightly.

By now, the water should be boiling. Set the bowl atop the pot of water. The bottom of the bowl should not touch the water. Let the steam from the water heat the bottom of the bowl and continue to whisk energetically. While whisking, scrape the bottom of the bowl regularly with the whisk to keep the egg from cooking on the bottom of the bowl. When the mixture starts to thicken, whisk in the wine a couple of ounces at a time until all of the wine is incorporated. Continue to cook until the mixture is the consistency of a thick salad dressing, roughly 10 minutes. Remove the bowl from the heat and continue to whisk until the bowl is cool to the touch. This may be served warm or chilled.

Note: If you would like a thicker custard-style dessert, simply reduce the amount of wine by 1/4 cup and cook 5 minutes longer.

. . . .

Croutons

Croutons are simply savory pieces of crispy baked bread. You can buy them at the supermarket, but making your own allows you to make them exactly how you like, or allows you to use up old bread.

Ingredients
- Bread (any kind), sliced or cubed
- Butter or olive oil, melted
- Salt
- Pepper
- Dried basil
- Dried thyme
- Dried oregano
- Paprika
- Granulated garlic or garlic powder

Directions

Preheat oven to 350 F. Croutons usually are made with stale leftover bread; use if you have it, but fresh bread works well too. Place bread in a large mixing bowl and add enough melted butter or olive oil to just coat. Sprinkle in liberal amounts of all spices and toss together completely. Lay bread in a single layer on a baking sheet and bake in oven until crisp and brown. This recipe is just a suggestion. You can slice the bread very thin for crostini, slice a little thicker for bruschetta, or dice for a bread salad.

. . . .

Bread Crumbs

Directions

Preheat oven to 250 F. While oven is warming, tear slices of bread into 1-inch pieces and place in the bowl of a food processor. Process until crumbs are the fineness you would like. Spread crumbs out on a cookie sheet and bake for 10 to 15 minutes, until bread crumbs are a pale golden color.

Stir once or twice during baking. Remove from oven.

. . . .

Remoulade

Remoulade is tarter sauce with a fancy name. There are countless variations and flavorings possible. This formula will work in most recipes.

Yields: Approx. 1 cup

Ingredients

1/2 cup good mayonnaise
2 tablespoons chopped dill pickle or pickle relish
1 teaspoon lemon juice
2 tablespoons chopped fresh herbs
1 tablespoon capers
Salt and pepper to taste

Directions

Mix together all ingredients.

. . . .

Poached Eggs

I'm constantly amused at the array of gadgets one can purchase to poach eggs. Poaching eggs is easier than frying and requires only two pieces of equipment — a shallow pan and a slotted spoon. Have a rummage sale and get rid of all that other stuff.

Ingredients

Eggs
Water
2 to 4 tablespoons vinegar, lemon juice or some other type of acid

Directions

Fill a shallow skillet or pan with a 2-inch depth of water. Bring to a boil over medium- high heat. Add a splash or two (2 to 4 tablespoons) of vinegar. Drop eggs one at a time into boiling water and gently tumble with a spoon to keep the eggs from sticking to the bottom of the pan.

Continue to cook in the boiling water until the eggs are the desired firmness. Scoop the eggs out of the pan with the slotted spoon and let the water drip off completely. Serve immediately.

Note: The vinegar in the poaching water keeps the egg white from spreading out. The more you add the tighter the white becomes. You should be careful about adding too much because it will flavor the eggs a bit.

. . . .

Panir Cheese

Panir cheese is sometimes called Indian tofu. It's easy to make and has the unique ability to be fried or cooked without melting. Dice or slice the cheese and brown in a little butter or oil and you have a terrific salad garnish, soup topper, or alternative to Parmesan cheese in a pasta dish.

Yields: 8 ounces

Ingredients

2 quarts whole milk
1/4 cup lemon juice

Directions

Heat the milk in a large pot over medium-high heat, stirring constantly while scraping the bottom of the pan to avoid scorching. Bring the milk to a full rolling boil and then reduce heat to low.

Immediately pour in lemon juice and gently stir for a few seconds. Remove the pan from the heat. Continue to stir until lumps of curd form. Let stand for 10 minutes.

Line a colander with several layers of cheesecloth. The cheesecloth should be large enough to overhang the edges of the colander. Pour the curd into the lined colander to capture the. Gather up the corners of the cheesecloth and twist until most of the liquid is squeezed out (be careful, it's hot). Rinse briefly under cold tap water. Twist again to remove any remaining liquid.

Set wrapped cheese in a large bowl and put a substantial weight on the cheese — a bowl of water, a pumpkin, a big rock — anything handy to compress the cheese. Compress the cheese for 1 hour. Unwrap and use or store for up to 1 week in the refrigerator.

. . . .

Basic Pie Dough

Be careful not to mix your pie crust too much, it will become tough. If making a two-crust pie, double the recipe.

Yields: 9-inch crust

Ingredients

2 cups all-purpose flour
Pinch of salt
1/4 cup cold butter, cut into small pieces
1/4 cup shortening cut into small pieces
3 tablespoons cold water

Directions

Sift flour into a bowl and then add salt to the flour. Add butter and shortening to the flour and work together with your hands. Continue to blend until mixture resembles bread crumbs. Sprinkle cold water onto flour and work in with a round bladed dough knife. Press together into a round ball, cover bowl and chill for at least 30 minutes. Roll out on a sturdy counter and cut into desired shape.

. . . .

Tempura Batter

The secret to success with frying batters is to keep them very cold. This is a very simple batter and may be flavored with a variety of herbs and spices.

Yields: 2 cups

Ingredients

1/2 cup flour
1/2 cup cornstarch
1 teaspoon baking soda
1 teaspoon baking powder
1 teaspoon sugar
1/2 teaspoon salt
1 egg
2/3 cup ice cold water

Directions

Combine dry ingredients in a mixing bowl and set aside. In a second bowl, lightly beat egg and combine with water. Stir in dry ingredients being careful not to overmix. Batter will be slightly lumpy.

. . . .

Espagnole (Brown Sauce)

Most of us don't have quantities of beef drippings or a pot full of beef bones hanging around to make a rich beef stock. If you do, I'm eatin' at your house. There are very good soup bases available at any supermarket that will allow you to make an acceptable stock as rich as you would like. Check the ingredients and make sure salt is not the first ingredient; this signals an inferior product. If you use a base, you may have to add a few drops of kitchen bouquet or caramel color to achieve the sought-after dark brown color.

Yields: 5 cups

Ingredients

1/2 cup butter or other fat
1/2 cup flour
1 quart rich beef stock
Salt and pepper to taste
1 tablespoon lemon juice
Optional: 1 tablespoon dried thyme

Directions

Bring stock to a boil in a small pot. Reduce heat and keep hot.

In a large stockpot, melt the butter over medium heat. Add the flour and stir together to form a paste. Continue to cook this mixture, stirring constantly, until it takes on a distinctive rust color. Add hot stock to the pot and stir vigorously until lumps of flour are smoothed out. Add thyme (if desired) and lemon juice. Adjust seasoning with salt and pepper. Bring sauce to a boil, reduce heat and simmer at least 15 minutes to completely cook the flour. The longer you simmer the sauce, the smoother and shinier the sauce becomes. It will keep for a week in the refrigerator or a year in the freezer.

. . . .

COOKING TECHNIQUES

Blanching and Shocking

Blanching simply is partially cooking food, typically vegetables, in boiling water or steam. Shocking is the method for stopping that cooking. We blanch and shock vegetables to prepare them for recipes, canning or freezing. This is a technique that can be useful for many vegetables.

Directions

Bring a pot of salted water to a boil.

Add vegetables in boiling salted water until softened slightly, yet still a little firm.

Snare a piece out of the pot and bite into it to check for doneness.

Place vegetables into a colander and completely drain off the hot water.

Immerse the cooked vegetables in a bowl of ice water to stop the cooking.

Once cooled, pat vegetables dry and use or set aside.

. . . .

Cooking Dried Beans

There are countless varieties of dried beans to try and they all have a little something different to offer. Cooking them is easy, but it takes a little time. The time comes from the long soaking, usually overnight, so you need to plan ahead. Many books will tell you that you can cook the beans from a dry state, but try to avoid this. My experience is that beans cooked directly from a dry state tend to get mushy on the outside and lose their skins before the insides are cooked. Here is a step-by-step outline.

Directions

Place beans in a colander and rinse with cold water. Sort through them and pick out any dry husks or debris.

Place beans in a large bowl or pot along with 3 times their volume of cold water. Do not add salt or any acidic ingredients (lemon juice, tomato juice). Cover to keep out debris and bugs. Soak at room temperature for at least 6 hours.

Drain beans and rinse in a colander. Place in a heavy-bottomed pot and cook in water twice the

volume of the beans. DO NOT ADD SALT, it will lengthen the cooking time and make the skins tough. Bring to a boil over high heat. Reduce heat and simmer for 1 to 3 hours depending on the beans and depending on how soft you want the beans. Taste them to judge if they are done.

Drain in a colander and rinse with cold water to stop the cooking. Use or store covered in the refrigerator for up to one week.

. . . .

Peeling and Seeding Tomatoes

Many recipes call for peeled and seeded tomatoes, however, in many cases this is unnecessary. Occasionally the seeds and skins can diminish the visual appeal of the dish. Peeling and seeding is especially appropriate when using raw tomatoes in a cold salsa or salad recipe. Removing the seeds leaves just the firm flesh, which keeps the sauce or salad from getting watered down. This technique is easy, but it does consume a little time.

Directions

Bring a large pot of water to a boil over high heat.

Cut out the cores from the tomatoes and cut a 2-inch cross over the opposite end of the tomatoes.

Drop the tomatoes into the boiling water and let sit until the corners of the cut start to peel away.

Remove the tomatoes with a set of tongs and cool under cold running water.

Grab the peeling corners with your hands or a knife and peel each corner back in one motion until completely peeled.

Cut the tomatoes in half along the equator. Scoop the seeds out with a spoon or, if you are going to roughly chop the tomatoes, simply squeeze them until the seeds fall out.

Roasting Peppers

You can roast any kind of pepper. The roasting tends to sweeten the flesh, but the real jackpot from roasting is the delightful richness that the charring and roasting brings to the pepper. You might get an argument from some foodies, but in my opinion the best result is realized when you char the pepper black and leave bits and pieces of the skin with that delicious char on the pepper. Choose any sweet or hot pepper, some are easier to skin than others, but they will all be delicious roasted.

Directions

Rub liberally with salad or olive oil.

Cook and char over direct flame, it is sexier and more authentic to roast them over a roaring wood or charcoal fire, but you can get very good results roasting over the flame from a gas range (it may be a little messy). You may also roast peppers under a very hot broiler.

Turn the peppers so that they char on all sides.

As you finish each pepper, slip them into a large bowl inside a large plastic bag while still hot.

Let the peppers sweat in the bag for at least 15 minutes.

After the sweat, pull the charred skin off the flesh. It should be fairly easy to remove, but don't be too fussy about getting every last bit.

Discard the stem and skin and scrape out the seeds from inside the pepper.

Peppers can be canned or will keep for a week in the refrigerator.

Making Vegetable Stock

All you need to prepare a vegetable stock is a large pot and any handy vegetable trimmings. It's best to have some type of onion in the stock, but all other ingredients are completely interchangeable. Garlic skins, herb stems, tomato and pepper cores and seeds, celery ribs and leaves, carrot peels, radish tops, chard stems, broccoli and Brussels sprout stems, bean stems, radish tops, chili pepper seeds (if you like it spicy) are all possibilities. You could also add mustard seed, cloves, citrus peel, or any variety of vinegar — the more items, the stronger the flavor.

Directions

Fill the desired size pot with cold water; determined by the amount of stock you wish to prepare.

Add 1 bay leaf, 1 tablespoon of peppercorns, salt to taste and the vegetable trimmings. Almost anything adds flavor to the stock.

Bring the stock to a boil, lower heat, and let simmer for no longer than an hour. The flavor will be extracted in that time and any longer will make the stock cloudy.

Pour the liquid through a fine sieve or cheesecloth. Use immediately or cool to below 40 F. This takes approximately 2 to 4 hours. It will keep a week in the refrigerator or freeze up to a year.

Tip: For any of you who are not vegan, here's a nifty trick. Break an egg or two, shells and all, into the stock while it simmers. This will clarify the stock.

· · · · · · · · · · · · · · · ·

Making Yogurt Cheese

Many Indian recipes call for the firm thick yogurt this preparation produces. The longer you let this sit, the thicker and firmer it will be.

Yields: approximately 1-1/2 cups

Ingredients

3 cups plain yogurt (any type)

Directions

Line a sieve or colander with a large double thickness of cheesecloth or place a large flat-bottomed coffee filter in the sieve or colander.

Spoon the yogurt into a cheesecloth or coffee filter, and place over a bowl to catch the liquid.

Cover with plastic wrap and set in the refrigerator for at least 8 hours.

Discard the liquid.

· · · · · · · · · · · · · · · ·

PRESERVING THE FLAVORS

7

If you are a CSA member, got a great deal from the local farmer or you have a large backyard garden, this may be the most important chapter in this book. Unless you have a large family or eat more than you ought to, you may have a hard time using all the produce you suddenly find yourself surrounded with. You may have five pounds of green beans. That's a lot of beans and no two-legged creature is going to eat that many beans before they spoil. What do you do with all those beans? During the high season, you may have to find a home for bushels of tomatoes. It kills you to watch them become compost.

And what about all those beautiful chili peppers? Preserving the harvest is necessary and rewarding. The work you put in during September (peak harvest season) will be repaid in March with peak flavors off the shelf.

Preserving food means three things: freezing, drying or canning. We'll deal with each separately. They all have advantages and disadvantages, but all will allow you to enjoy the abundance of September during the more austere days of February.

. . . .

Freezing

The most important tool for freezing is an efficient and reliable freezer. It must hold food at zero degrees Fahrenheit to stop organic activity completely and it is best if you set it for -10 F for extra safety. While perfectly acceptable, the small freezer in your kitchen will quickly fill up. If you prefer freezing, you will ultimately need a chest freezer.

Try to keep a chest freezer as full as possible for two reasons. No 1: It makes no sense to freeze empty space. No. 2: A full freezer ensures that you have a safety net if the power goes out. As long as you don't open the freezer door the food will stay frozen for up 48 hours just from the ambient temperature in the freezer.

While freezing is the simplest of the preservation methods, it does require some preparation. You will need a few large pots for blanching and/or, if you like, a steamer basket or strainer. You will also need a large colander or strainer to drain off the blanching water.

The larger these implements are, the larger the batches you can prepare.

You will also need air and watertight containers, wrap or bags. Air movement around food causes the ice crystals to evaporate and freezer burn is the result. Freezer burn is not dangerous but it is yucky. Do what you can to avoid it by using the proper containers.

Here are some container suggestions as well as containers to avoid:

Thick-walled plastic containers with an airtight lid. Try to match the size of the container with the amount of product you are freezing. Your containers should be full. This will minimize the amount of damaging air trapped in the container.

Glass canning jars. You must leave a 1-1/2-inch space between the top of the food and the lid to allow for expansion as the product freezes.

Thick plastic freezer bags. These are very good for saving space. They can be frozen in shapes that stack well. Be sure to squeeze the air out of these before you seal and freeze them.

Avoid:

- *Thin plastic bags. The plastic bags that you get in the produce department of your grocery store will not keep out air and tear very easily when they are frozen.*

- *Thin-walled plastic containers. The containers from cottage cheese or margarine are too fragile and prone to cracking under cold temperatures.*

- *Avoid glass jars with pronounced shoulders; these will get stressed and might crack while the contents expand during freezing.*

Freeze as soon after harvest as possible. Flavor and nutritional content deteriorate with prolonged storage in many foods.

To prepare many items for freezing, you should blanch or preferably steam the produce (see Appendix). This deactivates many enzymes that convert sugars to starch in vegetables. It also allows you to cook directly from frozen, which minimizes the flavor and texture damage from thawing.

Immediately after blanching or steaming, shock the vegetables in ice cold water to stop the cooking exactly at the point you would like, usually just a little underdone and crisp.

To freeze pieces individually, lay in a single layer on a cookie sheet and freeze a few hours. Place the frozen pieces in a container loosely. This allows you to use just the amount you want without thawing a whole frozen block of vegetables. As long as they are kept airtight, most fruits and vegetables can be frozen and used within a year.

If you need to thaw before using in a recipe, it is best to do it slowly in a refrigerator. It is safer and there is less flavor loss.

Drying

Drying is the oldest form of food preservation. In fact, I reckon the first person to discover dried food did it by accident. He likely left a fish and a handful of grapes on a rock somewhere in the hot central Asian sun and forgot about them. When he rediscovered them they seemed a little shriveled and ghastly but none the worse for wear. Because pre-biblical man was hungrier and less terrified of food-borne pathogens than we are, he ate them when everything else was gone. "Eureka, " he thought, "I can store food this way and eat grapes in the winter — Yum!" We've been eating raisins, dates, dried chilies and pemmican ever since.

All you need is dry weather, a hot sun and a little time.

Drying preserves food by removing one of the requirements for food spoilage —moisture. Once the moisture is removed, most biological action stops and food can be safely stored. Dried food has the advantage of not filling up limited and expensive freezer space. In some cases the drying concentrates and intensifies the flavor of the food.

Dried food is equally nutritious as frozen food and dried fruit, especially, is incredibly nutrient dense. Any fruit or vegetable can be dried but you will have the most success with those items that are not overly moist to begin with. Cucumbers and watermelons can be dried, but it will take a long time and they are not very good. Mushrooms, chili peppers, tree fruits, berries, beans, tomatoes and herbs are outstanding dried.

You can air-dry food, dry it in the sun or dry it in the oven but I don't do any of those things. I have cats and all these methods require having food lying around the house for long periods of time. Invariably the colorful trays of trinkets become cat toys. I could contrive to keep the cats away from the goodies but I have opted for the much simpler method of using a food dehydrator. They are relatively inexpensive and produce more consistent and controlled results than the other methods and they are usually enclosed so my cats can't get at them.

Most fruits can be dried raw but vegetables should be blanched and shocked (see Appendix) before drying. This takes some of the moisture out and slightly sets the color and nutrients. If you need to blanch an item for freezing, you usually should blanch it for drying. To rehydrate dried food, simply cover with boiling water and let steep for several hours. Cook the food in the steeping water or save as the base for vegetable stock.

Tips for Drying

Pick out a food dehydrator that you can store in your house. Some of them are the size of garages. Unless you have a large family a smallish dehydrator should fill your needs.

Consider the ease of cleaning your unit. Being able to clean in a dishwasher is a bonus.

Try to cut like items in consistent sizes. This allows you better control of the drying and the food pieces will finish at the same time.

Store dried foods in glass jars or plastic bags. It should be kept in a cool, dry, dark place; not in the refrigerator.

CANNING

Canning has fallen out of favor. It does require some equipment and a little time. And for many items, freezing is a better option. I think that most garden vegetables are stored better frozen. It allows more flexibility and convenience. But I still can because it allows me to prepare items with specific flavors. The huge array of pickles is an example, and most preserves, jellies and jams are required to be canned. The canning is an integral part of the recipe. A pickle wouldn't be a pickle unless it was canned in some way and the flavor of preserves develops in the jar.

Canning low acid foods, most of which are vegetables that are not pickled, requires a pressure canner. This book does not contain any recipes that require a pressure canner. Information about canning low acid foods is readily available. The main difference is that higher processing temperatures are required to eliminate pathogenic bacteria in low acid foods. The pressure in a pressure canner will raise temperatures to sufficient levels. There are several recipes for refrigerator pickles in this book. Because items are not processed they must be kept in the refrigerator. In many cases these items are much crisper and fresher tasting than canned items.

Canning Equipment

Water Bath Canner

A water bath canner is simply a covered pot large enough to hold your jars and an additional two inches of water. It should be wide enough across to allow space between the jars. A pot specially made for canning will usually come with a wire rack to keep the jars off the bottom of the pan and allow you to remove them all at once. You can buy the rack separately and use it in any pot that it fits in.

Canning Jars

It is best to buy your jars new but it is perfectly safe to reuse them if they are not chipped or damaged. There are many sizes of jars available but the most common are pint- and quart-size jars. These are available in standard and wide mouth profiles. Each has its preferred use, but in many cases either will do. Wide mouth jars are easier to fill and clean. You should not use old mayonnaise or commercial pickle jars because they are not fully tempered and may shatter during processing.

Canning Lids

You will still find old canning jars with rubber gaskets and wire bails. These are very attractive but it is difficult to find the gaskets and the jars will certainly have weakened over time. It is best to use the contemporary two-piece vacuum lid. They are comprised of a thin metal lid with a rubber seal molded to the underside of the rim. These are held in place with a screw band. The screw bands are reusable — the lids are not.

Wide Mouth Canning Funnel

This is not essential but it will save you a little growling and swearing. They are inexpensive.

Jar Tongs

If you have very strong hands you can fish jars out of boiling hot water with a regular set of tongs. For the rest of us, it is best to get a canning jar tongs. Many times you can find them at rummage sales and thrift stores for next to nothing

Canning Step by Step

Preparing and Filling Jars

1. Prepare the canner by placing rack in the bottom. Sterilize the canning jars in canner by filling jars with very hot tap water and placing in a canner filled with very hot tap water. There should be one inch of water over the top of the jars. Place over medium-high heat and bring to a boil; boil 10 minutes. Turn off heat and immediately place lids in canner wherever you can find room, and let sit in hot water until ready to use.

2. Carefully remove a jar and with tongs and drain off water. Remove one lid and shake off water. Fill with food allowing for required headspace.

3. Remove air bubbles with a rubber or wooden spatula while packing food a little more tightly.

4. Wipe rim of jar with a clean towel. Apply the lid and secure with the screw ring until seal is formed

5. Repeat all steps until all jars are filled.

Processing Jars

1. Reheat the water from sterilizing the jars to 180 F.

2. Place filled jars in canner making sure jars are not touching each other.

3. Add additional water to make sure water level is at least two inches above jars.

4. Bring water to a boil. Once fully boiling, reduce heat to a robust simmer and cover canner with lid.

5. Process (boil) the jars for the required amount of time starting from the point you reach a rapid boil.

6. Turn off heat and remove canning kettle lid.

7. Remove jars from canner with a tongs and place on an absorbent towel. Allow space between jars to cool completely.

RECIPE INDEX

recite index

Multi-Purpose

Techniques

Preserving

Vegetables Alphabetically

METRIC TABLES

Capacity

1/5 teaspoon	= 1 milliliter	4 quarts (1 gal.)	= 3.8 liters
1 teaspoon	= 5 milliliters	1 milliter	= 1/5 teaspoon
1 tablespoon	= 15 milliliters	5 milliters	= 1 teaspoon
	or 1/2 fluid ounce	15 milliters	= 1 tablespoon
2 tablespoons	= 1 fluid ounce	29.6 milliters	= 1 fluid oz.
1/5 cup	= 50 milliliters	100 milliters	= 3.4 fluid oz.
1 cup	= 8 ounces	240 milliters	= 1 cup
	or 240 milliliters	1 liter	= 34 fluid ounces
	or 240 grams of water	1 liter	= 4.2 cups
2 cups (1 pint)	= 16 ounces	1 liter	= 2.1 pints
	or 470 milliliters	1 liter	= 1.06 quarts
4 cups (1 quart)	= .95 liter	1 liter	= .26 gallon
4 cups (1 quart)	= .95 liter		

Weight

1 fluid ounce	= 30 milliters	100 grams	= 3.5 ounces weight
1 fluid ounce	= 28 grams	500 grams	= 1.10 pounds
1 pound	= 454 grams	1 kilogram	= 2.205 pounds
1 gram	= .035 ounce	1 kilogram	= 35 oz.
28.4 grams	= 1 ounce weight		

Cooking

16 tablesppns	= 1 cup	2 tablespoons	= 1/8 cup
12 tablespoons	= 3/4 cup	2 tablespoons + 2 teaspoons	= 1/6 cup
10 tablespoons + 2 teaspoons	= 2/3 cup	1 tablespoon	= 1/16 cup
8 tablespoons	= 1/2 cup	2 cups	= 1 pint
6 tablespoons	= 3/8 cup	2 pints	= 1 quart
5 tablespoons + 1 teaspoon	= 1/3 cup	3 teaspoons	= 1 tablespoon
4 tablespoons	= 1/4 cup	48 teaspoons	= 1 cup

RESOURCES

Chefs Collaborative
A national chef network that's changing the sustainable food landscape using the power of connections, education and responsible buying decisions.
www.chefscollaborative.org

FarmersMarket.com
Online support (with database) for the nation's farmers markets, as well as market customers.
www.farmersmarket.com

First Hand Harvest
CSA serving the Rockford, IL area.
www.firsthandharvest.com

Green America
Green America is a not-for-profit organization (formerly Co-op America) whose mission is to harness economic power (the strength of consumers, investors, businesses, and the marketplace) to create a socially just and environmentally sustainable society.
www.greenamerica.org

Local Harvest
Find farmers' markets, family farms, and other sources of sustainably grown food in your area.
www.localharvest.org

Midwest Renewable Energy Association
A non-profit organization founded to promote renewable energy, energy efficiency, and sustainable living through education and demonstration.
www.the-mrea.org

Maplewood Gardens
CSA located in Elderson, WI
http://sites.google.com/site/maplewoodgardens/home
Contact David Peterson at:
drgarlic@wittenbergnet.net

Randall Smith's Web Site
A professional resourse for responsible food choices.
www.cooklocalfood.com

Slow Food USA
Slow Food USA seeks to create dramatic and lasting change in the food system. We reconnect Americans with the people, traditions, plants, animals, fertile soils and waters that produce our food. We seek to inspire a transformation in food policy, production practices and market forces so that they ensure equity, sustainability and pleasure in the food we eat.
www.slowfoodusa.org

USDA Agricultural Marketing Service
Database for farmers markets, including a national farmers market search engine.
www.ams.usda.gov/farmersmarkets

Any state university extension program.

ABOUT THE AUTHOR

A chef for more than 20 years, Randall Smith is currently Executive Chef at the iconic Clocktower Resort in Rockford, IL. He is a Middle Wisconsin Chef's Association Chef of the Year nominee and winner of the Winnebago County Green Recipe Award. A columnist and contributor for magazines and newspapers, he writes about the importance of using local produce and is a tireless advocate for farmer's markets, CSAs and sustainable farms in Wisconsin and Illinois. In 2006, he visited Ireland to study ways that local foods might be sold and served. He also works closely with the Central Rivers Farmshed, The Wisconsin Local Food Summit and the Midwest Renewable Energy Association.

Randall believes in the importance of developing relationships with our food, the people who grow it, the people who prepare it and the people who eat it. He would love hear to from you at his website www.cooklocalfood.com.

Other Fine Books from F+W Media

QUICK-FIX HEALTHY MIX

Stop over-paying for foods loaded with toxins, unhealthy fats and sugars. Instead, make your own high-quality mixes at a fraction of the cost. *Quick-Fix Healthy Mix* has more than 225 easy-to-make recipes, made of easy-to-find, eco-friendly ingredients. Casey Kellar is the author of six books on living in a natural lifestyle and has consulted with small food companies to help them with their formulas.

ISBN 13: 978-1-4402-0385-5
softcover • 240 pages • Z5032

SOAP MAKER'S WORKSHOP

For generations people have enjoyed the pure cleanliness and moisturizing effects that come from hand-crafted soap This easy-to-follow book and bonus CD walks you through the soap-making process with step-by-step instructions for using everyday kitchenware to make soap, setting up a safe workspace, and easily preparing the necessary lye and oils. You'll also learn which oil to add for a rich lather, how to make liquid soap or shampoo, and more, with 30 recipes.

ISBN 13: 978-1-4402-0791-7
softcover • 160 pages • Z6423

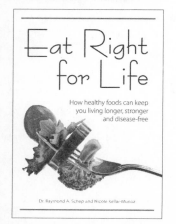

EAT RIGHT FOR LIFE

How Healthy Foods Can Keep You Living Longer, Stronger and Disease-Free *Eat Right for Life* is filled with scientific and practical advice for leading a healthy lifestyle. It shows how to use simple ingredients from the garden, kitchen or local supermarket to make delicious foods to enhance a healthy life. The book contains more than 125 natural foods, including vegetables, herbs and minerals. It discusses the "kitchen pharmacy" through disease prevention guidance and how to use ordinary natural foods to promote excellent health and clear, radiant skin.

ISBN 13: 978-1-4402-1132-4
softcover • 240 pages • Z7121

Visit our website at www.betterwaybooks.com